The Essential
Lapsit Guide

The Essential Lapsit Guide

A Multimedia How-To-Do-It Manual and Programming Guide for Stimulating Literacy Development from 12 to 24 Months

Linda L. Ernst

Neal-Schuman

An imprint of the American Library Association

Chicago   2015

LINDA L. ERNST has been a children's librarian for more than thirty-five years. Actively serving very young children and their caregivers has been an important part of her job and one of the most enjoyable ones. Just as parents are encouraged to keep it simple and start early to expose their children to the world of language and literature, Ernst offers assistance in applying this knowledge to the areas of library service and programming for very young children. She has given training workshops for the King County Library, Seattle Public Library, Everett Public Library, and the Sno-Isle Library System in Washington. She has also given workshops in Kentucky, Michigan, San Francisco, and Scottsdale, Arizona. Conference programs include the Pennsylvania Library Association and the Washington Library Association. She has guided and encouraged adults to discover, develop, and share the early literacy experience with very young children. The Children's and Young Adult Services Interest Group of the Washington Library Association awarded Ernst the 2004 CAYAS Award for Visionary Library Service to Youth. Ernst has served as chair of the Early Childhood Programs and Services Committee for the Association for Library Service to Children and was a member of the 2007 Caldecott Award committee. She is currently employed by the King County Library System in Washington. This is her fourth book on the topic of libraries and very young children. She can be reached at lindalernst@gmail.com

© 2015 by the American Library Association.

Printed in the United States of America
19 18 17 16 15   5 4 3 2 1

ISBN: 978-1-55570-761-3

Library of Congress Cataloging-in-Publication Data
Ernst, Linda L.
    The essential lapsit guide : a multimedia how-to-do-it manual and programming guide for stimulating literacy development from 12 to 24 months / Linda L. Ernst.
        pages cm
    Includes bibliographical references and indexes.
    ISBN 978-1-55570-761-3 (alk. paper)
    1. Children's libraries—Activity programs—United States. 2. Libraries and infants—United States. 3. Libraries and toddlers—United States. 4. Libraries and caregivers—United States. 5. Early childhood education—Activity programs—United States. 6. Literacy. 7. Infants—Development. 8. Toddlers—Development. I. Title.
    Z718.3.E77 2014
    027.62'5—dc23
                                                                            2014001003

Cover images © Shutterstock, Inc. Text composed in Minion Pro and Interstate typefaces.

♾ This paper meets the requirements of ANSI/NISO Z39.48-1992 (Permanence of Paper).

Contents

PREFACE   vii
ACKNOWLEDGMENTS   xi

Part I: Program Foundations

1. Fascinating Facts	**3**
What We Know and What We Have Learned	4
Biology: The Facts and Revelations	5
Language	6
Early Learning	8
Impact on the Library	8
Resources	10
2. Who Is Involved	**15**
The Children	15
The Adults	20
Families	22
Child-Care Providers, Early Childhood Educators, and Others	27
The Librarian/Presenter	27
Conclusion	28
Resources	29
3. Service Areas	**33**
In-House Services	33
Outreach Programs	39
Partnerships, Funding, and Grants	46
Resources	47

Part II: Program Building Blocks

4. The Play's the Thing—Books, Rhymes, and Programs	**53**
Things to Consider with Programming	54
Putting the Program Together	61
Resources	171

Additional content
can be found at
alaeditions.org/webextras.

Contents

5. Enhancements   177
   Music   178
   Flannel Boards   187
   Puppets   189
   Creative Activities   191
   Language   196
   Movement   198
   Props   199
   Play   203
   Displays   207
   Handouts   210
   Resources   215

   Appendix: Handouts & Templates   225
   Author/Title Index   251
   Theme Index   257
   Subject Index   273

Preface

The Essential Lapsit Guide is a compilation, revision, and update of two previous works: *Lapsit Services for the Very Young* and *Lapsit Services for the Very Young II*. "Lapsit" has become identified with public library programs and services aimed at serving very young children, younger than 24 months of age, and their adult caregivers or providers. These works developed out of the latest research findings in the areas of how very young children learn, acquire language, and develop physically and mentally. This book reflects the latest research findings and awareness of how early in life learning begins. The information in this book can be used to enhance the basic services, facilities, and programming that libraries offer to their communities. An age-appropriate annotated bibliography, rhymes, songs, and fingerplays make up the majority of the guide. To support the educational value of lapsit programs, the book includes suggested tips throughout the text that discuss how to encourage and actively engage program participants and offer brief statements relating to early literacy, brain research, language development, the importance of play, and related topics.

The Essential Lapsit Guide provides the conceptual framework, successful programming materials and activities, and resources that will enable the librarian presenter to be a role model for the adult participant. In this way, the ideas, materials, and knowledge presented will enable adults to re-create these fun learning experiences on their own with their very young children.

Overlapping fields of study, including education, health, library science, and others, create a need to exchange and even expand one's traditional role. Librarians may be called upon to teach, educators may need to develop a greater knowledge of biological development, and parents may want to learn and know it all. Partnership and networking have become commonplace through grant sharing and data gathering by librarians, schools, and government agencies. The very young child is now a major focus not only of parents but also of educators, librarians, politicians, and, yes, even commercial marketers. By expanding the fields of knowledge, understanding, and awareness that impact very young children, this population can be better served. The primary audience for this book is librarians who are currently employed in the field and students in library science who are planning to venture into programming and services for the very young.

The book is organized in such a way as to allow for easy access to the information needed. Part I presents information on the foundations for successful programming. Chapter 1 contains the biological data and facts about early literacy pertaining to the very young child. Chapter 2 focuses on the variety of participants who will be involved in the programs. The section concludes with chapter 3's examination of services other than programs and partnership possibilities. Part II covers the building blocks for creating successful programs. Chapter 4 examines concerns and questions that the presenter should consider prior to offering this type of program, outlines and formats for programs, and ready-to-go programs for children newborn to 24 months and their caregivers. This chapter also offers resources for those who prefer to create their own outlines or want to expand their current program selections. It contains a lengthy list of annotated books that work well with this age group, giving with most entries suggested topic headings, tips on how to encourage participant interaction, and very brief statements for adult education. It also provides a wide variety of rhymes with directions for participant interaction. Chapter 5 focuses on ways to enhance your programming through the use of additional materials and creative activities. Adding music, visuals, puppetry, and activities that the adults and children can do together will allow you to augment your core program and extend it beyond the allotted time. You can use some of these enhancements, such as music, flannel boards, and puppets, during the program and others, such as dancing to music, reading from lists, and naming things in the child's world, after the program to demonstrate things the participants can be doing at home to create a literacy-rich environment for their children. The use of these enhancements will also encourage adult-child interaction, enabling the presenter a chance to offer suggestions and support to individuals during the activity.

The book ends with an appendix that includes full-page sample handouts and templates (also available at alaeditions.org/webextras), and three indexes for authors and titles of the picture books and rhymes, program themes, and general subjects.

Why offer these programs and services for the very young? There is a variety of reasons ranging from philosophical and educational to those that are personal in nature. They serve as a valuable introduction to the wonderful world of language in which the very young child and adult together share a fun, learning experience that can be re-created independently. These experiences encourage

---

The performances available at **alaeditions.org/webextras** bring the content of chapters 4 and 5 to life. They demonstrate forty-seven rhymes and accompanying activities to encourage interaction with the audience. These rhymes can be used as ready-made parts for your program or they can serve as inspiration for encouraging adult and child interaction to promote early childhood learning.

early brain development with verbal, visual, and tactile stimulation. Language and learning become integral parts of these children's daily lives and prepare them for future success. With today's current economy, local libraries can provide families of all kinds with fun, intergenerational learning experiences and environments, often at little or no expense. Everyone involved benefits, with adults gaining confidence in their ability to share stories, interact more with their children, connect with others in their community, and find resources; the library gaining regular users and supporters; and the children developing in healthy ways. "Lapsit" storytime is an early literacy/learning experience that adults and very young children can share that also just happens to be a lot of fun.

Acknowledgments

It is only through the help of countless people willing to share their knowledge and expertise that a book like this can be created. My sincere and heartfelt thanks to all the children's librarians and early childhood educators who share the stories, rhymes, and songs in the public domain through the oral tradition, along with parents, grandparents, and other adults who have kept these alive for new generations.

I am particularly grateful to the children's librarians of the King County Library System in Washington and Scottsdale Public Library in Arizona who allowed me to observe their programs and examine their collections and who shared their ideas and concerns and served as sounding boards for my ideas and concepts.

Once again, I extend my thanks to Nancy Stewart of Friends Street Music and Sing With Our Kids for her willingness to share original materials and resources from *Little Songs for Little Me, Plant a Little Seed*, and her extraordinary websites.

Electronic communications have increased the sharing of ideas and resources, so I would like to thank and acknowledge the many electronic discussion lists and blogs that play such an important role in developing services and programs for the very young. These include but are not limited to the discussion lists of the Association of Library Services to Children, a division of the American Library Association (ALSC-L and PRESCHSVCS), and the Australian Library and Information Association Children and Youth Services (otherwise known as "aliaCYS"), and Amy Koester, for permission to include her blog, *The Show Me Librarian* (http://showmelibrarian.blogspot.com), as a resource in this text.

My family and friends have all my thanks for their encouragement and support. A special thanks to Cheryl Hadley who helps me find "my voice" and to my editor, Amy Knauer, for her patience.

Finally, this book is dedicated to the children and families who have shared so much with me throughout my career.

Part I

Program Foundations

Fascinating Facts

IN THIS CHAPTER

✓ What We Know and What We Have Learned

✓ Biology: The Facts and Revelations

✓ Language

✓ Early Learning

✓ Impact on the Library

✓ Resources

The field of early childhood studies has grown to encompass the realms of psychology, sociology, education, neurology, linguistics, politics, and even marketing. Due to developing research techniques and equipment, researchers are able to provide reliable data on how the brain develops and learning takes place. At the Institute for Learning and Brain Sciences (I-LABS; http://ilabs.washington.edu) at the University of Washington, advances in technology are enabling studies on how children learn and acquire language. In 2010, I-LABS acquired an MEG (magnetoencephalography) imaging machine that allows them to see a living brain in its entirety while actively at work.

Early childhood concerns also show up in the fields of education, health, and politics. In 2006, Governor Christine Gregoire of Washington State created the Department of Early Learning at the state level, thus highlighting the importance of early childhood education. John Diaz, Chief of the Seattle Police Department, and Sue Rahr, King County Sheriff, agree that early childhood education is valuable: "Research shows that every dollar spent on early care and education can generate returns of up to $10 in savings from reduced crime, corrections and other costs" (Diaz and Rahr, 2011). The American Academy of Pediatrics in 2011 recommended that pediatricians "discuss 'media limits' for babies and toddlers with parents, though they do not specify how much time is too much" (Carey, 2011), instead encouraging interactive play and strongly discouraging television viewing for children two years and younger.

Programming and services for very young children and their caregivers have become a primary part of many public libraries' mission statements rather than an exception. Some libraries have added an early childhood position to their staff to focus on and develop services for the very young. The Brooklyn Public Library (BPL; http://www.bklynpubliclibrary.org) in New York designed the program Brooklyn Reads to Babies and saturated the entire borough with the message that reading to very young children is important. In Colorado, the

Colorado Libraries for Early Literacy (CLEL; http://www.clel.org) is a statewide network that partners libraries and community organizations. The Association for Library Service to Children (ALSC; http://www.ala.org/alsc) and the Public Library Association (PLA; http://www.ala.org/pla), both divisions of the American Library Association, have developed programs and initiatives that spotlight the very young, including Born to Read (http://www.ala.org/alsc/issuesadv/borntoread) and Every Child Ready to Read® @ your library® (http://everychildreadytoread.org).

What We Know and What We Have Learned

Librarians have become increasingly aware that reading aloud, doing action rhymes, and talking to and interacting through play with very young children create an environment that stimulates and encourages brain development. This early learning environment does have an impact on how children do in school, and research supports this. This chapter provides an overview of the research into early brain development and its impact on libraries and parents. Keep in mind that this field of research is complex, is constantly developing, and encompasses many areas of study.

Armed with facts about the brain, child development, and how learning takes place, we are better able to create age-appropriate literacy programs. We can pass on educational bites of information to our community and help adults start their children on the road to success. Very young children often face major risk factors that impede their ability to succeed in life. In 1993, the National Education Goals Panel released *The National Education Goals Report: Becoming a Nation of Learners*, a report that listed the following as risks:

- Inadequate prenatal care
- Parents who are isolated/divorced, single, lacking family and community support, undereducated
- Substandard child care, two working parents, high turnover and insufficient training for child-care providers
- Poverty
- Insufficient stimulation of children by caring adults

These risks have not changed or disappeared. The current economic and political upheaval in the United States and around the world adds stress to the lives of many families. These stresses may crack the foundation a child needs to be physically, mentally, and emotionally healthy. Libraries can help reduce these risks. In free programs, librarians can teach parents how to create a stimulating learning environment for their very young children, act as role models for adults interacting with very young children, help child-care providers incorporate this stimulation into their daily routines, and give parents/adults a chance to develop support networks with others.

New technologies and research tools have helped establish basic facts regarding brain development in the very young child. Newborn children are no longer considered "blank slates" waiting for stimulation. Prenatal studies show that the fetus reacts to stimulation while still in the womb. After birth, it is the children's environment—what they eat, what they hear and feel, their sense of security, interesting things around them—that impacts how the brain connections develop.

Biology: The Facts and Revelations

Research shows that areas of the brain actively develop and mature at different times. This is why it is easier to learn certain things at certain times than at others. Given that children learn through all their senses, studies suggest that children have stronger connections between brain cells if they are held, touched, talked to, and played with on a regular basis by caring and involved caregivers. This is true of all children, be they hearing, hearing impaired, or with special needs. Talking, language, and communication are all very complex abilities to learn, and it is critical for adults to take active part in all aspects of children's growing experiences. Repetition is important to reinforce what children experience. Communicating and demonstrating skills gives children information as well as a role model to emulate, from using speech, to turning pages in a book, to any other skill the children are developing. Although children are born with an overabundance of brain cells and connections, over time only the ones with active exchanges survive—the old rule of "Use it or lose it."

When children are born, the major brain function is to sort out and become accustomed to their new world. By one year of age, children are actively engaged, seeking input from the environment and individuals that make up their world. It is important to remember that each child is a unique individual who develops at a unique pace and in areas that catch the individual child's interest. Even at this early age, the young child displays definite preferences and becomes a learning machine, albeit one limited by skills and abilities that need more time to develop. Chapter 2 examines this more closely in the section focused on children and in the related child development chart.

Helping children learn about themselves and the world around them is a primary responsibility of the parent and/or the primary adult caregiver. Learning about brain research can help adults guide children toward their full potentials by creating a stimulating, healthy learning environment. Current research indicates that children have the ability to learn even earlier than once believed. By using noninvasive methods and conducting behavioral studies, researchers gather data about electrical activity in the brain and stimulants preferred by the child, such as sounds or pictures, through the study of sucking patterns.

So, what are the basic facts?

- Children are born with 100 billion brain cells called neurons. There are 50 trillion functioning connections between neurons called synapses. This number increases during the first few years of life; then synapses that are not consistently being activated will be "weeded out," trimmed, or cut back as in pruning.
- "Wiring" between the neurons will increase significantly the first few months of life. However, pruning of unused synapses will take place over an extended time.
- Environmental factors have more influence on brain development than first thought, and they have a lasting influence.
- A child's early experiences help determine the brain's "wiring."
- The child's environment and the amount of stimulation received influence the vitality of the connections between cells, which are strengthened through constant sensory stimulation.
- Children's brains develop over time, with certain areas of the brain developing at different times and at different paces.
- At three years of age, the child has about twice as many connections in the brain as an adult does.
- There is a rapid rise in the number of synapses from 50 trillion to 1,000 trillion in the first few months after birth.

Language

"If parents spend the first year of their child's life worrying mostly about motor development, we devote the second to language" (Eliot, 1999, 351). Language is the main way people communicate with one another and learn about their world. Children develop this skill at different times, which often causes concern among parents when comparing their children to others' children of the same age. The grammar and structure of the language, the richness and volume of its vocabulary, and how words are pronounced all need to be learned. Children are able to comprehend what is being said before they themselves have mastered the actual skills and abilities needed to talk. Eliot notes, "Learning to talk is probably the greatest intellectual leap of an individual's life: it opens up a new universe of questions, reasoning, social communication on opinions (for better or worse!) that punch all the other types of learning into warp speed and make a child finally seem like a full-fledged person" (Eliot, 1999, 354). It is the foundation upon which intellect builds.

Children at birth are able to develop speech in any language and are considered "Citizens of the World" (Kuhl, 2007). Through hearing a language consistently, children learn to vocalize the sounds of that language by babbling. As they focus on what they hear around them, usually the primary language, their ability to hear and vocalize the sounds not present in the immediate environment diminishes. Still, an environment rich in sounds, words, and interactions provides young children with the tools necessary to master their primary language.

According to Golinkoff and Hirsh-Pasek in *How Babies Talk* (2000), scientific discoveries regarding brain development and language indicate the following:

- Silence is not golden. Very young children learn through all of their senses. Communication is essential for language development, whether it be auditory (hearing) or visual (sign language). Television cannot be a substitute because it does not demand interaction on the part of the child. A stimulating environment helps children remain interested in their world while learning about it. Interaction can be with the parent or an alternative caregiver. The important thing is to be actively engaging in communication with the child. Hearing-impaired children need stimulation as well, which can be done through the use of sign language, visual aids, touch, vibrations, and so forth. Working-class and professional parents talk more to their young children than do parents on welfare. Teen parents also tend to be unaware of the importance of talking to their children.

- New scientific methods can yield assessment tools, such as methods for determining learning loss.

- Children are learning more that you would suspect. Not only do little ones see and hear, but they also analyze and remember experiences. Overestimate, not underestimate, a baby's capabilities.

Early Learning

To help remember
the concept that
"PLAY = LEARNING,"
keep in mind the equation:

```
PLAY + LEARNING
      ▼
   PLEARNING
```

Thanks to the unknown creator of this term
at the 21st Century Learner Summit in 2003.

Learning happens when the brain makes new connections to what is already known and in place. Touching, talking, moving, singing, looking at things or people very closely, and sharing with others are all ways children learn. To learn from an experience, children need to be actively involved and using their senses. This is most often called "play" (Ernst, 2008, 11). When a child is actively engaged in doing something, learning comes more quickly and its complexities are more easily grasped. By copying what they see others doing around them, children gain control by doing it themselves. Movement helps children learn by increasing oxygen levels in the bloodstream, thereby energizing brain cells. In addition, an adult who has a caring relationship with the child can create an environment where the child feels safe and emotionally secure enough to try something new (e.g., the activities that take place in storytime). For more detailed information on learning, see The Children section in chapter 2.

Impact on the Library

With all that this "early brain research" is revealing, what implications does it have for libraries and librarians? Librarians, as early childhood educators, have the opportunity to educate and empower parents, no matter what their economic level, about best practices informed by brain research. This helps parents become the best teachers they can be—motivators and horizon openers, not just instructors—and to help them create an environment that gives their children a good start toward lifelong learning. It is also important for librarians and early childhood educators to be aware of conflicting or confusing interpretations of brain research. Terms such as "windows of opportunity" can be misinterpreted and cause parents to have unrealistic expectations for their children or to overreact to generalizations. Parents need to understand that a "window of opportunity" refers to what can be considered the optimum time for specific learning to take place, but it does not mean this is the only time that such learning can occur. In fact, what many parents enjoy doing naturally with their children, such as touching, talking, singing, and playing, is essential "food" for the brain.

How does the library respond to the latest scientific research? Libraries have increasingly emphasized the importance of reading aloud to the entire family, including the very young child. Librarians can be guides and role models for parents and caregivers on what and how to read to children (see, e.g., the Reading Aloud to Little Ones handout in this book's appendix); how to talk about characters, experiences, and situations; and how to create an environment where enjoyment and then learning take place.

> America's librarians who serve children and families know a wonderful secret that spurs them on despite budget cuts and staff shortages. They know that every time they share a story or a book, a game or song, with tiny children—infants, toddlers, or energetic three to five year olds—and their young mothers and sometimes fathers—they have a chance to light a flame of perception or [create] a memory that will remain with a human being forever, and may even make a difference in an entire lifetime.
> (Mathews and Somerville, 1996, 7)

Libraries and librarians are showing parents how to help their children build the foundation of literacy skills that they will further develop in school and use throughout their lives. Moving beyond traditional library patrons, librarians are offering storytimes for younger children, holding instructional workshops for adults who live and work with children, and collaborating with other agencies in the community to reach non–library users. Libraries are striving to be a true developmental resource for children and families, whatever their cultural origin or economic background, during the vital early learning years during which children will be able to develop lifelong reading habits.

How can libraries spread the word? How can libraries better link their capabilities and resources to the importance of language in early childhood? First, understand the participants involved: adult caregivers and very young children. Next, determine what plan is the most efficient for working with this group in a particular situation. For example, for in-library programs, librarians can network with other agencies in the community to find participants. In-library programs require organizing in-house resources for better accessibility and creating a more child-friendly environment (including changing areas). What should libraries do to present workshops for teen parents or other specific groups? Explore who will be the target audience, what materials are appropriate, and possible locations for these programs. Sites other than the library may be easier for mothers/primary caregivers to get to or feel more comfortable to them.

Science has shown the importance of language in the early years of a child's life. It is vital that libraries provide appropriate services to the very young and the adults who care for them.

Resources

Books

Note: Many of these texts are included on resource lists used by institutions of higher learning.

Aamodt, Sandra, and Sam Wang. *Welcome to Your Child's Brain.* New York: Bloomsburg, 2011.

Anderson, R. C., E. Hiebert, J. Scott, and I. Wilkinson. *Becoming a Nation of Readers: The Report of the Commission on Reading.* Champaign, IL: Center for the Study of Reading, 1985.

Bronson, Po. *Nurtureshock: New Thinking about Children.* New York: Twelve, 2009.

Brown, Stuart, with Christopher Vaughan. *Play: How It Shapes the Brain, Opens the Imagination, and Invigorates the Soul.* New York: Avery, 2009.

Byrnes, James. *Language and Literacy Development: What Educators Need to Know.* New York: Guilford Press, 2009.

Carnegie Task Force on Meeting the Needs of Young Children. *Starting Points: Meeting the Needs of Our Youngest Children.* New York: Carnegie Corporation of New York, 1994.

Eliot, Lise. *What's Going On in There? How the Brain and Mind Develop in the First Five Years of Life.* New York: Bantam Books, 1999.

Ernst, Linda L. *Baby Rhyming Time.* New York: Neal-Schuman, 2008.

Galinsky, Ellen. *Mind in the Making: Seven Essential Skills Every Child Needs.* New York: HarperStudio, 2010.

Golinkoff, Roberta Michnick, and Kathy Hirsh-Pasek. *How Babies Talk: The Magic and Mystery of Language in the First Three Years of Life.* New York: Dutton, 2000.

Gopnik, Alison, Andrew N. Meltzoff, and Patricia Kuhl. *The Scientist in the Crib: Minds, Brains, and How Children Learn.* New York: William Morrow, 1999.

Healy, Jane M. *Your Child's Growing Mind: A Guide to Learning and Brain Development from Birth to Adolescence.* Revised ed. New York: Doubleday, 1994.

Hirsh-Pasek, Kathy, and Roberta Michnick Golinkoff, with Diane Eyer. *Einstein Never Used Flash Cards: How Our Children Really Learn—And Why They Need to Play More and Memorize Less.* Emmaus, PA: Rodale, 2003.

King, Kendal, and Alison Mackey. *The Bilingual Edge: Why, When, and How to Teach Your Child a Second Language.* New York: Collins, 2007.

Koralek, Derry, ed. *Spotlight on Young Children and Play.* Washington, DC: National Association for the Education of Young Children, 2004.

Mathews, Virginia H., and Mary R. Somerville. *Kids Can't Wait . . . Library Advocacy Now! A President's Paper*. Chicago: American Library Association, 1996.

McGuinness, Diane. *Growing a Reader from Birth: Your Child's Path from Language to Literacy*. New York: W. W. Norton, 2004.

Medina, John. *Brain Rules for Baby: How to Raise a Smart and Happy Child from Zero to Five*. Seattle: Pear Press, 2010.

Schoonover, Carl E. *Portraits of the Mind: Visualizing the Brain from Antiquity to the 21st Century*. New York: Abrams, 2010.

Shonkoff, Jack P., and Deborah A. Phillips, eds. *From Neurons to Neighborhoods: The Science of Early Childhood Development*. Washington, DC: National Academy Press, 2000.

Shore, Rebecca. *The Baby Teacher: Nurturing Neural Networks from Birth to Age Five*. Lanham, MD: Scarecrow Press, 2002.

Sousa, Edward. *How the Brain Learns*. 2nd ed. Thousand Oaks, CA: Corwin Press, 2001.

Staso, William H. *Brain Under Construction: Experiences That Promote the Intellectual Capabilities of Young Toddlers*. Book Two of a Series: 8 to 18 Months. Orcutt, CA: Great Beginnings Press, 1997.

Tough, Paul. *How Children Succeed: Grit, Curiosity, and the Hidden Power of Character*. Boston: Houghton Mifflin Harcourt, 2012.

Zigler, Edward, Dorothy G. Singer, and Sandra J. Bishop-Josef. *Children's Play: The Roots of Reading*. Washington, DC: Zero to Three Press, 2004.

Articles

Berman, Jenn. "10 Reasons Play Makes Babies Smarter." Parenting.com. http://www.parenting.com/article/why-play-makes-babies-smarter?page=0,3.

Carey, Benedict. "Parents Urged Again to Limit TV for Youngest." *New York Times*, October 18, 2011.

Cohn, Jonathan. "The Two Year Window." *The New Republic*, December 1, 2011.

Diaz, John, and Sue Rahr. "Investing in Kids Reduces Crime, Trims Criminal-Justice Costs." *Seattle Times*, October 15, 2011.

Graman, Kevin. "From Research to Policy: Studies on Development Information Push for Early Learning." *Spokesman Review*, April 17, 2011.

Muha, Laura. "Your Baby's Amazing Brain." *Parenting*, Fall 1999.

Nicolopoulou, Ageliki. "The Alarming Disappearance of Play from Early Childhood Education." *Human Development* 53, no. 1 (2010): 1–4. http://psychology.cas2.lehigh.edu/sites/psychology.cas2.lehigh.edu/files/disappearance_of_play.pdf.

Oregon.gov. "Office of Child Care: Brain Research." Oregon's Child: Everyone's Business. http://www.oregon.gov/EMPLOY/CCD/pages/brain_development.aspx.

Puckett, Margaret, Carol Sue Marshall, and Ruth Davis. "Examining the Emergence of Brain Development Research: The Promises and the Perils." *Childhood Education*, Fall 1999: 8–12.

Simmons, Tim, and Ruth Sheehan. "Brain Research Manifests Importance of First Years." *The News and Observer*, February 16, 1997.

E-resources

For additional resources, check the Department of Education and/or Department of Early Learning websites for your state or country, websites for such national and local organizations as the Association for Library Service to Children and the Brooklyn Public Library, as well as statewide cooperatives like Colorado Libraries for Early Literacy.

Association for Library Service to Children. http://www.ala.org/alsc. Click on the categories "Online Learning" and "Professional Tools" for listings of resources.

Brooklyn Public Library. "Brooklyn Reads to Babies." The goal of this campaign, aimed at parents and caregivers of babies and toddlers, is to underscore the importance of reading aloud to children during the first years of life and to emphasize this unique bonding opportunity. http://www.bklynpubliclibrary.org/first-5-years/read/baby.

Colorado Libraries for Early Literacy. http://www.clel.org. This joint effort by Colorado's public libraries and its state library developed a comprehensive statewide approach to delivering and supporting early literacy services.

CYFERnet: Children, Youth and Families Education and Research Network. http://www.cyfernet.org. CYFERnet provides a database of research and reports related to children, youth, and families on such topics as child development and parenting. The site also offers practical research-based tools, curricula, and activities for working with these groups.

Institute for Learning and Brain Sciences (I-LABS), University of Washington. http://ilabs.washington.edu. The I-LABS center studies the "fundamental principles of human learning," with emphasis on learning in children. This site makes available for viewing presentations by Dr. Patricia Kuhl and Dr. Andrew Meltzoff on such topics as early learning, brain development, and language acquisition (http://ilabs.washington.edu/multimedia-resources). It also provides links to partnership sites where additional information can be found (http://ilabs.washington.edu/i-labs-early-learning-partners).

Kuhl, Patricia, "Early Childhood Development: Early Learning, the Brain and Society." The University of Washington Provost Distinguished Lecture Series, May 24, 2007. http://www.uwtv.org/video/player.aspx?mediaid=1574718530.

National Association for the Education of Young Children. http://www .naeyc.org/. This is the website of the world's largest organization advocating on behalf of young children and those who work with them. To find early learning information, enter the phrase "early years are learning years" in the search box at the top of the screen.

National Education Goals Panel. *The National Education Goals Report: Building a Nation of Learners*, Vol. 1: *The National Report*. September 1993. http://www2.ed.gov/pubs/goals/report/goalsrpt.txt.

National Network for Child Care. http://www.nncc.org. This network serves professionals and families who care for children and youth. Select "Articles and Resources" to access information.

National Research Council. http://www.nationalacademies.org/nrc/index. This nonprofit organization, composed of the National Academy of Sciences, National Academy of Engineering, Institute of Medicine, and National Research Council, works to provide advice and research on science, engineering, and health matters. This site includes reports such as the Colorado Department of Education's *Starting Out Right: A Guide to Promoting Children's Reading Success* (http://www.nap.edu/catalog.php?record_id=6014).

Public Broadcasting System. *The Secret Life of the Brain*. Educational Broadcasting Company and David Grubin Productions, 2001. http://www.pbs.org/wnet/brain/index.html. This link provides access to the program overview for each episode (baby, child, teenager, adult, aging), select clips, and resources regarding brain development and other related topics.

Saroj Ghoting, Early Childhood Literacy Consultant. http://www.earlylit.net/index .shtml. Visit this site to find library websites plus research references and handouts from early literacy programs held at the 2011 American Library Association annual conference.

Talaris Institute. http://www.talaris.org. Talaris provides easy-to-understand tools and information regarding early brain and behavioral development. The intended audience includes parents and others who interact with children, such as educators, child-care workers, and health professionals.

"TEDxRainer—Dimitri Christakis—Media and Children." TEDxTalks video, 16:12. Uploaded December 27, 2011. http://www.youtube.com/watch?v=BoT7qH_uVNo.

Virginia Early Childhood Foundation for the Virginia Early Childhood Advisory Council. *Milestones of Child Development: A Guide to Young Children's Learning and Development from Birth to Kindergarten.* Virginia's Early Childhood Development Alignment Project. Richmond, VA: Office of Early Childhood Development, Virginia Department of Social Services, 2013. http://www.dss.virginia.gov/files/division/cc/provider_training _development/intro_page/publications/milestones/milestones_one _document/Milestones_Revised.pdf.

Zero to Three: National Center for Infants, Toddlers, and Families. http://www.zerotothree.org. This organization "informs, trains, and supports professionals, policymakers, and parents in their efforts to improve the lives of infants and toddlers." The site offers research articles, podcasts, video clips, and handouts to download on such topics as early learning, brain development, self-esteem, crying, influence of the father on a young child's development, and other subjects of interest to those who interact with young children.

Who Is Involved

2

Providing services and planning programs for very young children and their caregivers requires some understanding of the individuals involved: the audience, children and their caregivers (be they parents, other family members, or early child-care professionals); the leader of the program, the librarian/presenter; and, in fact, the entire library staff, who provide support for these programs and services. Interaction between these groups and a good understanding of their makeup help to create a fun learning experience for all involved.

IN THIS CHAPTER
- ✓ The Children
- ✓ The Adults
- ✓ Families
- ✓ Child-Care Providers, Early Childhood Educators, and Others
- ✓ The Librarian/Presenter
- ✓ Conclusion
- ✓ Resources

The Children

The baby sleeps, wakes, cries, accepts food and a clean diaper, observes the world for a moment, and then falls asleep again. The pretoddler picks up a board book, tastes it, puts it back down, and then repeats the process. There is not much learning going on—or so it seems to the uninitiated. In fact, the connections in these young children's brains are multiplying and working full speed through repetition and experience, so learning is constantly taking place.

How do you go about planning programs that will help create appropriate stimuli for the very young to learn, and what kinds of programs are appropriate? Some formal background in child development, including a realistic understanding of the very young child's abilities, skills, and needs, is important. For further education in these areas, look to college or community college courses and/or classes on topics such as children's mental and emotional development offered through local hospitals, clinics, or early childhood associations. As active promoters of emerging literacy experiences for the very young, librarians are in a unique position to help educate adults about creating stimulating learning environments for the children in their care.

When planning programs, it is important to consider the needs of both the little ones and the adults involved in their lives. Librarians should function as experts on how to read aloud, what to read aloud, and the benefits of reading aloud to very young children, but this requires more than merely demonstrating how and what to read. Our work includes talking with children and adults, encouraging children to imagine, to put their own words to pictures and link their own experiences and feelings to words. In short, we help children learn to derive meaning from words and pictures that relate to them, and we assist parents and other adult caregivers in encouraging this learning in their children. We are not, however, the experts in supplying diagnoses or evaluations of individual children. Still, we can direct the adults to information sources, support groups, and the real experts who can assist them.

When planning services and programs for very young children, it can be challenging to decide how to form the groupings. Should it be by actual age or by the children's abilities? Who decides where the child should be placed: the presenter or the parent? Throughout this text, and to keep things simple, I define the various age groups in the following manner:

- **Infant:** birth–12 months
- **Pretoddler:** 12–24 months
- **Toddler:** 24–36 months
- **Preschooler:** 3–5 years
- **Adult:** the primary parent or caregiver who has significant contact with the child at the program or elsewhere

For an alternative suggested grouping, one can refer to the classification of the National Association for the Education of Young Children, the world's largest organization that works on behalf of young children, which lists the age ranges as follows:

- **Infant:** birth–15 months
- **Toddler:** 12–36 months
- **Preschool:** 30–60 months (2.5–5 years)
- **Kindergarten:** enrolled in *any* public or private kindergarten

Classification available at: http://www.naeyc.org/files/academy/file/clarificationOnGroups.pdf.

The term "lapsit" has been used by libraries for storytime programs directed at the very young child and implies that an adult lap needs to accompany each child who attends. The ages for such programs can range from birth to 24 months.

This covers a wide range of developmental stages as well as the various abilities of each child. Some children are still observing their world from a static position, others have discovered their own mobility, and still others are ready for the "Me do!" of toddlerhood. The pretoddler child is at times defined as the period between the infant's total dependency on adults and the toddler's striving for independence. Getting ready to venture out into the world, the pretoddler still requires strong and immediate connection with the primary caregiver. This is why the adult is such an important participant in lapsit programs. Together the adult and child venture into the fascinating world of language.

Physically, children develop and master the large-motor skills first. Thus, little ones have more success with large movements, such as waving an entire arm, than with fine-motor skills, such as counting on fingers. For example, the rhyme "Eency Weency Spider" is easier for them to act out if it is changed to "The Great Big Spider," which allows them to use their whole bodies instead of trying to control only their fingers. These children are able to manipulate large objects, such as chunky crayons, to some degree.

Between the ages of 13 and 18 months, the child's brain starts to connect sounds, symbols, and concepts to the physical world. Children in this period can follow simple instructions, such as "Bring me the book" or "Stop," but their attention span is short. They are beginning to identify and name objects and to communicate using gestures and simple, one- or two-word sentences, but their verbalization skills are still limited: They can comprehend far more than they can verbalize. It is within this time period that most children begin determinedly manipulating the physical world around them.

Between 18 and 24 months of age, pretoddlers attain much greater control of large-motor movements and are able to do more with the physical world around them. They can jump on two feet, climb stairs, and explore their fine-motor skills. This is also when they start to concentrate on language and communication. Many children of this age become frustrated due to their inability to verbalize what they are feeling or want to know, which can lead to insecurity on the part of the children. However, they are developing speech and language skills more rapidly at this age than at any other, and they often have a vocabulary of about twenty words or more. The child needs extensive exposure to language, to practice and experience it, which can be accomplished through conversations with their caregivers, by listening to rhymes, songs, and stories, and by creating conversations with their toys or even themselves.

It is important for the adult to understand the child's methods of communicating. This can be done by "reading" the child's body language. Crying, turning away, wiggling, avoiding eye contact, and even falling asleep will let the adult know the child has had enough stimulation for now. Smiles, babbling, and gestures can be interpreted as things are going well. Some basic sign language can even been taught to the very young, the use of which seems to relieve some communication frustrations. For example, the sign for "more" is tapping the fingertips and thumbs of both hands together and the sign for "no" is snapping the pointer and middle finger down onto the thumb (as if imitating a duck's quack)—two words that, when used, help very young children communicate their needs to the adults around them. By giving the child time to examine and contemplate what is going on around him or her, an adult can make learning language skills a positive experience. Brief conversations, looking at one picture or page in a book, reciting a rhyme at bath time, or singing a lullaby at bedtime are ways of incorporating mini language-learning experiences throughout the child's day.

The adult also needs to be patient, giving the child time to take in what is going on around him or her, process it, and respond to it. To all very young children, the world is completely new, and they deserve the time needed to understand it. The Washington Research Institute uses the abbreviation C.A.R. (comment, ask, respond) to help adults remember this fact (for more information, see http://www.walearning.com/products/language-is-the-key/car-strategies). This skill can be demonstrated to a group by using a lift-the-flap or other participatory books. Before lifting a flap, ask simple questions about who or what might be under the flap; name something in the illustration and allow the children to discover it for themselves. Encourage the adults to take the children's lead and go through the story at their pace.

A child will often concentrate on a specific skill, giving it priority over others for a period of time. This may cause other skills to seem to recede for a while. This often continues until the specific new skill is mastered and is incorporated into the child's daily life. This is all part of the child's learning how to be a separate individual—a challenging and sometimes scary venture. The child will look to the familiar caregiver for support and reassurance, so separation anxiety is likely when the child is put into an unfamiliar situation or with strangers. Familiar routines, environments, and people, however, will help the pretoddler gain confidence and mastery of his or her world.

The Developmental Stages chart included here is a simple chart of basic developmental skills for children 12–24 months of age. Other versions are available in books and online, or through your state health department, local hospitals, early childhood agencies, and the like. For more information, check out the resources at the end of the chapter.

	Ages 12-18 months	Ages 18-24 months
Physical Development	• Can stand and sit alone • Crawls • Can bend over and pick things up • Can go up and down stairs–up by holding on to someone or something, and down by backing down the stairs on knees • Throws a large ball with two hands, and can also roll it	• Can kick a large ball • Can jump with two feet together • Begins to try running • Pulls pull-toys • Climbs on and into things, such as boxes • Can walk up and down stairs with assistance
Fine-Motor Skills	• Can carry objects when walking • Can push push-toys and cars along • Gestures or points to indicate things • Turns pages in a book but not individually • Loves to sort and dump things from containers • Scribbles using whole-arm movement • Begins to gain competency with thumb and forefinger pincer grasp • Waves bye-bye • Starts using spoon	• Able to throw smaller balls • Can build towers out of three to four blocks • Scribbles on paper, with arm movements tending to be a more vertical (up and down) action • Begins to manipulate objects, such as puzzle pieces, to fit in required space • Can use a spoon without help • Turns knobs
Intellectual and Language Development	• Has a vocabulary of 10-20 understandable words • Imitates others' words • Understands simple commands when given one step at a time • Starts to name and identify objects • Develops comprehension ahead of verbalization skills • Prefers the familiar • Is very sensory oriented–feel and touch • Babbles, incorporating real words and sounds • Begins to identify parts of body • Sees books as toys • Uses language to get adult's attention	• Has a vocabulary of several hundred words • Points to and identifies body parts • Identifies and names pictures of objects • Starts to overcome obstacles, such as opening a closed door • Can follow two or three simple directions • Remembers routines and patterns • Likes to echo people and repeats things • Starts to show preferences in making choices • Begins to notice time in such ways as to "now" and "later" • Likes to "read" or tell story to adult • Still invents words and is learning rules of grammar • Asks questions–lots of questions!
Social and Emotional Development	• Exhibits separation anxiety when separated from parent or other primary caregiver • Plays alone • Enjoys being held and read to, and feeling secure • Imitates others' actions • Likes to have an audience and applause–showmanship • Prefers individual, one-on-one attention • Starts to claim own possessions and space–"MINE!"	• Still has difficulty sharing • Self-centered • Likes to take short walks • Will play alongside other children doing the same things–parallel play • Starts to show sense of independence–"NO!" • Wants everything now • Tries to do things without assistance • Can get physically aggressive when frustrated

Reach Out and Read (http://www.reachoutandread.org) is a nonprofit organization that promotes reading aloud to children. A free developmentally appropriate book and parental advice about the importance of reading to children, especially the very young, is prescribed by the pediatrician at each checkup. Using the exam room and the waiting room, pediatricians and their staff can promote this program, which is available in English, Spanish, Chinese, and Vietnamese.

The Washington State Department of Early Learning offers a child developmental chart covering birth to six years of age (http://www.del.wa.gov/publications/esit/docs/PrescreenChart_English.pdf). Its Early Support for Infants and Toddlers (ESIT; http://www.del.wa.gov/development/esit/Default.aspx) provides access to a variety of resources related to child development. Under "Related Information," click on "ESIT publications and documents" to download the child development chart in other languages, such as English, Spanish, Chinese, Cambodian, Lao, Korean, Vietnamese, and Russian.

The Adults

What about the adults? How can understanding them help us create services and programs? The child does not grow in a vacuum. It is imperative that a caring adult act as a guide and participant in the child's life. It is necessary for the very young child's brain to be stimulated in order to develop and grow. This can only happen when someone creates a positive developmental climate for the child.

The term "adults" in this book will most often refer to parents. These can be first-time parents, experienced parents, teen parents, working parents, low-income parents, undereducated parents, or parents who speak a language other than English. If not a parent, then the adult is someone who cares for the child or has major ongoing responsibility for the child, perhaps a grandparent who has taken on this responsibility, willingly or not. Whoever the adults may be, they all have one thing in common: they want the best for their children.

Parents today find themselves pulled in many directions. Stress levels are often high, and some parents place unbearable pressure on themselves regarding their children's development. Many other parents may not be aware of the influence these few months have on the rest of their children's lives. "Welfare parents talk less to their toddlers than do either working-class parents or professional parents. According to the observational data, the average welfare child heard only 616 words per hour, the working-class child, 1,251 words per hour, and the professional child, 2,153 per hour" (Golinkoff and Hirsh-Pasek, 1999, 142). Parents for whom English is a second language (often referred to as ESL) may have reservations about their ability to speak English to their children or may feel self-conscious when they do. Teen parents may have difficulty reconciling their new role as a parent with that of being a teenager. Grandparents are often the ones providing day care, yet they may be unsure of what to do with the very young child in regard to today's standards. Many parents feel pressured because they want to "do it right" and at the right time, but they are sometimes unsure of what "it" is. They create their own tension, which needs to be minimized before the children can have a healthy and stimulating environment in which to learn and grow.

Adult caregivers need to be made aware that what children experience will influence their self-identity and social wellness as well as what they learn and how they grow. Emphasize to the adults how important it is that they do the following:

- Read to the children at least 15 minutes a day. It does not have to be done all at one time or even all from the same material. Read recipes, stories, the newspaper, grocery lists—anything and everything! Include songs and rhymes for variety.
- Incorporate books into a daily routine such as bedtime or after a meal, but find other times to share books as well.
- Use eye contact to involve the children, especially when sharing language through rhymes and songs.
- Be a role model for the children. Let very young children see how books are held and pages turned. Children should see the adult reading books, magazines, and newspapers. Sturdy board books and old catalogs will help children practice the skills they observe. Remember that children are copycats during this period.
- Make the experience fun. Be expressive while reading aloud, and allow the children to interact with them.
- Point to the printed text as it is read and identify words and letters.
- Use the public library. Economics as well as space considerations can make it difficult to have an extensive home library. Adults need to know what materials can be borrowed from the public library, how the library can direct them to needed services/agencies, and that there is no charge for these services, at least in the United States. Borrowing library materials is also a good way to sample books, audio material, or DVDs before purchasing. Children most often long to possess a much-loved, often-read favorite book.
- Give the children time to respond. Enthusiasm is wonderful, but adults need to remember that children's brains need time to process and absorb what is happening.

Families

The term "family" has changed, or, rather, it has expanded beyond its "traditional" definition. All families, diverse as they are, should be respected, not only for their differences, but also for their similarities to what had once been defined as the "average family." Families that have children with special needs, bilingual families, those in shelters or other emergency housing, teen parents, grandparents raising grandchildren, and other family groups all need support for giving their children the best possible environment in which to learn.

The Special-Needs Family

Mainstreaming has become the norm in American public schools, and the public library is required by law to provide access for children with special needs to attend programs, as stated in the Americans with Disabilities Act of 1990. (To read the ADA and its amendments as of 2008, use this link: http://www .ada.gov/pubs/ada.htm.) Quite often libraries include notices on program flyers requesting those requiring special accommodations to contact the library prior to the program. More often than not, however, special-needs children do not attend public programs. Ideally, libraries will create special programs, either in house or as outreach, to serve this group.

When developing such a program, you must first locate those families with special-needs children in your area. Check the local telephone book or other directories for listings of local chapters of national organizations, hospitals, or health centers that may have parent support groups, and then contact them to learn which programs and services you already offer may be of interest to them. Learning about their specific needs also enables you to adapt your existing program presentations to include these children. Other resources include mental health centers, community health centers, societies for the blind or hearing impaired, Easter Seals, programs for the developmentally delayed, community service centers, social services agencies, local school districts, and specialized schools. Librarians sometimes are uncomfortable with this area of service due to a lack of experience and training specific to special needs. The most important thing to remember is that, in many ways, all children are identical in their needs: They all need security, attention, exposure to developmental and language-building experiences, and a caring adult to guide them along the way. Consider offering workshops on the importance of reading to the very young for teachers at special-needs schools and agencies. Invite the families, too, who will also find such workshops informational and fun.

It can sometimes be challenging to select material to use in a program for special-needs groups. Often you can use the same resources as for the "average" children, but with greater sensitivity to how special materials or assistance might make the program more accessible. For example, when presenting a story program to deaf or hearing-impaired children, incorporate some sign language and/or enlist the aid of an interpreter. You may need to enlarge illustrations and include more tactile material, such as flannel-board stories, puppets, movable books, and the like. Allowing the children to touch story props, to give the bear puppet a hug, for example, or giving them the space and time to react to the story expands "storytime" to include more than spoken words. Some children need to know what is coming up next, so try to introduce the next segment with a picture. The adult may need to hear the presenter give the "okay" to step out of the room with the child for a moment to allow the child to "refocus" if overstimulated by the program. Accepting the children and interacting with them as they are is vitally important. Parents of special-needs children are often already very involved with their children. The presenter's ability to relax and display a positive attitude will let the adults know that sharing books and building language-learning experiences should be part of their children's lives as much as any other children's.

Following are some ideas for helping children strengthen certain skills by using fingerplays, rhymes, and songs found in a storytime. For words and directions, see chapter 4.

- Practicing standing and balance:
  - "Pop! Goes the Weasel" involves standing upright, hopping, and turning.
  - "Hickory, Dickory, Dock" involves standing upright, bending, and clapping.
- Developing visual tracking:
  - "Two Little Blackbirds" uses flannel-board pieces that are placed on a board and then moved, or puppets that change location.
  - The rhyme "Roly-Poly" can incorporate a puppet/doll or storytime mascot that is moved to various locations (e.g., "up," "down," etc.).
  - "Humpty Dumpty" is another rhyme that can be used for visual tracking of "up" and "down."
- Sitting upright:
  - "1, 2, 3, 4, 5, I Caught a Fish Alive" gives the children brief moments of sitting independently, reinforced with a positive hug.

- Naming parts of the body:
  - "Head and Shoulders, Knees and Toes"
  - "These Are Baby's Fingers"
- Identifying and moving body parts and learning different rhythms: Include musical activities. Integrate dance and movement so the children and adults have a positive interaction with sounds and rhythms. Remember to include large body movement especially; try different styles of music, and dance around the room.
- Developing hand-eye coordination: Provide large flannel pieces that children can select and then place on a flannel board: "Lots of Cars," a song from *Plant a Little Seed* by Nancy Stewart, is an example of what works well. Make simple felt car shapes in bright colors that the children can place on the flannel board themselves, with minimal assistance from their caregivers.
- Participating in activities and recognizing materials: Use titles that offer lots of repetition and rhyme: *Brown Bear, Brown Bear, What Do You See?* by Bill Martin Jr. is a good example, especially if used at every program.
- Creating bonds between children and adults: Encourage touch between the adults and children by using interactive rhymes, fingerplays, and songs.
- Practicing eye contact: Some special-needs children shy away from human eye contact. Use puppets to help bridge the gap between presenter and participants: "Here Comes a Mouse," from *Catch Me and Kiss Me and Say It Again* by Clyde Watson, can be performed with a mouse puppet that the presenter then uses to give each child a little tickle.

Programs alone are not the only ways to serve families with special-needs children. Having material from special-needs agencies available at programs helps families become aware of the services available to them. Families may need assistance in finding these resources, whether online, in print, or organizational. Some states have councils or committees that offer grants to further inclusion; for example, the New York State Developmental Disabilities Planning Council (http://ddpc.ny.gov) supplies grants to public libraries to support this area of service.

Daily life can be very stressful for special-needs families. What better way to serve them than to provide a fun, supportive, and caring environment and programs in which they can participate? Even if an adult caregiver and child simply observe from the back of the room, they are still part of the group and can glean things to share at home.

The Bilingual Family

American society has been enriched by the many cultures that have come together to create it. It is important that these various cultures be respected and preserved. Some children hear their parents speaking only in their native, non-English language at home, some adults cannot read English, and some adults live secluded from the greater community. The sounds that make up the English language can be heard throughout the storytime program, and participation is encouraged. The librarian should be aware that a word or phrase in English may have a different meaning or connotation in another language and be sensitive to those cultural cues whenever possible. In the United States, libraries offer storytimes in English, with some being able to offer them in other languages. In these cases, when possible, the program presenter should be someone with a good command of the specific non-English language; if this is not practical, an interpreter should be on hand. In either case, careful planning and rehearsal prior to the program will help keep the presentation organized.

Immigrant families who attend programs for the very young can benefit in a number of ways:

- The programs expose them to simple English vocabulary, and they will sometimes recognize the easy-to-follow storylines as being related to folktales from their own background. Sharing fingerplays, action rhymes, and songs is a wonderful way to share cultures.
- Reading simple stories and repeating rhymes and songs with the children are entertaining ways to practice English. The adults can gain confidence in their language abilities, and the positive reinforcement they receive from the nonjudgmental children adds fun to this language-building experience.
- The programs provide a comfortable setting for networking between the adults in attendance. This is a very attractive opportunity for immigrant families who may often feel quite isolated.

For a diverse program, display books in languages other than English and direct the families to them. Reading a story in English and then having the same story available in a patron's native language builds a bridge between the two languages. If you plan to use your usual English materials, remember to speak clearly and slowly, but naturally. Demonstrate with words and actions, use visuals, and, most important, relax and smile to put your participants at ease.

Programs for those new to the English language are sometimes designated in the literature as ESL (English as a second language), EFL (English as a foreign language), and ELL (English-language learners) or ESOL (English for speakers of other languages). The EFL Playhouse (http://www.esl4kids.net/index.html) is an online resource for preschool and elementary teachers that provides links to many other ESL and EFL sites for fingerplays, language resources, and teaching tips.

Teen Parents

The teen parent population in the community can be located through vocational schools, alternative high schools, welfare centers, health clinics, Head Start centers, and other child-care facilities. Teen parents need information about basic child development, parenting strategies, and how to deal with the stress in their lives due to child-rearing demands. They often have little or no idea of the important role that language and interaction play in their children's lives. They often did not have the childhood experience of regularly being read aloud to, and it is also likely that they are not readers either. The librarian can become their role model. Since childhood for these parents is not in the distant past, some may remember a story, rhyme, or song. They need to be encouraged to share these memories with their children. Teen parents often respond well to hands-on experiences, and programs for the very young child are exactly that. Teens learn as they teach their children. Some communities have mentor programs for teen parents, and through training, the mentors can learn to pass along the importance of reading aloud to very young children.

Grandparents

Many more grandparents are taking on the role of full-time or part-time child-care providers. This group of adults needs the materials, services, and support of the public library because grandparents often have limited resources. The library's storytime programs become a way for them to provide very young children with a social and educational experience. The library can also support grandparents as they try to help their grandchildren navigate this new contemporary world, which is so different from when they were parents. Parenting strategies they once firmly believed in may now be questioned. "Don't pick the baby up, or you'll spoil him" has given way to the realization that little ones need the physical closeness of caring adults. These programs help them refresh their own memories of stories, rhymes, and songs and can educate them about the new research regarding the importance of the first years of life. Grandparents may be overwhelmed by the wealth of current child development information available. The librarian can make this information-rich, new world more manageable.

Grandparents may also have more time to spend interacting with their grandchildren, creating a stimulating learning environment and a better chance for future success in school and in the world than they or their children had. Be aware of things that might unintentionally make it difficult for grandparents to participate. Be conscious that something as simple as having chairs in the room, around the edge of the group, is helpful for participants with physical limitations. When demonstrating action rhymes, offer alternatives so that senior caregivers feel included; instead of having them lift the children up in the air, suggest that they raise just the children's arms. Provide these caregivers with resources and materials they will find useful, including information about legal, educational, support, and community agencies.

Child-Care Providers, Early Childhood Educators, and Others

The very young child may at times be brought to a program by a non–family member. Nannies, babysitters, and child-care workers may welcome services and programs that help them connect with the children and develop a support network. Some may not speak the same language at home as the children they care for here, may be unfamiliar with the customs of the area, or may not have an early childhood background. Providing access to materials, services, and caring individuals helps them create an environment that enriches young children's lives and their own. These caregivers will find at these programs opportunities for further education and networking with others working in the field of early childhood through continuing education programs offered in house, resources provided by the library's website, or talking with other program participants.

Time and resources are often limited for this group, so outreach is also important. Through mailings, workshops, free materials, and services, they can gain confidence, receive support, and develop the ability to serve their youngest clients better. Your efforts will reach further into the community than you might imagine.

The Librarian/Presenter

The children's librarian has been the usual person assigned to serve the very young and their caregivers, although the teen librarian or other staff librarian is at times the presenter. A nonprofessional, an early childhood caregiver/educator, or even a volunteer may have to take on the role. No matter who the presenters are, they all require information, training, and the right attitude to make a successful program.

A basic understanding of early childhood development can be obtained through formal classes, attending workshops covering the topic, and reading the literature. Observing lapsit programs and gaining practical experience by presenting programs expand that knowledge. Though the presenter's expertise may not necessarily be early childhood, the presenter needs the ability to connect caregiving adults with materials and resources in the field that will help them create an environment and foundation their children can build on. Staff members need to be aware of not only print and electronic resources but also the local referral agencies in the area.

Recognizing materials that are age appropriate is the presenter's responsibility. The adult participants will become familiar with what works best to give the child an enjoyable language experience. Learning what is age appropriate can help overzealous adults relax and enjoy the stage their children are in now, rather than rushing on to the next one.

Conclusion

Today's families are all unique and face many challenges. The stress and pressure come from all sides: economic hardships such as poverty, poor diet, homelessness; global conflicts; adult family members absent due to work schedules, incarceration, or military service—to name a few. Even families that do not face these hardships feel an impact from them. Stress can also come from the intense pressure parents put on themselves to ensure their children have the best start possible. Constantly comparing their children's skills and abilities to others' can lead to dissatisfaction with their children's development. All parents want to help their children gain the skills and knowledge to be successful in life. By understanding the families you serve, or hope to serve, you can better design your services to meet their needs.

Programming for the very young requires the library to accommodate a wide variety of participants, with children at many levels of development and having different backgrounds and needs. Children in the age range of 12–24 months benefit from the stimulation provided by interaction with the adults, which helps strengthen brain connections and thereby helps develop children's skills and emotional responses. Each child proceeds through experiences at a unique pace. The adults share a positive language experience with their children that they can re-create on their own at home. Storytimes for the very young are far from just entertainment. They are language-learning experiences shared by child and adult that just happen to be a lot of fun. They empower and educate the parent/adult caregiver toward developing the child's full potential.

Resources

Development

Carlson, Frances M. *Essential Touch: Meeting the Needs of Young Children.* Washington, DC: National Association for the Education of Young Children, 2006.

Diamond, Marian, and Janet Hopson. *Magic Trees of the Mind: How to Nurture Your Child's Intelligence, Creativity, and Healthy Emotions from Birth through Adolescence.* New York: Dutton, 1998.

Golinkoff, Roberta Michnick, and Kathy Hirsh-Pasek. *How Babies Talk: The Magic and Mystery of Language in the First Three Years of Life.* New York: Dutton, 1999.

Hannaford, Carla. *Smart Moves: Why Learning Is Not All in Your Head.* Revised ed. Alexander, NC: Great River Books, 2007.

Hirsh-Pasek, Kathy, and Roberta Michnick Golinkoff, with Diane Eyer. *Einstein Never Used Flash Cards: How Our Children Really Learn—and Why They Need to Play More and Memorize Less.* Emmaus, PA: Rodale, 2003.

Morgan, Linda. *Beyond Smart: Boosting Your Child's Social, Emotional, and Academic Potential.* Seattle: ParentMap, 2010.

Stokes, Beverly. *Amazing Babies: Essential Movement for Your Baby in the First Year.* Toronto, ON: Move Alive Media, 2002.

Stoltz, Dorothy, Marisa Conner, and James Bradberry. *The Power of Play: Designing Early Learning Spaces.* Chicago: American library Association, forthcoming.

Stoppard, Miriam. *First-Time Parents: What Every New Parent Needs to Know.* New York: DK Publishing, 2006.

Language and Literacy

Apel, Kenn, and Julie J. Masterson. *Beyond Baby Talk: From Sounds to Sentences: A Parent's Complete Guide to Language Development.* Roseville, CA: Prima Publishing, 2001.

Associated Press. "Unraveling How Kids Become Bilingual So Easily." MSNBC, updated July 20, 2009. http://www.msnbc.msn.com/id/32013276/ns/health-kids_andpar.

Blakemore, Caroline J., and Barbara Weston Ramirez. *Baby Read-Aloud Basics: Fun and Interactive Ways to Help Your Little One Discover the World of Words.* New York: AMACOM, 2006.

Galinsky, Ellen. *Mind in the Making: The Seven Essential Life Skills Every Child Needs.* New York: HarperStudio, 2010.

Golinkoff, Roberta Michnick, and Kathy Hirsh-Pasek. *How Babies Talk: The Magic and Mystery of Language in the First Three Years*. New York: Dutton, 1999.

McGuinness, Diane. *Growing a Reader from Birth: Your Child's Path from Language to Literacy*. New York: W.W. Norton, 2004.

Medina, John. *Brain Rules for Baby: How to Raise a Smart and Happy Child from Zero to Five*. Seattle: Pear Press, 2010.

Sousa, David. *How the Brain Learns to Read*. Thousand Oaks, CA: Corwin Press, 2005.

Steiner, Naomi, and Susan Hayes. *7 Steps to Raising a Bilingual Child*. New York: AMACOM, 2008.

Grandparents

Johnson, Craig. "Economy Sends More Kids to Grandma's House." CNN.com, July 28, 2011. http://www.cnn.com/2011/LIVING/07/28/grandfamilies.census.rise/index.html?iref=allsearch.

E-resources

American Association of Retired People. http://www.aarp.org. AARP offers information for seniors in many areas, including grandparenting. On the homepage, click on "Home and Family" and then "Family and Friends." The AARP website also has a search box where you can search for the term "grandparent." Subjects covered include raising grandchildren, family relationships, financial health, and providing child care for grandchildren. Also included are links to sites that offer statistics and reports in this area of interest.

American Library Association. http://www.ala.org/. Born to Read, http://www.ala.org/alsc/issuesadv/borntoread, a site created by the Association for Library Service to Children (ALSC), provides tips for reading, book sharing, websites, information on emergent literacy, and booklists that can be shared with parents. Every Child Ready to Read® @ your library®, http://www.everychildreadytoread.org/, is a joint project of the ALSC and the Public Library Association, both of which are divisions of the American Library Association. This site provides workshop information, handouts, and research on the topic of early literacy.

Child and Family WebGuide, Tufts University. http://www.cfw.tufts.edu. This directory lists sites presenting childhood development research and advice that have been evaluated by graduate students at Tufts University.

CHAPTER 2: Who Is Involved

Frank Porter Graham Child Development Institute (FPG). http://www.fpg.unc
.edu/about-fpg. The FPG studies important issues facing young children
and their families, using this information to enhance policy, improve
practice, and inform.

Institute for Learning and Brain Sciences (I-LABS), University of Washington.
http://ilabs.washington.edu. I-LABS "is an interdisciplinary center
dedicated to discovering the core principles of human learning, with
special emphasis on work that will enable all children from 0 to 5 to
achieve their full potential."

Talaris Research Institute. http://www.talaris.org. This website provides easy-to-
understand research and information on brain and behavioral development
for parents and other adults who interact with young children and their
families.

Washington State Department of Early Learning. http://www.del.wa.gov.
This site offers links to downloadable development charts, for example, one
that covers birth to six years of age (http://www.del.wa.gov/publications/esit/
docs/PrescreenChart_English.pdf).

Young Children, National Association for the Education of Young Children.
http://www.naeyc.org/yc. This professional journal of the NAEYC
concentrates on topics and issues related to the field of early childhood
education.

Zero to Three. http://www.zerotothree.org. This national, nonprofit,
multidisciplinary organization informs, educates, and supports adults
who influence the lives of infants and toddlers.

Service Areas

3

IN THIS CHAPTER

✓ In-House Services

✓ Outreach Programs

✓ Partnerships, Funding, and Grants

✓ Resources

Programming tends to be the primary focus when considering services for the very young, but serving children 12 to 24 months old and their caregivers needs to extend beyond that. Library in-house services should include child-friendly facilities, trained staff, and a collection that is appropriate for this age group. Outreach programs need to respond to the needs of the underserved community. Networking with outside agencies, both public and private, helps tie programs into local and national efforts. Partnerships with public, private, and governmental groups will strengthen services to the very young.

Examining all the possibilities of service can leave you overwhelmed and feeling responsible for library services that seem to be growing exponentially. Keep in mind your library's mission statement. Try to learn the needs and characteristics of the target community prior to initiating services. Then evaluate in-house and outreach programs to determine how well they meet the needs of the community. This chapter will help demystify service delivery and direct you in this area. It will also demonstrate that the librarian does not have to do it all alone.

In-House Services

It is important to consider the resources you currently have before developing or expanding services for the very young and their caregivers. Services include staffing, the physical area and layout, collections, and any "extras" your library/ school or care facility intend to provide. After this self-evaluation, you can make decisions concerning future service plans.

Staffing and Training

Staffing has a direct impact on the amount and kinds of services that can be offered. In many cases, there is one professional who has training and experience in children's library services along with some background in child development. This person should be familiar with the developmental stages and needs of children, be knowledgeable about children's literature, have a basic understanding of early literacy, and possess the ability to interact positively with children and their caregivers. However, this person is only one member of the team that supports and encourages people of all ages to use the library and venture into the world of language. The entire staff, professionals and nonprofessionals, should be aware of patrons' needs and their possible misgivings about visiting the library. One of the roles of the specialist is to help staff members who do not usually serve children understand why serving the very young is an important part of the library's mission. Inform them about the role they play in creating a welcoming and friendly environment for both children and adults. Make sure the staff is aware of the lifelong educational impact such programs and services can have on children's lives. Often people, especially those who do not directly serve children, view lapsit programs as simply "fun time," but these programs are much more: they are "purposeful play," a term used by Baltimore County Public Library to describe its intention behind Storyville (http://www.bcplstoryville.org/storyville_about .html). Build understanding and strong support for children's services among the staff by helping them to understand that programs and services for the very young help develop lifelong learners and readers. Incorporate a mini training session as part of a staff meeting or during an informal conversation. Use handouts or e-mails to share facts and tips on early literacy. Make sure the staff is aware of what is happening in children's services, be it an upcoming program or new toys in the children's area. It takes the whole staff to promote programs and services for the very young, to point out and encourage the use of age-appropriate materials, and to spread the word about the importance of reading aloud to very young children. All staff can do several things to support this area of service:

- Point out where the board books are located.
- Reassure an adult that checking out the same picture book for the "umpteenth time" is absolutely okay because children learn through repetition.
- Offer a storytime flyer to an adult with a baby or young toddler.
- Assure the adult that "some days are like that" while offering a sticker to a fussy child.
- Display booklists with suggested titles for reading aloud or on topics of interest, such as early literacy or potty training.

Facilities

The actual physical area and layout influence how this clientele is served. Is the area visible to the staff for supervision? If there is a separate parenting collection, is it close enough to the children's books for parents to maintain supervision over their children? Parents should not leave children alone, even "just for a moment," while they are busy elsewhere. Look at your area to see if it is appealing and encourages reading experiences between the children and adults. A variety of chair designs can encourage parent-child pairs to cuddle up and share stories. Styles range from comfortable overstuffed chairs, rocking chairs, and soft foam chairs to beanbag chairs and floor pillows. Be sure to examine the seating options monthly as a safety precaution. If the space available is not suited for furniture, a brightly colored rug can help define the reading area. Some facilities can accommodate large pieces, such as a playhouse or a giant stuffed toy to lean upon. Companies that specialize in early childhood equipment offer a variety of interactive centers with age-appropriate activities, such as sliding beads, turning gears, letter blocks, mirrors, and so on. These centers can be freestanding or attached to a wall or bookcase. Part of many pediatricians' waiting rooms for years, they now have begun to find their place in the library. Some libraries have centers designed specifically for their space and decor and feature activities that help develop early literacy skills. For example, the Arabian branch of the Scottsdale Public Library in Scottsdale, Arizona, has a freestanding wall with cushions and curves to allow people to wander around and try the various activities. Some facilities will design and create an entire area with very young children in mind. Baltimore County Public Library's Storyville, at the Rosedale and Woodlawn branches, is one such center: "a place where books and purposeful play come together to provide valuable experiences that nurture young children and support parents and caregivers in their role as their child's first and best teacher" (http://www.bcplstoryville.org/storyville_tour.html). By searching the Internet using the words "early learning centers in libraries" or "early literacy centers in libraries," you can find an assortment of learning centers from the simple to elaborate.

Specifically designed centers are not the only way to designate space for the children's area. Posters, especially bright, colorful, story-related designs, are wonderful additions and relatively affordable; for durability, laminate them, if possible. Remember that children love to look at photos and illustrations of other children. Place some of the decorations at a child's-eye level. You can also use fabric to define the children's area. Drape brightly colored yardage across a wall, or use chiffon so that the colors change where they overlap. To ensure safety, make sure whatever you use is securely in place and out of the reach of curious children.

Next, you should consider how accessible the collection is. Board books are best suited for this age group. Can the children reach them, sort through them, and replace them? Are they kept on low shelves or are they in boxes on top of the bookcase? If children cannot reach the books, what good are they? In fact, it is quite likely that children will try to climb the shelves in an attempt to reach the books. To head off such a potentially dangerous situation, organize board books at a child's-eye level. Place them in colorful plastic boxes or crates or in book racks that can be left on low tables. The decision as to how to catalog board books can also affect how they are stored; for example, there is a difference between a generic browsing collection and one that is organized by authors' last names. See the following Collections section for more information.

It should not be considered a luxury to have additional types of in-house materials beyond board books, as these will help children to develop language and reading skills. For example, we added a simple stacking toy to the children's area in our library that the children can enjoy without creating too much noise, and also while practicing skills such as sorting, hand-eye coordination, and object manipulation. It is made of vinyl, so it is also easy to keep clean. Some locations have enough space for building blocks, not necessarily made of wood, but of cardboard, vinyl, or foam. Puzzles with just a few pieces (four to six) are another fun activity that gives the child a sense of accomplishment. Puppets and dolls encourage dramatic play and storytelling by both the child and the adult. I have often seen a puppet serve to initiate a dialogue between generations. You can include items that can be used for "purposeful play" (e.g., Baltimore County Public Library's Storyville) in the learning area.

When creating a child-welcome and child-friendly environment, remember to ensure that the area is also a safe one. Check regularly for small or sharp objects that might find their way into little mouths. Cover electrical outlets with safety covers (available at many grocery, department, and hardware stores). Keep cords out of the reach of inquiring fingers. Cushion sharp corners with foam or commercially available plastic bumpers. Toys or puppets in the area should be suitable for the children under three and clean; check them regularly, discarding or repairing as necessary.

You should also look at other areas of your facility, the restrooms in particular, to determine if they are suitable for serving the very young and their caregivers. Something as simple as having changing tables/areas in both the men's and women's restrooms will make bringing children to the library more convenient for either parent.

Collections

The collection holds the treasures that children and adults seek, so it should include a good representation of books suitable for ages 12 to 24 months (see chapter 4 for recommended titles). Board books will make up the majority of this collection because children this age have not yet developed the fine-motor skills necessary for turning thin paper pages. Fingerplay books, Mother Goose titles, and audio materials add depth to the collection. All of these materials help the adult expand the language "lessons" with sight and sound, touch and action, enabling the child to have a total sensory experience with language, thereby reinforcing perceptions and concepts to help develop communication skills. Some libraries use colored dots to identify the age-appropriateness of books; if you do this, do not forget to provide a key to explain what the colors mean.

The following are common characteristics of books appropriate for this age group:

- Sturdy pages that can stand up to rough usage without ripping
- Illustrations that are clear, bright, and colorful and include pictures of other children
- Sized to fit in a child's hand
- Brief text and simple plot that may reflect a child's daily activities or experiences
- White space on the page that provides a sort of "rest spot" for the child, making it easier to examine and absorb what is pictured

Child-care providers and educators can place a high demand on the collection, so it may be advisable to present or package the collection in nonstandard ways. For example, Washington's King County Library System maintains *Books to Grow On* and *Books to Grow On for Toddlers*, theme kits consisting of age-appropriate books, curriculum ideas, adult support materials, and some type of enhancement (e.g., a puppet or toy). Originally created for day-care providers and early childhood educators, these collections have proven to be very popular with the community at large, especially parents.

Collection guides help the adults access materials. Printed guides and online resources can include the following:

- Booklists of recommended, age-appropriate titles for the very young
- Lists of board books and suggested authors
- Lists of nonprint materials recommended for children that include information on how to use them appropriately

- Guides to books on parenting skills and such concerns as reading aloud to children, discipline, toilet training, anger management, knowing your one-year-old, sibling rivalry, and so forth
- Activity sheets of fingerplays, songs, and crafts that the adults and children can use at home to create a language experience
- Titles on such topics as fingerplays, music, child safety, and so on, to help adults who work with children

Expand the collection to include nonprint material, such as CDs that include traditional songs, nursery rhymes, children's stories, lullabies, and even classical music. Try to keep this collection close to the children's area to encourage browsing by the adults without their having to leave their children alone. Parents can use these nonprint materials to encourage interaction with their children and as an introduction to new artists and material.

Access to the collection is important. Signage, including floor plans, can provide visual clues to the collection's contents and layout. Handouts describing the children's collection are also useful takeaways for adults. Be sure to include the various collections on the library's website, highlighting new or innovative collections and services. This electronic information needs to be accessible, intuitive, and navigable, so design the website accordingly. Doing so may even inspire adults to visit the library.

Programs

Programming for the very young should be integrated into the overall mission statement for the organization. Create programs for different audiences. The most familiar type of program is the storytime, in which adults and children participate together. Because storytime is an obvious program choice, the majority of this book focuses on helping you to design your own. You can, however, also develop workshops for adults only on such topics such early literacy, the importance of reading aloud, and so forth.

Including very young children in programs usually reserved for older children is another possibility. Although summer reading programs are traditionally aimed at older children, adding a component for the very young does not need to be complicated. Theme and artwork can be the same for both age groups, but you can target the very young by including toddler-friendly activities rather than just counting minutes or books to show progress. Create record forms that resemble a bingo card or the path on a game board, with activities repeated to match the form you have created. Each time a child completes an early literacy activity, it can be checked off in some way. Possible activities include these:

- Visit the library and check out a book.
- Look at a book together.
- Read a story about going to the farm/zoo/store and then go there.
- Point out the first letter of the child's name found in the words of a story.
- Meet the children's librarian.
- Sing a song.
- Do an action rhyme.
- Play with sounds and words (Dr. Seuss works great for this).

If rewards are part of the summer reading program, select something that is safe for very young children. Incentives could be a board book, bib, baby "sippy" cup, or growth chart. Many commercial companies will personalize items with your organization or program name and logo. For more ideas on activities for developing readers and brain games to play with the very young, see the resources in chapter 5.

"Leave No Pre-Schooler or Toddler Behind: Summer Reading Programs and Our Youngest Patrons," a paper presented by Pamela Main-Diaz, Sharon Deeds, and Debbie Noggle at the Public Library Association's 2006 conference, focused on summer programming for the very young. PLA offers a DVD of the recorded session with the handouts that is available for purchase at http://www.associationarchives.com/SITES/pla. You can find information about this presentation on blogs as well, including the official *PLA Blog* at http://plablog.org/2006/03/leave-no-preschooler-or-notes-in-your-hotel-room-behind-part-deux.html. For additional program suggestions, see *Children's Services: Partnerships for Success* by Betsy Diamant-Cohen (2010).

Outreach Programs

On the whole, library programs and collections are used by those who already know about them and have the inclination to take advantage of them. However, not everyone in the community is a reader or library user. It is not enough to create wonderful in-house services and programs; we need to expand beyond the confines of the library walls. It is the nonusers and nonreaders who especially need to hear the message about how important reading is in a child's first few years of life. They need to become aware of how the library can help them to interact with their very young children and to supply enjoyable language-building experiences during those crucial first years of life.

Who Are "They"?

Most of us would like to reach everyone, but limited staff and resources make it necessary to set priorities and determine a target audience, for example, parents with very young children who are "at risk." Often these include teen parents, families new not only to the area but to the United States, families who do not speak English or understand the concept of a "free" library, families at or below poverty level, migrant workers, and so on. Helping an adult and a very young child discover a new world of language together may influence not only the child but the entire family.

Teachers and caregivers of the very young are an important target group as well. Private and government agencies can pinpoint target audiences within their service areas. For example, some agencies offer a mentoring program that pairs an individual or family with a support person. These mentors, when trained, can promote and disseminate information about the importance of talking and reading aloud to very young children. Libraries can offer literacy workshops for agency staff, programs for the families they serve, and/or handout materials explaining the importance and many benefits of reading to very young children.

Transportation is an almost insurmountable obstacle for some families, especially low-income ones. Consider providing outreach in areas that have limited public transportation or are underserved by other agencies that could promote the importance of reading aloud to very young children.

Once a target group is decided upon, you need to connect with them. It is essential not to assume anything. Many people have no concept of what a library is or does. Just the fact that one can borrow a book and take it home might amaze some people. When meeting with these groups, the simpler the program presentation, the better it is likely to be received. Keep a conversational tone throughout your presentation. Provide handouts, written in the audience members' native languages, if possible, to enable the participants to review what you have presented at their own pace.

Where Are They?

You can find your target audiences by checking in the local yellow pages, with the state child-care licensing department, with social service agencies, and with other education and child development organizations to determine area needs. Conferences for child-care providers and early-childhood educators also provide a way to locate people who would benefit by connecting with the library. Community colleges that offer early childhood development classes for adults and children are another source, as they may have long wait lists; if so, you will have identified a need in your area. Groups that might be interested in working with the library include these:

- Child-care centers
- Professional associations
- Parent support groups
- Head Start and Early Head Start sites
- Family support agencies
- Relocation or immigrant centers
- Alternative high schools and adult education facilities
- Community colleges, especially those with child-care centers and/ or child-development degree programs
- Hospitals, pediatricians, and family clinics
- Early childhood educators
- Food banks
- Recreational agencies, such as the Boys and Girls Clubs of America

What Can We Offer?

Since outreach implies "going out," be aware of the impact this will have on the collection, staffing needs, and other services already in place in the library building. Extending a service or program that cannot be supported tends to undermine good intentions. Some services may require extensive planning time. Others place further demands on staff and resources at a location other than the library. Professional librarians may be the only qualified presenters for certain programs, whereas volunteers might be trained to do other programs. Before reaching out, ask the difficult questions and evaluate what already exists:

- Is the program to be part of a series or a one-time event?
- What do you currently offer in the way of programs and services for families with very young children?
- Do other programs already exist in your community but with waiting lists to attend?
- What do the local demographics tell you about the community?
- What agencies in the community are serving the very young and their caregivers?
- What is the biggest obstacle preventing families from attending in-house programs and taking advantage of your services?
- Are there statistics to support the need for outreach programs and services?
- What is the purpose and goal of outreach?

Possible Outreach Services

Quite often, libraries use newsletters as a way to disseminate information about their materials and services, either in "hard copy" on paper or via an electronic medium, such as e-mail. The paper variety requires staff time to develop, write, print, proof, and mail, but sometimes a paper copy is the most appropriate format to give out. Costs associated with staff time, supplies, and postage make electronic newsletters an increasingly more attractive option, and they are faster to produce, update, and distribute. Be sure to take into account how an electronic newsletter will look and function when downloaded and printed out because you, and those on your e-mailing list, may want to have this option. Content for newsletters should include basic information about library services and programs. In addition, child development, books, rhymes, songs to share, and suggestions of ways to enhance the language-learning experience are all possible topics for inclusion.

Mailing lists are also easier to create and maintain electronically. Develop a mailing list of those involved with the lives of very young children. Newsletters sent to child-care agencies, pediatricians or family health clinics, early childhood education centers, and so forth, will keep those communities aware of the library and how it reinforces their objectives of supporting families with young children.

Community events are great forums for spreading the word that the library is for little ones. Events take place in community centers, parks, YMCAs, hospitals, shopping malls, schools—just about anywhere. They may celebrate family or culture or be a promotion of some kind, perhaps focusing on child safety or back-to-school readiness. Taking part in these events provides an opportunity to remind parents, caregivers, early childhood educators, health professionals, and others that the library is part of their team to help children develop to their highest potential. Such events are excellent opportunities to reach out to the non–library user. Host a table or booth displaying library materials and services for the very young, and provide a fun activity, such as making bookmarks, getting a sticker, or hearing a story on site. Consider distributing free local parenting newspapers and magazines at the library, and get on their e-mail lists to receive announcements about community events for families.

Creating collections specifically for outreach is another good option. Locating a collection at an Early Head Start center, for example, allows the librarian to connect with the director and teachers when collections are replenished or rotated, ideally leading to an ongoing relationship. Since it is difficult for sites with large enrollments and many staff to get to the library, having the library members come to them is often very much appreciated. You can place picture-book collections in private and public child-care centers, Head Start program sites, shelters, and food banks on a rotating basis. Some organizations have programs that train volunteers to read aloud to children in doctors' waiting rooms, food distribution centers, shelters, and so on. Training these volunteers is one way librarians can reach out into more areas of the community.

Outreach can also mean varying or expanding a traditional service. Bookmobiles extend the library materials and services to those who are unable to get to the library building. The King County Library System (KCLS) in Washington State has created two mobile outreach services specifically aimed at young children and those in child-care settings. ABC Express is a bookmobile-type bus that visits child-care centers and neighborhoods in the KCLS service area. Provided once a month at selected sites, it gives children and their caregivers an opportunity to select books, music, movies, and other materials they find interesting. Library2Go! is a relatively new service, similar to ABC Express but using specially outfitted vans rather than larger, bus-sized vehicles. Staffing is shared by community libraries and Central Outreach Services. These mini bookmobiles visit smaller family home day cares and community sites. Enhancements such as handouts, newsletters offering literacy tips, activity suggestions, and booklists of resources are being developed. When time allows, the KCLS staff on board demonstrates action rhymes or share songs or a story to augment the library experience.

Give-away programs are highly visible ways to do outreach. Most popular is the book give-away program for new babies. It encourages new parents to read to their children and lets them know they are welcome to visit the library with babies in tow. Cost, however, is a major factor with this type of program, so outside funding may be needed. For example, in Washington State, the Read Me a Story program was funded by a coalition of the King County Library System, the Bellevue Friends of the Library, and the local Overlake Hospital Medical Center. New parents in the hospital's birth center received a bib printed with "Read Me a Story," a coupon redeemable for a free board book at the Bellevue Public Library, and information on the reasons to read to your baby, how to make time for reading, and where to read, as well as suggestions for rhymes and songs. Some libraries have adjusted the target age for programs like this to include the "older" child (12-plus months). Such programs may have an increased impact on the interaction between adult and child, depending on the child's stage of development. Board books, CDs of children's rhymes or songs, bibs, and so forth, are all possible give-away items. KCLS also created a DVD to promote reading aloud to children; it explains what prereading skills are and what library storytime is all about and includes a sample story read aloud. KCLS distributes copies of this DVD to pediatricians' offices, clinics, health departments, and so on, and they are free for people to take home and keep.

Presenting workshops for early childhood educators and child-care providers can enable the librarian to enlist more people in the drive to promote early foundations for literacy and the importance of the early years for mental and emotional development. Workshops may cover an introduction to library services and materials, how and what to read to very young children, and how to incorporate language-learning experiences into daily routines. Other possible topics for workshops include those that support certification requirements for child-care providers and early childhood educators. Library materials and their use, for example, are part of the national curriculum guidelines for certification as a Child Development Associate. Requirements for becoming a qualified instructor vary by state, so be sure to investigate the requirements for your area. It may be easier to host such courses at your location using outside instructors. In any case, the librarian has the opportunity to spread the word that reading to very young children and conversing with them about books are important, and that the library is available to assist in the venture. For example, Multnomah County Library in Oregon offers a variety of educational programs for parents (https://multcolib.org/parents/programs-parents) and educators (https://multcolib.org/early-literacy-programs-educators), and KCLS hosts at various locations STARS (State Training and Registry System) programs that meet the state's continuing education requirements for early child-care providers and educators. Another option is to offer workshops to PEPS (Program for Early Parent Support) and other parenting groups at community centers or religious sites.

Story programs that are prepared for use in the library can also be used for outreach. The participants have a chance to see an actual role model demonstrating how to read aloud to children, what kind of materials are developmentally appropriate while still being fun, and what activities can encourage reading. Locales for such programs can include the following:

- Social service agencies
- Food banks
- Shelters
- Development centers
- Alternative schools—teen parent classes
- Health clinics
- Welfare offices
- Corrections facilities
- Migrant camps
- Head Start/Early Head Start sites
- ESL centers or relocation centers

These programs, usually presented by a children's librarian, can place a high demand on the librarian's time, and in-house services may be disrupted. To counter this, train volunteers to present story programs out in the community, thus increasing the availability of this kind of program without placing additional stress on staff. Multnomah County Library uses trained volunteers for its Books While You Wait program, which takes children's books and reading aloud (including multilingual materials) to waiting rooms in agencies where parents and children go for medical or social services.

Outreach programs created by private and national organizations are another option for local libraries. Although there are costs involved, the program components come already designed and manufactured, thus saving time and costs in the long run. Start by investigating some of the following programs and websites:

- Born to Read—It's Never Too Early to Start!, www.ala.org/alsc/issuesadv/borntoread/. This program is from the Association for Library Service to Children, a division of the American Library Association.
- Every Child Ready to Read® @ your library®, www.everychildreadytoread .org/. This parent education initiative is a joint effort of the Public Library Association and the Association for Library Service to Children, both divisions of the American Library Association.
- Reach Out and Read, www.reachoutandread.org/index.aspx. This is a national pediatric literacy program fostered by the Department of Pediatrics at Boston Medical Center.
- Center for the Book in the Library of Congress, http://read.gov/cfb. An act of Congress created the CBLC to stimulate public interest in books, reading, and libraries and to encourage the study of books and print culture. It has thirty-six state affiliates that offer a wide variety of programs. One affiliate is MotherGoosePrograms.org, which offers a variety of literacy programs, including one titled *Beginning with Mother Goose* (www.mothergooseprograms.org/index.php).
- Head Start/Early Head Start National Resource Center, https://eclkc .ohs.acf.hhs.gov/hslc/tta-system/ehsnrc. This site is from the Administration for Children and Families, a division of the U.S. Department of Health and Human Services.
- First Book, www.firstbook.org/. This organization is dedicated to giving children in need the opportunity to read and own their first new books.

Partnerships, Funding, and Grants

Creating partnerships can be advantageous not only to cover costs but also to develop networks with the organizations and agencies that strive to help children and families succeed in life. Each partner brings its own agenda and expertise to the table, so clarity of purpose and appropriate division of responsibilities are essential. Communication between partners is also essential to ensure clarity of purpose. National organizations such as the American Library Association and the Association for Library Service to Children provide information about partnerships on their websites.

Many types of partnerships are possible. Traditional partnerships have included these:

- Friends of the Library groups
- Library foundations
- Local financial institutions, such as banks, credit unions, and so forth
- Community foundations
- School districts

Nontraditional partners might include the following:

- Chambers of Commerce, including local, regional, and various ethnic organizations
- United Way
- Civic organizations such as Rotary, which emphasizes literacy, Elks, or Kiwanis
- Departments of Education—local, state, or federal
- Retail stores—local or national
- Endowment organizations such as those for the arts or humanities (e.g., National Endowment for the Arts/Humanities)
- Restaurants
- Sports teams—local or national
- Institutions of higher education

Many organizations and partnerships look to grants to obtain funds for their programs. When creating grant proposals, your writing needs to be detailed, evaluative, and specific. There are many resources available to help you write a proposal, with a basic Internet search being the best resource for current descriptions, criteria, and availability of possible partnerships and funding. Some national organizations have offered conference programs to assist those venturing into grant writing. The American Library Association, at their July 2011 annual conference, had a presentation titled "Show Me the Money!" that was aimed primarily at academic libraries but also offered basic guidelines, questions to ask, tips, and important things to keep in mind when creating a grant proposal (http://www.ala.org/acrl/sites/ala.org.acrl/files/content/conferences/ confsandpreconfs/national/seattle/papers/110.pdf). The 2012 Public Library Association's conference included a preconference on winning grants, understanding what your specific community needs and wants, as well as programs on collaborating with child-care providers and library-museum partnerships (http://www.ala.org/pla/education/placonference/past/2012).

Be on the lookout for online classes and discussion groups that cover these topics. ALA has offered a facilitated online class titled "Community Partnerships: How to Raise Money and Build Relationships." The Redmond branch of the KCLS houses the Nonprofit and Philanthropy Resource Center, which has extensive print and online resources, with over 200 links to websites dealing with nonprofit and fundraising topics (http://guides.kcls.org/content .php?pid=108819andsid=818670). For additional information, see the following Resources section.

Resources

Services

Arnold, Renea, and Nell Colburn. "Read to Me! Summer Reading for Preschoolers." *School Library Journal* 53, no. 7 (July 2007): 25.

Baltimore County Public Library. "Virtual Tour of Storyville." http://www .bcplstoryville.org/storyville_tour.html.

Blake, Barbara, Robert Martin, and Yunfei Du. *Successful Community Outreach: A How-To-Do-It Manual for Librarians*. Book and CD-ROM. New York: Neal-Schuman, 2011.

Cerny, Rosanne, Penny Markey, and Amanda Williams. *Outstanding Library Services to Children: Putting the Core Competencies to Work*. Chicago: Association for Library Service to Children. Chicago: American Library Association, 2006.

Diamant-Cohen, Betsy. *Children's Services: Partnerships for Success*. Chicago: American Library Association, 2010.

Ernst, Linda L.. *Baby Rhyming Time*. Book and CD-ROM. New York: Neal-Schuman, 2008.

Feinberg, Sandra, and James R. Keller. *Designing Space for Children and Teens in Libraries and Public Places*. Chicago: American Library Association, 2010.

Main-Diaz, Pamela, Sharon Deeds, and Debbie Noggle. "Leave No Pre-Schooler or Toddler Behind: Summer Reading Programs and Our Youngest Patrons." Paper presented at the Public Library Association 2006 Annual Conference. http://www.eshow2000.com/pla/2006/handouts_audiotapes.cfm.

Middle Country Public Library. "Family Place Libraries." http://www.middlecountrypubliclibrary.org/children/early-childhood/family-place-libraries/.

Public Library Association. "Every Child Ready to Read @ your library Sneak Peek Webinar." Originally presented May 4, 2011. http://www.ala.org/alsc/ecrr/sneakpeekwebinar.

Walter, Virginia A. *Children and Libraries: Getting It Right*. Chicago: American Library Association, 2001.

Partnerships and Funding/Grants

Arnold, Renea, and Nell Colburn. "Howdy, Partner: Community Alliances Can Help You Reach the Next Generation of Readers." *School Library Journal* 52, no. 5 (May 2006): 37.

Becker, Bill. "Library Grant Money on the Web: A Resource Primer." *Searcher* 11, no. 10 (November/December 2003). http://www.infotoday.com/searcher/nov03/becker.shtml.

Harris, Dianne. *The Complete Guide to Writing Effective and Award-Winning Grants (Step-by-Step Instruction with Companion CD)*. Ocala, FL: Atlantic Publishing Group, 2007.

Kepler, Ann, ed. *The ALA Book of Library Grant Money*. 8th ed. Chicago: American Library Association, 2012.

Landau, Herbert B. *Winning Library Grants: A Game Plan*. Chicago: American Library Association, 2010.

MacKeller, Pamela H., and Stephanie K. Gerding. *Winning Grants: A How-To-Do-It Manual for Librarians with Multimedia Tutorials and Grant Development Tools*. Book and Multimedia DVD. New York: Neal-Schuman, 2010.

McCune, Bonnie. "Early Literacy: A Sustainable Statewide Approach." *American Libraries*, September 2010. http://americanlibrariesmagazine.org/features/08172010/early-literacy-sustainable-statewide-approach.

Smallwood, Carol, ed. *Librarians as Community Partners: An Outreach Handbook*. Chicago: American Library Association, 2010.

Staines, Gail M. *Go Get That Grant!* Lanham, MD: Scarecrow Press, 2010.

E-resources

American Library Association. "Awards, Grants, and Scholarships." http://www.ala
.org/awardsgrants/. Click on "Grants and Fellowships" to browse an
alphabetical list of available grants.

Association for Library Service to Children. "Awards, Grants and Scholarships."
http://www.ala.org/alsc/awardsgrants. Categories include Book and Media
Awards, Children's Notable Lists, Professional Awards, and Scholarships.

King County Library System, Redmond Library. Nonprofit and Philanthropy
Resource Center. http://guides.kcls.org/content.php?pid=108819andsid
=818670. This website offers over 200 links to other sites dealing with
nonprofit and fundraising topics. It is part of the Cooperating Collections
Network, which provides information on private philanthropic giving to the
grant-seeking public.

Reach Out and Read. http://www.reachoutandread.org/. This national nonprofit
promotes early literacy by making books a routine part of pediatric care,
including placing books in pediatric waiting rooms. It trains doctors and
nurses to advise parents about the importance of reading aloud and provides
books to give children at pediatric checkups from six months to five years of
age. Children growing up in poverty are its primary focus.

Toys, Furniture, and Other Supplies

Check the websites for international contact information.

Community Playthings (early childhood furniture, storage, toys, etc.). http://www
.communityplaythings.com/. Mail: 359 Gibson Hill Road, Chester, NY
10918-2321. Phone: 1-800-777-4244.

DEMCO (library furniture, learning materials, library supplies, etc.). http://www
.demco.com/. Mail: PO Box 7488, Madison, WI 53707-7488. Phone
(customer service): 1-800-962-4463.

Environments, Inc. (early childhood classroom equipment, furniture, educational
toys, and curriculum materials). http://www.eichild.com/. Mail: PO Box
1348, Beaufort, SC 29901-1348. Phone: 1-800-342-4453.

Gaylord (library furniture, learning materials, library supplies, etc.).
http://www.gaylord.com/. Mail: PO Box 4901, Syracuse, NY 13221-4901.
Phone: 1-800-448-6160.

International Playthings LLC (puzzles, games, educational toys from around the globe). http://www.intplay.com/. Mail: 75D Lackawanna Avenue, Parsippany, NJ 07054. Phone (consumer information): 1-800-445-8347.

Lakeshore Learning (educational products such as puzzles, toys, musical instruments, etc., that support early childhood and elementary curriculum, including the areas of language and literacy). http://www.lakeshorelearning.com/. Mail: 2695 East Dominguez Street, Carson, CA 90895. Phone: 1-800-778-4456.

Learning Resources (educational products in language arts, reading, ESL, early childhood, etc.). http://www.learningresources.com/. Mail: 380 North Fairway Drive, Vernon Hills, IL 60061. Phone: 1-800-333-8281.

School Specialty (educational products in language arts, reading, ESL, early childhood, etc.). https://store.schoolspecialty.com/OA_HTML/ibeCZzpHome.jsp?minisite=10206. Mail: PO Box 1579, Appleton, WI 54912-1579. Phone: 888-388-3224.

Part II

Program Building Blocks

The Play's the Thing– Books, Rhymes, and Programs

4

IN THIS CHAPTER

✓ Things to Consider with Programming

✓ Putting the Program Together

✓ Resources

Programming for very young children, in the age range of 12 to 24 months old, has become standard for many libraries throughout the United States and in other countries around the world. Parents are increasing their demands for such programming because of their desire to give their children the best and earliest start possible for developing mental, social, and language skills. Libraries are striving to serve the whole family and have discovered that serving this age group encourages many families to become regular library users. Using this service as an outreach program for such groups as teen parents, non-English speakers, and others often draws in non–library users by appealing to the adults' desire to benefit their children and share experiences through either entertainment or education—the two being one and the same for small children.

An additional benefit from programming for the very young is that the adults have an actual role model who demonstrates what and how to read aloud to and communicate with their children. By being expressive, adding appropriate sounds, varying the length of the story, and talking about the illustrations, the librarian encourages the adults to do likewise. Learning about and seeing quality books that are age appropriate for their children gives the adults' the confidence to select books on their own, and reading aloud to their children also enables the adults to practice and improve their reading skills.

Many parents/adults are so often overwhelmed with the primary needs of day-to-day life that reading to their children often falls by the wayside. Librarians can demonstrate how and when reading aloud and developing imagination, curiosity, and language skills can fit into everyday living experiences inside and outside the home.

Things to Consider with Programming

The increasing popularity of programming for the very young creates a few major concerns that libraries must address. Each library will be unique in terms of its facility, staffing, and policies, so no one answer is absolute. Instead, libraries need to create a variety of options, of which only one may meet their particular need.

Age Divisions

How do you decide what age grouping to use for your program? Some libraries define age groups as infant (newborn–12 months), young toddler (12–24 months), toddler (2–3 years), and preschool (3–5 years). Others use infants (baby in arms), "waddlers" (those starting to move around under their own power), toddlers (2–3 years), and preschool (3 years and older). You can include this information in the program descriptions used for publicity. For some examples, see Program Descriptions for Publicity Flyers in the appendix. Then there's also the concern of the children having older siblings who attend as well. Frequently the decision is dictated by both staffing and scheduling. One presenter doing all the programs and having to fit programming into a full schedule of other responsibilities might mean using wider age groups. In many cases, the younger children can be put together in one group for ages 2 and younger. The presenter must decide how to divide the groups, be it by chronological age or by developmental abilities. Mixed age groups seem to be becoming more likely as the presenter's available time is evaluated in relationship to in-house services, outreach, and other demands, including those imposed by economic restrictions.

Attendance

What if no one comes? Publicity is one area to focus on when trying to attract program participants. Investigate what types of publicity are available, how and where such materials are distributed, who the target audience is, and what options are currently being used to get the word out. Many places use a printed monthly calendar or program flyer distributed inside the library. Others will educate the community about programs for the very young through news articles in a local paper, newsletters to day-care centers, preschools, and so forth. Publicity can perhaps target health clinics or hospitals in the area, local early-childhood education groups, or community colleges that offer parenting classes. Keep in mind your target audience. If you want to reach families at risk, you might want to focus on social agencies or alternative high schools. Although traditionally paper has been the primary medium of publicity, electronic media such as websites, e-newsletters, e-alerts, and so on, increase the speed of delivery and access to program information. Word of mouth is another way to get the information out, and do not look just at participants to spread the word; engage the rest of the staff to promote these programs and services as well. For those with successful publicity campaigns who find themselves suffering from overwhelming crowds, keep reading.

Crowds/Registration

Often in striving to build a clientele, librarians end up facing the challenge of what to do when there is not enough room for everyone who wants to attend. When crowd control becomes an issue, you need to set some limits. These limits are not arbitrary; they are important to ensure a fun and memorable learning/literary experience for all who attend. Keep in mind that these programs are not designed simply to keep the little ones busy for a while.

Look first at what you actually have as usable program space. The size of the room will dictate the maximum number of attendees for safety reasons. Check the fire code for the room/space you would like to use. In how many areas can programming be done, and how many staff members will be involved? The presenter needs to feel comfortable working with the number of participants and also be able to maintain "control" of the program. These storytimes are always pretty lively, but you do not want them to become utter chaos.

Here are some solutions for crowd control:

- Require participants to register, either in advance or upon arrival. Registration, although time-consuming, has some benefits. It gives you a definite number of participants who will attend, which is useful when preparing materials for the program. It also provides a record after the fact of how many people actually attended and their contact information (name, phone number, e-mail address, etc.). Create a waiting list that will help you to evaluate the impact of this program and to decide on the number of times it should be offered and when. People who register tend to commit themselves to attending the program on a regular basis. Registration is also useful if you want to follow up or develop a connection with program participants, such as through sending out an electronic newsletter.
- Offer two classes back-to-back so that the same program material can be used with two different groups of participants. Two morning classes or even two early evening classes may be a possibility. If you

try this, be sure to include in your publicity that both classes are identical and attendance at only one is allowed. A poster stating this at the program room's entrance will serve as a good reminder.

- Provide tickets on a first-come, first-served basis. Create as many tickets as needed to match the number of attendees that you can accommodate, and make sure the program title, location, time, age group, and so forth, is included on them. Use different colors for each program and collect them as participants enter the room. When the maximum number of participants has been reached, be firm in turning away others. Post a sign saying the program is full and to please attend the next one or speak to the librarian/presenter after the program about other program times. Hopefully you will not have to post a staff member at the door to enforce this rule.

- Offer this class as a series for a limited number of weeks. Registration would help to ensure that a different group has a chance to sign up for the next series and will give you the ability to serve more people.

- Check with other libraries in your area to see if they are interested in collaborating on a program. Each library could offer the program once a month on a different day and at a different site, or each library one could take one week a month to offer storytimes for the very young, with each one deciding which week during the month works best for them. Many such arrangements are possible, but the goal should be to provide programs each week for the very young children in the area.

- Set up a program that targets a specific group to help thin the crowd at your regular program time. Some participants may be part of another group, such as a play group or mother-support group, and setting up a program just for them may free up some space in the regular program.

Too large a crowd can also occur because more than just the target audience is present, for example, when older or younger siblings tag along. Restricting the program to a particular age child and an accompanying adult ensures one-on-one interaction between each pair and with the rest of the group without distractions. If using this approach, make sure that your publicity materials clearly state this. If older siblings attend and you allow it, remind the attendees that the program is aimed at the very young child and that is where your attention will be focused. You can suggest that siblings use a doll or stuffed toy to be their "little one" during the program.

Overcrowding can inhibit attendees' involvement with the programs components. For example, being unable to hear the story or see the illustrations, having no room to move around, having too many distractions to focus on what's happening, and lacking interaction with the presenter are only a few of the problems that can arise. Explaining to the adults why there are restrictions will help them to be more understanding and accepting of them. They might even become more supportive of programming and services for the very young.

Latecomers

Latecomers can be a distraction and can disrupt the program. You may find it necessary to speak with chronic latecomers personally to put an end to the problems caused by their late arrivals. Indicate first that you appreciate that they are making the effort to attend but that some adjustments need to be made because their tardiness affects the other program participants. Find out the reason why they are always late and make suggestions that might help them overcome the problem; for example, suggest that they return all of their books after, rather than before, the program. To encourage punctuality, make sure the publicity materials clearly state the starting time and approximate duration of the program. You can also post a sign, include the information in your guideline handouts, and even verbally express to the participants, "We start on time." Remember that repetition helps people learn things, even being on time.

Nametags

Using nametags is not mandatory, but they can be helpful in many ways. Having the children wear nametags allows the presenter to call them by name, which helps to direct the children's focus. Seeing their names on a nametag also increases the children's letter awareness. The adults should also have nametags, and these should include the names of both the adult and the child to help the presenter easily recognize who belongs together. Nametags can also be helpful in attendance taking for statistics. At the conclusion of the program, the children can place their nametags in a box or basket, either held by the presenter or placed on another table, so that they can be counted. Another idea could be for the presenter to collect the nametags from the children, counting aloud while doing so.

Challenges using nametags can include time, materials, and money. Making nametags, even with such time-savers as the Ellison die-cut machine, takes time, whether the presenter's or a volunteer's. Perhaps instead of using a new nametag for every program, you could create one to use for the entire series. You can make nametags from index cards or a simple shape, such as the outline of a teddy bear or bird, on laminated paper, heavy-weight paper, or cardboard, or you can use sturdier material that is vinyl on one side and fabric on the other, similar to outdoor tablecloths. Since most nametags become playthings for the very young child if placed within reach, tape or pin the nametag on the back of the child's shirt. For safety reasons, do not use yarn to hang the nametag around the child's neck. Cost may also affect what materials you choose to use for the nametags. You can enhance simple, self-stick nametags from office supply stores by using colorful stickers or stamps to decorate them.

Pace

The format and many of the materials used for a program for the very young are usually reused at every program, which can lead to more active participation by the children and a fun-filled time for all. A word of caution: do not let the pace of the program get away from you. This will be new material for most of the children and even for some of the adults. Give them time to process what they are hearing, seeing, and doing. Yes, have fun, but do not try to do so many stories, rhymes, songs, and activities that the pace becomes overwhelming for everyone. Remember that pausing can be important too. Adding between-activity comments, such as "Wow! We rowed the boat so fast! Now let's slow down a little with this story" or "I need to take a breath after climbing that tall apple tree—let's all take a big breath together," enables the group to avoid rushing from one rhyme/song/story to the next. Pausing also gives the presenter a chance to interject comments that help connect the individuals in the group to what is taking place. For example, if a child calls out "Cat!" when you turn to the page with the purple cat on it in *Brown, Bear, Brown Bear, What Do You See?* by Bill Martin Jr., it would be better to pause and say, "Yes, you're right; that is a cat!" than to read on without acknowledging the child's contribution to the reading of the story. As the presenter develops familiarity with the participants, pacing of the program activities will become easier with knowing when to slow things down or move things along.

Participation

Many presenters have concerns regarding the adults' participation in the program. In some cases, problems arise because the adults are self conscious, unsure of what their role is, or assume that the program is "just for the little ones." The presenter can easily rectify this at the beginning of each program by stating that (1) adults should focus on their children, (2) their children believe they have the greatest voice/face/actions in the world, and (3) this is a program for everyone. Sometimes the adults get so busy talking among themselves that they become a distraction to the group, especially the presenter. How does one mend this problem? The simplest way is to involve the adults directly with the literary experience and the children. Establish at the start of the program that the "rule" is that the children can watch but the adults must participate. Reassure the adults that the children are learning or being made aware of words, rhythm, and rhyme by just being there.

If you find yourself needing to reclaim your adult audience, you can try varying the volume and pitch of your voice to draw them back; for example, lowering the volume of your voice makes their voices more noticeable so they may become aware of their being disruptive and stop talking. Sudden narrative changes or sounds work as well; for example, whistling like a bird or barking like a dog while reading Bill Martin Jr.'s *Brown Bear, Brown Bear, What Do You See?* is one attention getter. If need be, remind the adults that there will be time after the program for talking among themselves. One of my favorite ways to bring adults back into the program is to ask the little ones if the big people are asleep: "They must be asleep," I say, "because I don't hear them joining in! Let's help them!" Another method is to have the children get the adults' attention by asking them to do a rhyme's actions with the adults; for example, have the children touch the adults' bodies when reciting "head and shoulders, knees and toes," be the cobbler and tap on the adults' shoes, or climb onto the adults to use as boats for "Row, Row, Row Your Boat." The more you actively engage both the children and the adults in the experience, the less chance there is for disruptive conversations to take place. When all else fails, the presenter may have to talk to the offenders before or after the program. Some adults may not understand exactly what the program is about, others may need some extra assistance in learning the rhymes and songs, and still others may not realize the importance of their involvement or the availability of "chat time" after the program. Always try to approach the situation with diplomacy and tact.

Role of the Librarian/Presenter

As programs and services for the very young have increased during the years, librarians have found themselves in a quandary. Many of us have little to no early childhood education or development background, and yet the adults look to us as the "experts" or "teachers." Through classes and self-study we have become better educated in the areas of early childhood, but we still do not feel comfortable referring to ourselves by these titles. Some librarians/presenters have even said to me, "Why should parents listen to me? I don't even have kids!" However, we are, as librarians, the experts in helping those same adults find materials, resources, and information regarding their concerns and questions. Our vocation centers on children and those with whom they interact. What better reasons do we need to accept our role as guides for our families and communities?

Room or Space Arrangement

The location and size of the group may dictate the arrangement of the group. One common arrangement is the circle, with the presenter either in the center or included as part of the circle. This works only if you have the necessary space and has the drawback of the presenter possibly needing to move around to prevent having his or her back to one part of the group. Another option is to have participants all facing the same way with the presenter in the front, similar to a standard classroom situation. The presenter should be higher than the group, if possible, so that visibility is not hindered. Although chairs are useful when bouncing rhymes are done, they may prove to be an obstacle during marches, impossible to fit with a large group, or too time-consuming to set up and take down. One compromise is to have the majority of the participants sit on the floor, chairs placed around the sides and back of the room, and the presenter positioned in front with a place to keep materials, such as a table, box, and so on. It's a good idea to post a sign to indicate that a program is in progress, and when cold and flu season arrives, you might also want to post a sign asking people not to attend if they are ill (see the two sign templates provided in the appendix).

Scheduling

There are many things to take into account when scheduling programs. Who will your target audience be? If you want to encourage working parents to attend, consider an evening or Saturday morning program time. If your focus is stay-at-home moms, dads, or caregivers, a weekday morning might be best. Would once a month work with the resources you have? Are there other libraries in the area with which you can create a "round robin" program series, with each library taking a specific week? Such an arrangement works well where the libraries involved are close enough to one another and have reciprocal agreements if not in the same system. For example, a group of four libraries agrees that each one will host one program on an assigned week during the month, giving the communities in their region an opportunity to attend programs each week of the month but at different locations. The libraries could also agree either to have their own staff present the program or, depending on the makeup of the system, to have one person do each program at all libraries. Having a year-round program for the very young held on a weekly basis may be your goal, but perhaps a four- to five-week series once a quarter, or a few months throughout the year, may be more practical.

Putting the Program Together

Format

Programs can be as unique and as individual as their creators, although there is a general format or framework to build upon, which is the focus of this section. The average length of programs for the 12-to-24-month age group is 20 to 30 minutes, but this can be expanded by allowing time before and after the class for participants to interact. The presenter should have enough material prepared to allow for flexibility in the program. A very active group may need more action rhymes and songs, whereas a quieter group may be able to listen to more stories. Once the presenter gets started and if everyone appears to be having fun, it may be tempting to extend the duration of the program. My advice is: Don't do it! Children this age can become overstimulated, and you do not want the experience to devolve into a crying, chaotic mess.

These are the four basic program sections:

- **Part 1:** Setting the stage
- **Part 2:** The storytime
- **Part 3:** Adult education
- **Part 4:** Bonus

Part 1: Setting the Stage

This is the time to create an atmosphere so that the adults can relax and become familiar with the group. It is sometimes useful to let participants introduce themselves and their children, including mention of the ages of their children. Quite often, even within an age span of 12 months, there will be children at many different developmental levels. By finding out what ages are present, the presenter can tailor the program to feature the best age-appropriate rhymes, stories, songs, and activities. Adults tend to compare their own children to the other children in a group setting, so having an awareness of the age range may help them to avoid this habit. Making a simple statement about each child being a unique individual, developing at his or her own pace, prior to starting the program may also defuse the adults' tendency to compare. Often adults interpret early childhood "milestones" or age charts as giving the exact ages for a child to be able to master something, for example, standing or talking. In reality, these are suggested age ranges; children can master skills sooner or later depending on their own growth development.

Adults in many cases are as new to this kind of experience as the children. Giving some guidelines as to expectations of behavior and activity may reassure them, allowing them to relax and enjoy the program. Here are some ways to present these program guidelines:

- Simply state the guidelines to the group at the beginning of each program.
- Write the guidelines clearly on a poster and display it at each program. Laminating this poster will increase its durability.
- List guidelines on a handout that can be distributed to participants. You may want to incorporate this into a handout that also includes fingerplays and other program-related material.
- Reproduce the guidelines provided in the two Program Guidelines handouts in the appendix or create your own using these handouts as templates.

Some basic concepts that I generally include are these:

- I don't expect the children to sit still, but I do expect the adults to keep them safe. If a child seems overwhelmed, cries, or generally "loses it," the adult should feel free to step outside to regroup and then return to the program or try again next week. Caregivers should talk with the presenter about any concerns they may have regarding their children's behavior. If the presenter has any concerns about the children's behavior, it is best to talk with the caregivers outside the program time.
- Please put toys, food, and other distractions away and silence your cell phones during the program. Bottles or other "not-to-be-parted-with" items are okay but should be used discreetly. This also applies to breast-feeding.
- We start the program on time while the children are "fresh." Time is set aside prior to and after the program for participants to interact and share.
- Big people take part! The children's participation in all the activities is not expected. However, they get their cues from their caregivers. The goal is to have fun with words in books, rhymes, songs, and other language-building play, so join in!

Part 2: The Storytime

Creating a fun-filled experience with language and literature for the participants as well as being a role model for reading aloud are the presenter's goals for this part of the program. The storytime segment consists of books suitable for the age group, finger rhymes, songs, and activities.

It is important to be ready with more material that you will actually need. You can vary the duration of the program by changing the number of finger rhymes, songs, and stories that you use. This is useful when you have to adapt to the group dynamics.

The general format of the storytime is as follows:

1. Opening song or rhyme
2. Finger rhyme/action rhyme/bounce/song
3. Finger rhyme/action rhyme/bounce/song
4. Story
5. Finger rhyme/action rhyme/bounce/song
6. Finger rhyme/action rhyme/bounce/song
7. Story
8. Finger rhyme/action rhyme/bounce/song
9. Finger rhyme/action rhyme/bounce/song
10. Story
11. Finger rhyme/action rhyme/bounce/song
12. Closing song, activity, or rhyme

The storytime should always include one story read aloud, with the possibility of adding others as time and group dynamics permit. Repeating a story, rhyme, and/or song during the same program is absolutely okay because both children and adults learn through repetition. Try not to compress too many literary experiences into the planned time frame. Children need time to absorb and process what they are hearing and doing. Presenting a fun language/literacy-learning program that can be duplicated at home will not only motivate the adults to do so but also give them the materials and know-how to do it.

For more actual program outlines, see the later sections Theme Index for Books, Theme Index for Programs, and Sample Program Outlines—A Baker's Dozen in this chapter.

Part 3: Adult Education

The presenter may sometimes find this section to be a stumbling block. The adult-education portion of the program has wonderful entertainment value, but it is also a language-learning experience. One of its major purposes is to create library users and promote literacy. It should also serve as an empowerment experience for the parents or caregivers.

Educational moments can be approached in many ways and are best kept simple. A table set up by the entrance with handouts, booklists for suggested reading, flyers from community agencies, and so forth, that can be easily picked up is a good place to start. Make sure your contact information is on any handouts you create, and don't forget to include general handouts about library services, such as open hours, special events, library card applications, and so on. Expand the subjects for book displays to include such topics as taking care of one's self, job searches, dealing with challenging children, and other personal needs.

During the storytime portion, the presenter can interject a comment if it relates directly to an educational fact. For example, after singing a song, state that "singing songs and reciting rhymes help children learn rhythm, and that is part of learning language." Think of them as "info bites" or "sparkles" or information you can toss out to the group like seeds in a garden.

You can create a small informational display by placing a miniposter (the size of a large index card) on an acrylic easel or book holder. You can vary the poster's content for each program by simply changing the miniposter. On each card, print a literacy, educational, or developmental fact. Laminate these miniposters/cards so you can use them multiple times. See the Interesting Facts and Tips handout in the appendix.

Part 4: Bonus

This section includes the time allowed for interaction and dialogue among the participants, both adults and children. Due to work schedules, transportation issues, language barriers, and other challenges, this may be the only activity for parents to participate in with their children. If so, a program such as this gives them a chance to see their children interact with others the same age and to meet families who may face similar situations with whom they can network. It might also give adults an opportunity to see how other adults interact with very young children and motivate them to do the same. Some ideas might be to bring out a collection of board books, blow bubbles while music plays, or offer some activity that the children and adults can do together. Having a chance to visit one-to-one with other people can be a welcome diversion, especially for stay-at-home moms, new immigrants learning English, and even those who are new to the neighborhood. The presenter should be available during this follow-up time to answer questions, talk individually with the adults, give a tour of the facility, and supply resources. This time makes the adults and children feel welcome and helps create a positive experience for everyone.

Tips

Here are some suggestions to help your program be the best it can be:

- Wear comfortable clothing. This program requires a lot of movement. I have found that pants work very well, especially ones with pockets. You can use pockets to hide finger puppets, a "cheat sheet" (an index card with a list of stories, rhymes, and songs that you plan to use), and a tissue (runny noses are often in attendance). Some people may be more comfortable with a storytelling apron or smock, which can serve the same function.

- Consider limiting the jewelry and accessories that you wear. Children are attracted to things that are bright, shiny, and eye-catching. They have a tendency to grab for such items and get distracted from the program.

- Include materials that you are comfortable with and have experience using, especially when first starting to do these programs. This is true for using puppets, picture cards, audio equipment, and any other prop. Practice with the props prior to the program.

- Limit the number of presentations in one program. Using six to eight different puppets or many different CDs that require changes can be difficult to do and will give your program a cluttered or cramped feeling. You want to keep the program flowing smoothly, so some variation is okay, but you should avoid an elaborate production.

- Select books carefully. Size can be an important factor; for example, using a small board book with a large group may prove difficult. Having multiple copies for the entire group would enable each adult-child pair to look at it together while the story is read aloud. Remember to keep the time of the program in mind; an evening program may best end with a "quiet" story, such as *Goodnight Moon* by Margaret Wise Brown, instead of *Wide-Mouthed Frog* by Keith Faulkner.

- Keep materials out of the children's reach. Displaying books is a nice idea, but a child may want to take a book to show to a caregiver, who may then try to return it, which may then produce a loud protest from the child. Be sure to arrange any audio equipment so that the cords are out of reach whenever possible.

- Examine the program area with an eye toward safety before opening the doors. Quickly check the floor for sharp objects, stacks of chairs that could be climbed on or tipped over, dangling curtain cords, and open electrical outlets that need to be covered. Remind adults prior to beginning the program that they are ultimately responsible for keeping their child safe while in the program area.

- Read expressively and use facial expressions. Varying the pitch and volume of your voice is a great way to gain the group's attention and can even help to regulate it. Children this age get many of their cues from body language, so be aware of what you are doing.

- Use a "cheat sheet" if you need one. You can write on an index card or small sheet of paper the stories, songs, rhymes, and activities you intend to use during the program. This can help you stay focused, so keep it close by (I keep mine in my pocket).

- Do not be afraid to change words, make up your own tune, or, in general, make a mistake. First of all, the program participants will probably not even notice. Second, it is a perfect example of how the adults can do the same things. By relaxing and accepting that mistakes happen, you give the adults permission not to do everything perfectly correct all the time.

- Keep your program simple. When introducing new material, first demonstrate it. Do not assume that everyone knows the rhyme or song, for example. You may want to create a poster that includes the words for the rhymes or songs used during the program and put it on display (for the text of the English rhymes included later in this chapter, go to alaeditions.org/webextras). You can also write out the words on a large pad, create a handout, or simply do the new piece a number of times throughout the program.

- Repeat, repeat, repeat! Do not be afraid to repeat the material more than once. A favorite rhyme the children love is always fun to do.

- Give the program a framework. Children like routines and start to anticipate what is coming up next in the program. Start and end the program the same way, every time. For example, make the first book you read always the same one; I always use *Brown Bear, Brown Bear, What Do You See?* by Bill Martin Jr.

- Respect the children. Keep the pace of the program moving along, but do not rush it. Children can process and absorb only so many things around them so fast. Let the children know what you are going to do next. For instance, I ask the children, "Would you like to hear a story?" or tell them, "I brought a book to read to you today" before I pick up the book. Eye contact also helps you connect with the child and adult. If a child tends to be shy, I start by interacting with the adult, giving the child time to observe and become familiar with me; given time, the child then gets involved when he or she is ready.

To Theme or Not to Theme

Librarians' programs are as variedly creative as the librarians themselves. The major difference in many cases is that some librarians use a thematic approach, while others do not. Some feel that a theme is necessary to create a program that flows evenly and helps in selecting materials. Other librarians insist that themes are unnecessary and prefer to create more of a potpourri of activities for their programs. Some do not want to be compared to schools that follow themes. The age group with whom we are working, children 12 to 24 months old, in reality does not need a new theme with every program. However, adults are often able to remember more if a theme is evident, which may lead them to continue the literary experience outside the program itself. Themes can also give order to a program. So the answer to the question "To theme or not to theme?" is easy—either way works. It is up to the presenter to decide which is more comfortable and which goes over best with program participants. In general, you can plan a core, consistently used program pattern that includes an opening and closing with one story and rhymes/songs. You can then create a thematic program by adding your selected stories, rhymes, and songs, if that is your style. The entire program does not need to be completely new every time. Remember, this age group is comfortable with a familiar routine once it is established.

Titles That Work

Annotated Bibliography

The following is an annotated bibliography of more than 180 titles, arranged alphabetically by author, that have been successfully used by librarians in storytimes with this age group. Each entry includes the bibliographical data, a brief summary, notes of interest, and suggested themes for which the book can be used. Tips to engage the participants are included wherever possible. The subject index that groups these titles by themes then follows in the section Theme Index for Books. Every effort has been made to verify that the books are still in print at the time of this text's publication. Resources for storytime books and programming appear in the Resources section at the end of the chapter.

Adler, Victoria. *All of Baby Nose to Toes*. New York: Dial Books for Young Readers, 2009.
> This rhyming text celebrates everything about a beloved baby, from eyes to toes. **TIP** Have the adult tap the child's body part (nose, ears, etc.) and hug the child each time the phrase "Me! I do!" is read. (Babies/Body/Stories in Rhyme)

Alborough, Jez. *Duck in the Truck.* New York: HarperCollins, 2000.

Large illustrations and rhyming text make this story fun to share. Duck and the other animals try to get the truck out of the muck. (Animals/Ducks/Stories in Rhyme/Things That Go/Trucks)

Allen, Jonathan. *"I'm Not Sleepy!"* New York: Disney Hyperion Books, 2010.

Ever argumentative, Baby Owl is definitely not ready for bedtime. Why does everyone seem to think Baby Owl is sleepy? He's not! He's really not! He's . . . "Zzzzzz." (Bedtime/Birds/Owls)

Anderson, Peggy Perry. *Chuck's Truck.* Boston, MA: Houghton Mifflin, 2006.

All the barnyard animals jump into Chuck's truck when he decides to go into town. The truck breaks down just as they get there. With Handyman Hugh's help, the truck is fixed like new. The bright colors and rhyming text help this story come to life. Sound effects are easy to incorporate as it is being read. **TIP** Animal sounds and sound effects will bring the audience into the story. (Animals/Farms/Stories in Rhyme/Things That Go/Trucks)

Asch, Frank. *Just Like Daddy.* New York: Simon and Schuster, 1981.

Going fishing with Daddy is a lot of fun, especially because Little Bear can do things "just like Daddy." This book is good to share with a group because most scenes are a two-page spread. (Bears/Families/Fathers)

Baicker, Karen. *I Can Do It Too!* Brooklyn, NY: Handprint Books, 2003.

The little one reminds everyone that what the big people in her life do, she can too! **TIP** Having everyone raising their arms and joining in with the phrase "I can do it too!," the reader encourages adults and children to join in the story. (Daily Life/Families)

Baker, Keith. *Big Fat Hen.* New York: Harcourt Brace, 1994.

The familiar counting rhyme with large beautiful pictures is perfect for group sharing. **TIP** Clap along to the rhythm of the text or put action into it. For example, pat a shoe, clap to shut the door, mime picking up sticks, stretch out arms side to side, or touch fingertips to make a big round belly. (Chickens/Counting/Numbers/Poetry/Stories in Rhyme)

Bang, Molly. *Ten, Nine, Eight.* New York: Mulberry Books, 1983.

A little girl gets ready to sleep with a quiet countdown routine to bedtime. (Bedtime/Counting/Numbers/Stories in Rhyme)

Barry, Frances. *Duckie's Splash.* Cambridge, MA: Candlewick, 2006.

This fun-filled pop-up book introduces opposites to the youngest reader. Duckie likes to do things her way, which just happens to run contrary to all her friends. The last page turn brings a surprise, as Duckie jumps in and the fish jump out! The illustrations are bright, colorful, and simply drawn. (Concepts/Ducks)

Bell, Babs. *The Bridge Is Up!* **New York: HarperCollins, 2004.**

A long line of vehicles waits for the drawbridge to come down so they can go across it. This cumulative story has a repeating line that is fun for all to join in on. There are numerous ways the line "So everyone has to wait!!" can be expressed. **TIP** *The Bridge Is Up!* can be told as a flannel-board story and can also vary in length, by including all the vehicles that are waiting while the bridge is up or leaving some of them out to shorten the story. (Animals/Flannel Board/Things That Go)

Berger, Barbara. *Grandfather Twilight.* **New York: Philomel Books, 1984.**

As Grandfather Twilight takes his evening stroll, nighttime approaches. Children will notice many things happening in the illustrations that add to this story, which are meant to be shared. This is a beautiful bedtime story with delightful artwork. (Bedtime)

Bloom, Suzanne. *The Bus for Us.* **Honesdale, PA: Caroline Press, 2001.**

A little girl asks, "Is this the bus for us?" as different vehicles drive up. Finally, the school bus arrives and everyone gets on. Pages are large enough for sharing with groups, and the story has possibilities as a flannel-board story. **TIP** In *The Bus for Us* you can add the response "Nooooo" to answer the story character's question. Encourage the adult to ask the child, "What is that? [Pause.] It's a _____!" Do this even if a child is too young to reply verbally by asking the adult to say the answer. (Buses/Things That Go)

———. *Treasure.* **Honesdale, PA: Boyds Mills Press, 2007.**

Goose sets off in search of buried treasure with Bear right behind. (Animals/Bears/Birds/Friends/Play)

Bornstein, Ruth. *Little Gorilla.* **New York: Clarion Books, 1976.**

All the animals in the jungle love Little Gorilla, even when he grows up and gets bigger. **TIP** This is a story filled with hugs between adult and child participants. (Animals/Animals, Jungle/Birthdays/Growing Up/Size)

Boynton, Sandra. *Good Night, Good Night.* **New York: Random House, 1985.**

All the animals on board a boat get ready for bed. Clear, bright cartoon illustrations bring a visual sense of play to this rhyming text. (Animals/Bedtime/Stories in Rhyme)

Braun, Sebastien. *Meeow and the Big Box.* **London: Boxer Books, 2009.**

Little cat Meeow finds a big brown box, paints it, and gathers things to put into it. What is it supposed to be? Clues provide hints to his creation. The illustrations are in bold primary colors on bright-white pages and large enough to share with a group. **TIP** This book can be made into a flannel-board story. (Animals/Cats/Imagination/Things That Go)

———. *Meeow and the Pots and Pans.* New York: Boxer Books, 2010.

Everyone is curious about what can be done with all the stuff they find in the kitchen cupboard. Meeow decides to get creative, and all his friends join in. TIP After reading the story, bring out various kitchen items and then read the story again with sound effects! (Music/Play/Sounds)

———. *On Our Way Home.* New York: Boxer Books, 2009.

Daddy and Little Bear go for a walk before bedtime, told from Little Bear's point of view. Text uses great vocabulary to describe the things they do and see along the way. (Animals/Bears/Bedtime)

Brown, Margaret Wise. *The Golden Egg Book.* New York: Golden Press, 1947.

A little bunny is all alone when he finds an egg. After trying to open it, he falls asleep, only to awaken and find a friend. (Animals/Ducks/Friends/Rabbits)

———. *Goodnight Moon.* New York: Harper, 1947.

This is the classic story of a little one needing to say "Goodnight" to everyone and everything before closing his eyes to sleep. (Bedtime/Rabbits/Stories in Rhyme)

———. *Home for a Bunny.* New York: Golden Press; Racine, WI: Western Publishing, 1956.

Bunny needs to find a home, but every place he looks is already taken. (Animals/Friends/Rabbits)

Browne, Anthony. *I Like Books.* New York: Dragonfly, 1988.

This little monkey loves all kinds of books, be they funny, fat, song, scary, and so on. (Animals/Books/Monkeys)

Bruss, Deborah. *Book! Book! Book!* New York: Arthur A. Levine Books, 2001.

When all the children go back to school, the farm animals have nothing to do. Hen leads them all into town to find "something to do" at the library. TIP Encourage the participants to make each animal's sound along with you by pausing after saying "All she hears is . . ." (Animals/Books/Farms/Sounds)

Butler, John. *Whose Nose and Toes?* New York: Viking, 2004.

Each question page shows a different baby animal—whose nose and toes? Turn the page for the answers. Illustrations of jungle animals and farm animals alternate. This title is similar to Butler's *Who Says Woof?*, but more of a challenge because the clues are primarily visual and include more "exotic" jungle animals. (Animals/Question-and-Answer Stories)

Butterworth, Nick. *Just Like Jasper!* Boston: Little, Brown, 1989.

Jasper goes to the store to buy a special toy. Pages are a nice size for sharing with groups, and the text is simple. Illustrations are clear and brightly colored. (Cats/Toys)

Carle, Eric. *From Head to Toe.* **New York: HarperCollins, 1997.**
> This book encourages children to mimic the actions of animals.
> **TIP** Have participants copy each movement throughout when reading aloud.
> (Animals/Exercise/Movement/Participation)

———. *Little Cloud.* **New York: Philomel Books, 1996.**
> In a bright blue sky, a little white cloud tries out different shapes till it decides
> to join the rest of the clouds and rain. **TIP** Ask participants what they see in
> the cloud. (Clouds/Rain/Shapes/Weather)

———. *The Very Quiet Cricket.* **New York: Philomel Books, 1990.**
> Little Cricket tries to talk to other animals but is unable to make a sound
> until the very end. **TIP** This story can be shortened to meet the attention
> span of the group. Have participants rub their hands or wrists together
> every time the little cricket rubs his wings. Pausing before turning to the
> last page seems to draw everyone's attention, creating a quiet moment. The
> reproduced cricket sound plays at the end of the book. (Animals/Bugs/Sounds)

Carlson, Nancy. *I Like Me!* **New York: Viking Kestrel, 1998.**
> With positive thinking and a good self-image, this pig proves that you can
> be your own best friend and have fun on your own. (Animals/Friends/Pigs)

Carter, David. *If You're Happy and You Know It, Clap Your Hands! A Pop-Up Book.* **New York: Scholastic, 1997.**
> This is a wonderful book to sing along with. Tabs are easy to manipulate on
> sturdy pages. **TIP** Do the actions asked for in the text. (Movable Books/Music/
> Response Books/Songs/Stories in Rhyme)

———. *Says Who?* **New York: Simon and Schuster, 1993.**
> This is a pop-up book of animal sounds. (Animals/Games/Movable Books/Response
> Books/Sounds)

Cauley, Lorinda Bryan. *Clap Your Hands.* **New York: G.P. Putnam's Sons, 1992.**
> This book includes rhymes to act out: clap your hands, roar like a lion, and
> other fun activities. (Movement/Participation/Play/Stories in Rhyme)

Chorao, Kay. *Knock at the Door and Other Baby Action Rhymes.* **New York: Dutton, 1999.**
> This title includes beautiful illustrations of twenty action rhymes. The
> directions for movements appear next to the line in a small box. Illustrations
> of the directions use simple line drawings that are clear enough to
> understand without words. This book can be used to present rhymes visually
> or as a resource book for finger rhymes. (Participation/Poetry)

Church, Caroline. *One More Hug for Madison.* **New York: Orchard Books, 2010.**
> Madison keeps asking Mother for one more thing to hold off bedtime.
> (Animals/Bedtime/Mice/Night)

Cimarusti, Marie Torres. *Peek-a-Moo!* New York: Dutton's Children's Books, 1998.

This oversized, lift-the-flap book has a different farm animal illustrated on each page. It is wonderful for encouraging interaction between reader and participants. **TIP** When reading *Peek-a-Moo!*, making the animal sounds is a must. (Animal/Farms/Games/Interactive Books/Lift-the-Flap Books/Sounds)

Cony, Frances. *Old MacDonald Had a Farm.* New York: Orchard Books, 1999.

This movable book of tabs, flaps, and dials shows the animals singing along with the reader. Pages are sturdy and fairly easy to manipulate.

(Animals/Animals, Farms/Farms/Movable Books/Songs)

Costello, David Hyde. *I Can Help.* New York: Farrar, Straus and Giroux, 2010.

When a little duckling gets lost and a monkey helps him find his way, a chain reaction starts in which all the young animals help one another solve their individual problems. **TIP** Ask participants how each animal helps out. Clap and cheer after the phrase "I can help" is read. (Animals/Friends/Helping)

Cousins, Lucy. *Hooray for Fish!* Cambridge, MA: Candlewick Press, 2005.

This rhyming romp follows along as Little Fish names and gives descriptions of all the different fish in the sea. (Fish/Ocean/Stories in Rhyme)

———. *Maisy Dresses Up.* Cambridge, MA: Candlewick Press, 1999.

Maisy, the little mouse, needs to find a special costume for a dress-up party. Illustrations use bright primary colors and are very simple. (Animals/Clothes/Fall/Mice/Parties/Seasons)

———. *Maisy Drives the Bus.* Cambridge, MA: Candlewick Press, 2000.

Maisy is the bus driver and picks up riders at each stop. Illustrations use bright primary colors and are very simple. (Animals/Buses/Mice/Things That Go)

———. *Maisy's Morning on the Farm.* Cambridge, MA: Candlewick Press, 2000.

Maisy, the little mouse, takes care of the animals on the farm one morning. Illustrations are bright and clear. (Animals/Farms/Mice)

Cowell, Cressida. *What Shall We Do with the Boo-Hoo Baby?* New York: Scholastic Press, 2000.

The animals try everything to get Baby to stop crying, but nothing works! **TIP** Have the participants join in with the animal sounds, and vary the volume till the last set is just a whisper. (Animals/Babies/Helping)

Craig, Lindsey. *Dancing Feet!* New York: Alfred A. Knopf, 2010.

Listen to the sounds of dancing animal feet, follow the tracks across the page, and discover whose feet they belong to. Rhyming text adds a bounce to dance to as it is read. Illustrations of hand-painted paper cut into primary shapes create a collage of different animals. **TIP** Act out the various ways that the animals dance. (Animals/Elephants/Movement/Question-and-Answer Stories)

———. *Farmyard Beat.* **New York: Alfred A. Knopf, 2011.**

> The chicks start dancing to a beat that gets louder as each of the other farm animals join in, and finally Farmer Sue wakes up and joins the party. **TIP** This story lends itself well to clapping along as it is read. (Animals, Farm/ Bedtime/Farms/Movement/Stories in Rhyme)

Crews, Donald. *Freight Train.* **New York: Greenwillow Books, 1978.**

> Bright colors and brief text name the parts of a freight train as it moves along on its journey. **TIP** Add a few "toot toot" sounds throughout the reading, and make believe you are pulling on a train whistle cord. (Colors/ Flannel Board/Things That Go/Trains)

Cronin, Doreen, and Scott Menchin. *Stretch.* **New York: Atheneum Books for Young Readers, 2009.**

> This rhyming text explores all kinds of stretches and things you can do with them. Stretching out wide to fly, stretching your mouth to roar, and stretching together are only a few of the fun exercises the children (and adults) can do during the reading of this story. (Animals/Movement/Sounds)

Demarest, Chris L. *Honk!* **Honesdale, PA: Boyds Mills Press, 1998.**

> Searching for her mother, Little Goose hears all the other animals reply to her question with their own sound. (Animals/Animals, Farms/Families/Farms/ Mothers/Movable Books/Sounds)

Dodd, Emma. *I Love Bugs!* **New York: Holiday House, 2010.**

> Easy-to-read rhyming text and bright illustrations depict all kinds of bugs and the things they do. **TIP** Throughout the story add action (e.g., squirm around, jump, etc.) to the text as it is described. (Bugs/Stories in Rhyme)

Ehlert, Lois. *Snowballs.* **San Diego: Harcourt Brace, 1995.**

> A snow family decorated by items one can find around the house makes this a pleasant winter story to share. Since each snow person is a full, vertical, double-spread illustration, this works well with groups and is fun to use with children 12 to 24 months old. **TIP** Crush tissue paper into balls and let children toss them around. (Families/Snow/Stories in Rhyme/Winter)

Elgar, Rebecca. *Is That an Elephant Over There?* **London: Levinson, 1995.**

> A simple question asked for which lifting the flap gives the animal answer. Children enjoy saying "NO!" until finally the elephant appears. This is in board-book format but its size is okay for group viewing. (Animals/Animals, Jungle/Elephants/Games/Movable Books/Question-and-Answer Stories/Response Books)

Emberley, Ed. *Go Away, Big Green Monster!* **Boston: Little, Brown, 1992.**

> Clever cutouts help a colorful monster appear and disappear piece by piece as the pages are turned. **TIP** During *Go Away, Big Green Monster!*, have the audience wave their hands and say, "Shoo, shoo, shoo" each time a part of the monster is told to "Go away." (Colors/Interactive Books)

Faulkner, Keith. *The Wide-Mouthed Frog: A Pop-Up Book.* New York: Dial Books for Young Readers, 1996.

> While the wide-mouthed frog is hopping around eating flies, he asks the other animals what they eat. See how tiny he can get when he finds out one of them wants him for lunch! (Animals/Food/Frogs/Movable Books)

Fernandes, Eugenie. *Kitten's Autumn.* Toronto, ON: Kids Can Press, 2010.

> Kitten explores the outside world, watching all the forest animals eating before they go to sleep for the winter. Rhyming couplets tell the story using wonderfully descriptive words like "slurp," "snap," and "chomp."
> **TIP** Demonstrate the American Sign Language sign for each animal mentioned in text. See the Language section in chapter 5 for more resources and websites to help you with this. (Animals/Cats/Fall/Farms/Food/Sign Language/Sounds)

———. *Kitten's Spring.* Toronto, ON: Kids Can Press, 2010.

> Kitten discovers the sounds and sights of spring while exploring the outside world of the farm. Rhyming text and mixed-media artwork add to this simple and delightful tale with Kitten hiding on the page. (Animals/Cats/Farms/Sign Language/Sounds/Spring/Stories in Rhyme)

Ferri, Francesca. *Peek-a-Boo.* Hauppauge, NY: Barron's Educational Series, 2005.

> This large, lift-the-flap book encourages the child to play peek-a-boo with all the farm animals. Half the page features the flap covering half the animal's face; when the flap is lowered, the full face appears. **TIP** Have the children cover their eyes before lowering the flap so they can play peek-a-boo along with the story. (Animals/Farms/Games/Lift-the-Flap Books)

Flack, Marjorie. *Ask Mr. Bear.* New York: Macmillan, 1932.

> Danny asks the animals to help him give his mother a gift. Mr. Bear has the perfect answer. This can be done as a flannel-board story or with puppets.
> **TIP** Have the children give the adults they are with a hug at the conclusion. (Animals/Bears/Birthdays/Flannel Board/Mothers)

Fleming, Denise. *Barnyard Banter.* New York: Holt, 1994.

> Looking and listening to the animals on the farm, Goose is hiding on every page. The book uses wonderful and brilliant-colored illustrations.
> **TIP** Encourage everyone to use their voices to join in the chorus of animal sounds. See http://denisefleming.com/ for more ideas. (Animals/Animals, Farm/Farms/Response Books/Sounds/Stories in Rhyme)

———. *Beetle Bop.* Orlando, FL: Harcourt, 2007.

> This rhyming text with illustrations describes a wide variety of bugs and beetles. See http://denisefleming.com/ for activity ideas. (Bugs/Stories in Rhyme)

———. *In the Small, Small Pond.* New York: Henry Holt, 1993.

> This story presents a frog's-eye view of how the seasons change the pond where it lives. (Animals/Outside/Seasons/Stories in Rhyme/Water)

————. *In the Tall, Tall Grass*. **New York: Henry Holt, 1991.**

This rhyming text gives a bug's-eye view of what one may find in the grass when exploring. Terse verse and pulp painting (papermaking technique using cotton fiber, stencils, and accents) illustrate the bright colors and moods found on a hot summer day. **TIP** Use action to bring the text to life; for example, stretch your hands up high as the phrase "tall, tall, grass" is read aloud. Have the participants follow your actions. (Adventure/Animals/Bugs/Outside/Stories in Rhyme)

————. *Lunch*. **New York: Henry Holt, 1992.**

Mouse is hungry and makes a mess while eating his lunch. The large pages include brilliant-colored illustrations. **TIP** Have props/pictures of each item Mouse eats to hold up or put on a flannel board. See http://denisefleming.com/ for patterns and ideas. (Colors/Flannel Board/Food/Manners/Messes/Mice)

————. *Mama Cat Has Three Kittens*. **New York: Henry Holt, 1998.**

Kittens learn from their mama, but little Boris has his own way of learning. (Babies/Cats/Families/Mothers)

————. *Sleepy, Oh So Sleepy*. **New York: Henry Holt, 2010.**

Quietly this story circles the world as various baby animals are lulled to sleep. The repetitive line of "sleepy, oh so sleepy" seems to be a croon urging the little ones to doze off. This is a perfect bedtime routine as the day winds down. Illustrated with pulp painting, a papermaking technique using colored cotton fiber poured through hand-cut stencils and accents added with pastel pencils, the pictures have a textured look. (Animals/Bedtime)

Fox, Mem. *Ten Little Fingers and Ten Little Toes*. **New York: Harcourt, 2008.**

No matter where children are born in the world, they have something in common. This simple theme comes to life with a text that compares two little ones and shows their similarities. Helen Oxenbury's illustrations help show that comparison with multicultural little ones from all parts of the world. **TIP** Have adults tickle the children's fingers and toes whenever the lines "had ten little fingers / and ten little toes" are read. (Babies/Body/Daily Life/Multicultural Stories)

————. *Time for Bed*. **New York: Harcourt, Brace, Jovanovich, 1993.**

The animal parents get their children ready to go to bed. (Bedtime/Families/Stories in Rhyme)

————. *Where Is the Green Sheep?* **New York: Harcourt, 2004.**

The reader can find all kinds of sheep, but the green sheep seems to be missing. Illustrations are simple and bright. **TIP** Each time the question is asked, look in different places, such as your pocket, under a blanket, on your head, and so on. (Animals/Colors/Concepts/Farms/Sheep)

Gag, Wanda. *The ABC Bunny*. New York: Coward-McCann, 1933.

> Bunny explores the world around him one fine day. This alphabet rhyming story has been around a long time and is an easy story to memorize. (Animals/Rabbits/Stories in Rhyme)

Galdone, Paul. *The Little Red Hen*. New York: Houghton Mifflin, 2011.

> Whenever there is work to be done around the house, the little red hen ends up doing it all herself and gives herself a reward when it is finally completed. (Animals/Chickens/Helping/Work)

Garcia, Emma. *Tap, Tap, Bang, Bang*. London: Boxer Books, 2010.

> Animated tools demonstrate what they can do with sound effects to help out. Bold colors illustrate this story on pages large enough to share with groups. **TIP** Use body parts to demonstrate the tools' uses and sounds; for example, twist your wrist for a screwdriver, bang your fists together or on a knee to demonstrate a hammer, and so on. (Construction/Sounds/Tools)

———. *Tip, Tip, Dig, Dig*. London: Boxer Books, 2010.

> Animated trucks are busy at work cleaning up a huge mess and creating something children will enjoy in its place. Sound effects add to the busy feeling the text evokes. **TIP** Use body parts to demonstrate what each truck does and the sound it makes; for example, raise your hands up in the air as the crane lifts, roll your hands around each other as a mixer, and so forth. (Construction/Sounds/Things That Go/Trucks)

George, Lindsay Barrett. *Maggie's Ball*. New York: Greenwillow Books, 2010.

> The wind blows Maggie's ball down the hill, and the little dog tries to find it. There are lots of round shapes in town, but not her ball. When all seems lost and sad, the ball is found by a child and the two become friends. Alternating scenes that focus on Maggie's search and a bird's-eye view of the town encourage readers to look for the ball along with Maggie. (Animals/Dogs/Friends/Play/Toys)

Ginsburg, Mirra. *Across the Stream*. New York: Greenwillow Books, 1982.

> A bad dream chases Mother Hen and her chicks, but when they are rescued by Mother Duck and her ducklings, the bad dream has a happy ending. Illustrations are in bold colors and the text is brief. (Adventure/Animals/Chickens/Ducks/Water)

———. *Good Morning, Chick*. New York: Greenwillow Books, 1980.

> This simple story of a newborn chick's first day on the farm includes the repeating line "like this," which brings attention back to story. Illustrations are bright and clear. (Animals/Animals, Farm/Chickens/Farms)

Gravett, Emily. *Dogs.* **New York: Simon and Schuster Books for Young Readers, 2010.**

There are so many different kinds of dogs to love! This fun book of opposites with lively illustrations brings to life the many wonderful breeds, their behavior and temperament, found in the world of dogs. There is a twist at the end that will surprise everyone. (Animals/Concepts/Dogs/Opposites)

Gray, Nigel. *Time to Play!* **Cambridge, MA: Candlewick Press, 2008.**

A lift-the-flap book adds a dimension of fun to a simple story of a child looking for someone to play with. The searchers trek through the house gathering playmates as they go, and they all end up in the parents' bed to play together. (Families/Lift-the-Flap Books/Play/Stories in Rhyme)

Hacohen, Dean, and Sherry Scharschmidt. *Tuck Me In!* **Somerville, MA: Candlewick Press, 2010.**

When each little animal is asked, "Who needs to be tucked in?" and answers, "I do!," simply turn the adjoining half page and "tuck" the little one into bed. **TIP** Adults can "tuck" their children by holding them on their laps, or have the children tuck the adults with a hug. (Animals/Bedtime/Lift-the-Flap Books)

Hale, Sarah Josepha. *Mary Had a Little Lamb.* **New York: Scholastic, 1990.**

Bruce McMillan has updated this familiar rhyming story of Mary's little lamb. This photo-illustrated version is in a contemporary setting and uses children of many cultures to tell the story. (Poetry/Sheep/Songs/Stories in Rhyme)

Hall, Michael. *My Heart Is Like a Zoo.* **New York: Greenwillow Books, 2010.**

Hall uses heart shapes to create a menagerie of animals that can be used to encourage talking about feelings, shapes, counting, and colors. Vary length by reading only as many pages as the attention span of the audience allows or by selecting the number of pictures shown to the group. **TIP** A simple hands-on activity is to distribute hearts of various sizes and let participants create their own animal using glue sticks and construction paper. (Animals/Colors/Counting/Feelings/Numbers/Shapes/Zoo)

———. *Perfect Square.* **New York: Greenwillow Books, 2011.**

A perfect square is torn to shreds, punched with holes, crumpled, and changed. With each transformation to something new, the changed square is just as happy not being perfect. (Concepts/Feelings/Shapes)

Halpern, Shari. *Little Robin Redbreast: A Mother Goose Rhyme.* **New York: North-South Books, 1994.**

This traditional rhyme is wonderfully illustrated using bold colors, white space, and paper. (Birds/Cats/Poetry/Spring/Stories in Rhyme)

Henkes, Kevin. *Birds.* **New York: Greenwillow Books, 2009.**

A little girl describes all the different birds she sees outside her window and while walking around outside—not only physical descriptions but also what kinds of pictures they create in the sky, in trees, and on wires. (Birds)

————. *A Good Day.* New York: Greenwillow Books, 2007.

As four small animals confront the challenges of a day, everything turns out just fine. This is a quiet story for sharing. (Animals/Birds/Dogs/Feelings)

————. *Kitten's First Full Moon.* New York: Greenwillow Books, 2004.

When Kitten sees the full moon for the first time, she mistakes it for a bowl of milk. After trying to reach it, she ends up tired, wet, and hungry. Returning home, Kitten finds a surprise that makes everything better. (Cats/Moon/Night)

————. *Little White Rabbit.* New York: Greenwillow Books, 2011.

Little Rabbit heads out on an adventure and imagines what it would be like if he could be like the world around him. The full-color illustrations help us picture him as green as the grass, tall as the fir tree, hard as a rock, and fluttering like a butterfly. (Animals/Concepts/Imagination/Rabbits)

————. *Oh!* New York: HarperCollins, 1999.

Waking up in the morning to a snow-white world, everyone wants to play. (Animals/Play/Seasons/Snow/Winter)

————. *Old Bear.* New York: Greenwillow Books, 2008.

Sleeping through the winter months, Old Bear dreams of spring and being a young cub. This is a quiet story about the seasons as they change. (Animals/Bears/Seasons)

Hill, Eric. *Where's Spot?* New York: G.P. Putnam's Sons, 1980.

The original "lift the flap" book presents the story of Spot playing hide-and-seek. The simple story follows Mom as she looks for puppy Spot, who has missed his dinner. Children love to give the answer "NO!" after each flap is lifted. **TIP** Add a few more "NO!" responses after you open the flap and encourage the attendees to join in. (Dogs/Lift-the-Flap Books/Movable Books/Question-and-Answer Stories/Response Books).

Hillenbrand, Will. *Spring Is Here.* New York: Holiday House, 2011.

Mole wants Bear to wake up and celebrate spring, but Bear keeps sleeping. He finally comes up with a delightful and yummy plan. **TIP** Everyone can join in on the sound effects that are built into the text, such as tooting a horn. Hand motions can help illustrate gathering, churning, and mixing. (Animals/Friends/Seasons/Spring)

Hills, Tad. *Duck and Goose Find a Pumpkin.* New York: Schwartz and Wade Books, 2009.

Duck and Goose look all over for a pumpkin, and with some help from a friend, they do find one. (Animals/Ducks/Fall/Question-and-Answer Stories/Seasons)

Hopgood, Tim. *Wow! Said the Owl.* **New York: Farrar, Straus and Giroux, 2009.**

Wondering what daytime looks like, a little owl takes a long nap so she can stay awake all day. She can only say "Wow!" at each new color she sees till night sets in once again and the beautiful stars brighten the night. **TIP** Prompt the audience to respond with "Wow!" each time the owl says it. (Birds/Colors/Owls)

Horáček, Petr. *A New House for Mouse.* **Cambridge, MA: Candlewick Press, 2004.**

Mouse is looking for a new house in which the big yummy apple she found will fit. Die-cut holes throughout the pages allow readers to join Mouse on her search for a new house. **TIP** Insert questions such as "Do you think this will fit?" while reading *A New House for Mouse*, and wait for replies. These replies will come mostly from the adults, but usually after the adults and children have talked about it. Shake your head to demonstrate the body action for the word "NO! (Animals/Apples/Houses/Mice)

Hubbell, Patricia. *Pots and Pans.* **New York: HarperCollins, 1998.**

This is a great story about how baby gets into the pots and pans, creating a glorious concert of sound. The size of the book allows for group viewing, and the rhyming text is fun to read aloud. **TIP** Clap hands or pound fists on floor to the rhythm of the story—remember to keep it steady or it will pick up speed! (Babies/Games/Messes/Music/Play/Sounds)

Hughes, Shirley. *Giving.* **Cambridge, MA: Candlewick Press, 1993.**

A little girl and her brother discover you can give all different kinds of things, some of which make you happy and others not. (Giving/Sharing)

Hutchins, Pat. *Titch.* **New York: Macmillan, 1971.**

Titch may be little, but he certainly shows his big brother and sister that being little is special too. (Families/Gardens/Growing Up/Toys)

Isadora, Rachel. *Peekaboo Morning.* **New York: G.P. Putnam's Sons, 2002.**

A toddler plays peek-a-boo from the moment he wakes up. The last illustration is "I see you!" **TIP** With *Peekaboo Morning*, try incorporating a mirror as a prop. Have adults play peek-a-boo with the children when indicated by the text. (Babies/Daily Life/Games/Multicultural Stories)

————. *Uh-oh!* **Orlando: Harcourt, 2008.**

What has the little one been up to? We find out by turning the page to see what mischief the toddler is doing now. This suspenseful story moves along and will bring laughter to familiar events in daily life with a toddler. **TIP** Have adults chime in on the "Uh-oh" with a wide-eyed, surprised expression, and the children will imitate. (Babies/Daily Life/Families/Multicultural Stories)

Jonas, Ann. *Splash!* **New York: Greenwillow. 1995.**

Everyone into the pond! But how many are in their splashing around? Identify and count them all. (Animals/Counting/Numbers/Water)

Kalan, Robert. *Blue Sea.* New York: Greenwillow, 1972.

Little fish, big fish, bigger fish, and biggest fish meet up in the blue sea. (Concepts/Fish/Size/Water)

————. *Jump, Frog, Jump!* New York: Greenwillow Books, 1981.

This cumulative story always follows the frog, wondering how he got away from all who are after him. Does he catch the fly? Bright, bold colors make this a fun sharing story, and it is also available in big-book format. **TIP** Clap hands for each word in the chant "Jump, frog, jump!" (Animals/ Frogs/Participation/Play/Response Books/Water)

————. *Rain.* New York: Greenwillow Books, 1978.

This story describes a rainstorm using brief text and illustrations in bold colors. **TIP** Chant "Rain, rain, rain" before turning the page. You can increase the volume as the story progresses till the last page, when the chant changes to "Rain, rain, rainbow!" (Colors/Rain/Seasons/Weather)

Katz, Karen. *Where Is Baby's Bellybutton?* New York: Simon and Schuster Books for Children, 2000.

This lift-the-flap book engages the reader by asking him or her to locate different parts of baby's body. The anniversary edition, published in 2010, is oversized (8.5-by-10 inches) and can be used with groups. **TIP** Have adults tickle the children's body parts as identified during the reading of *Where Is Baby's Bellybutton?* (Babies/Concepts/Games/Lift-the-Flap Books)

Kraus, Robert. *Whose Mouse Are You?* New York: Macmillan, 1970.

Aruego's bold illustrations bring this simple story to life. In response to the question, the little mouse connects with his family and has an adventure on the way. (Adventure/Babies/Families/Mice)

Krauss, Ruth. *The Carrot Seed.* New York: Harper and Row, 1945.

A little boy plants a carrot seed that no one thinks will grow. Available in a big-book format, this story can be done as a flannel board or with props. (Gardens)

Kuskin, Karla. *Under My Hood I Have a Hat.* New York: HarperCollins, 2004.

Getting dressed and undressed to play in the snow becomes more fun with this simple poem. Bright illustrations clearly show what item of clothing is being discussed. **TIP** Offer the different items of clothing to try on as an activity. This story may also be told using a flannel board. (Clothes/Flannel Board/Play/Seasons/Winter)

Kutner, Merrily. *Down on the Farm.* New York: Holiday House, 2004.

This one is a keeper! Simple rhyming text with clear, bright illustrations shows life on a farm. Repeated refrain is "Down on the farm." **TIP** For *Down on the Farm,* repeat the line "Down on the farm" twice each time and encourage participants to chime in with you, clapping on "down" and "farm." (Animals/Farms/Participation/Stories in Rhyme)

Langstaff, John. *Oh, A-Hunting We Will Go.* **New York: Atheneum, 1974.**

This is a fun story to sing along with. The story can be modified as to length and animals "caught." It works well as a flannel-board story also. **TIP** By incorporating actions such as clapping hands, lifting feet, and so forth, throughout the story, you can have participants act out the story from beginning to end. (Adventures/Animals/Songs/Stories in Rhyme)

———. *Over in the Meadow.* **New York: Harcourt, Brace, 1957.**

Lovely illustrations go along with this familiar counting song of childhood. **TIP** This childhood song works well as a flannel-board story. (Animals/Counting/Numbers/Songs/Stories in Rhyme)

Lawrence, Michael. *Baby Loves.* **New York: DK Publishing, 1999.**

Find out what baby loves best in this fun romp through baby's day. The pictures are fun for all; even adults will laugh at what baby is actually illustrated doing. (Babies/Daily Life/Families)

Lear, Edward. *The Owl and the Pussycat.* **New York: Clarion, 1987.**

Paul Galdone's cartoon illustrations help tell the story of Lear's poem. Pages are big enough to share with a large group. (Animals/Birds/Cats/Owls/Poetry/Stories in Rhyme)

———. *The Owl and the Pussycat.* **New York: G.P. Putnam's Sons, 1991.**

Jan Brett has created a wonderfully detailed illustration of Lear's story-poem set in the Caribbean. The brilliant colors fill the pages, and the story is easy to memorize. (Animals/Birds/Cats/Owls/Poetry/Stories in Rhyme)

Lewis, Kevin. *Chugga-Chugga Choo-Choo.* **New York: Hyperion Books, 2001.**

This story describes a freight train's day from dawn till night, all from the viewpoint of a toy train. It includes bold artwork. **TIP** Make *Chugga-Chugga Choo-Choo* an interactive story by having the audience repeat the refrain "Chugga-chugga, choo-choo" and adding a few "train whistles" for fun. (Stories in Rhyme/Things That Go/Toys/Trains)

Lewison, Wendy Cheyette. *Raindrop, Plop!* **New York: Viking, 2004.**

A young girl and her dog count the things they play with outside and inside on a rainy day. Read the whole story or read it as two shorter stories when divided as only the outside time (counting 1–10) or the inside time (counting 10–1). (Rain/Stories in Rhyme/Weather)

Light, Steve. *Trains Go.* **San Francisco: Chronicle Books, 2012.**

This board book is filled with lots of different kinds of trains and the different sounds they make. (Sounds/Things That Go/Trains)

Litwin, Eric. *Pete the Cat: I Love My White Shoes.* **New York: Harper, 2010.**

Pete the Cat sings as he strolls down the road about how much he loves his white shoes, no matter what. His positive attitude does not change even when the shoes change color! **TIP** Participants should join the chorus of "Goodness, no!" every time he steps in something, clapping and singing along with Pete's song. The song is available online at http://www .harpercollinschildrens.com/feature/petethecat/. (Animals/Cats/Colors/Concepts/ Messes/Music/Participation/Songs)

Lobel, Anita. *Hello, Day!* **New York: Greenwillow, 2008.**

From sunup to sundown, each farm animal greets the day with its own unique sound. **TIP** Have adults repeat the animal sounds after the reader. (Animals/Farms/Sounds)

Macken, JoAnn Early. *Baby Says "Moo!"* **New York: Disney Hyperion Books, 2011.**

Baby's answer is always the same when asked what people or dogs or horses or birds say: "MOO!" This rhyming text takes us along looking for the animal that makes Baby's sound. Simple and bright artwork makes this a fun book to share. (Animals/Sounds)

MacLennan, Cathy. *Chicky Chicky Chook Chook.* **New York: Boxer Books, 2007.**

After a morning rumpus of action and sounds, the chicks, bees, and kitties settle down for a quiet rest until a nasty storm wakes them up. Through the use of energetic pictures and words, this text is a delight to read aloud. Playing with language is clearly evident in this book. **TIP** Children can act out this simple story and give voice to the sounds that fill this fun book. (Animals/Bugs/Cats/Chickens/Farms/Rain/Stories in Rhyme/Weather)

Martin Jr., Bill. *Brown Bear, Brown Bear, What Do You See?* **New York: Holt, Rinehart and Winston, 1967.**

A popular title for this age group, this question-and-answer rhyming story uses bold artwork and encourages the listeners to join the storytelling. **TIP** Incorporate sign language while telling *Brown Bear, Brown Bear, What Do You See?*; this story can also be done as a simple flannel-board story. (Animals/Colors/Flannel Board/Participation/Question-and-Answer Stories/Response Books/Sign Language/Stories in Rhyme)

———. *Here Are My Hands.* **New York: Henry Holt, 1985.**

This simple text in rhyme focuses on discovering parts of the body. **TIP** Touch each part of the body as it appears in the text. (Body/Stories in Rhyme)

———. *Kitty Cat, Kitty Cat, Are You Waking Up?* **New York: Marshall Cavendish, 2008.**

Getting ready for school takes Kitty Cat such a long time because of all the other things going on around the house. (Animals/Cats/Daily Life/Stories in Rhyme)

———. *Ten Little Caterpillars.* **New York: Beach Lane Books, 2011.**
> We follow the adventures of ten little caterpillars as they explore the world around them. This is a storybook, counting book, and information book all in one, with amazing illustrations by Lois Elhert. Additional information, including what type of butterfly each turns into, is at the back of the book. (Bugs/Caterpillars/Counting/Outside/Stories in Rhyme)

McDonnell, Christine. *Dog Wants to Play.* **New York: Viking, 2009.**
> All the other animals on the farm are too busy to play with Puppy until someone who has finished his chores comes looking for a playmate. **TIP** Use your voice and facial expressions to create a sense of increasing frustration and sadness that resolves by the end of the story. (Animals/Dogs/Farms/Friends/Games/Stories in Rhyme)

McDonnell, Flora. *I Love Animals.* **Cambridge, MA: Candlewick Press, 1994.**
> All the animals on the farm are loved by a child who identifies each one. Illustrations are the perfect size to share with a group. **TIP** In *I Love Animals*, use animals sounds after naming each animal; use when singing "Old MacDonald Had a Farm" or "When Cows Get Up in the Morning." (Animals/Animals, Farms/Farms)

———. *Splash!* **Cambridge, MA: Candlewick Press, 1999.**
> Baby elephant comes up with a great idea to cool off all the animals on a really hot day. Large pages are good for group sharing. (Animals, Jungle/Elephants/Play/Water)

Miller, Margaret. 2009. *Baby Faces.* **New York: Simon and Schuster.**
> This board books offers some classical facial expressions, such as smile, sad, pout, and so on, that adults can try to have little ones mimic. **TIP** Have adults make the facial expressions described while the children and adults are looking at each other. (Babies/Body/Daily Life)

———. *What's on My Head?* **New York: Little Simon, 1998.**
> This book features wonderful photographs of infants with different objects on their heads. This board book is a good size for midsized groups. **TIP** Act out *What's on My Head?* by putting the objects shown on your head or on the doll/puppet/animal's head, if using one. (Babies/Body/Photographs)

Miller, Virginia. *Ten Red Apples: A Bartholomew Bear Counting Book.* **Cambridge, MA: Candlewick Press, 2002.**
> This is a simple story about collecting apples that can also be used as a counting book. This book is large enough to share with groups and can be done as a flannel-board story. **TIP** *Ten Red Apples: A Bartholomew Bear Counting Book* works well as a flannel-board story. (Animals/Apples/Bears/Counting/Fall/Numbers/Seasons)

Murphy, Mary. *Caterpillar's Wish*. New York: DK Publishing, 1999.

Caterpillar wishes to fly as her friends do, but she cannot, until she turns into a butterfly. Bold, clear, colorful illustrations complement the very simple text. (Bugs/Caterpillars/Seasons/Spring)

————. *How Kind!* Cambridge, MA: Candlewick Press, 2004.

A circle of kindness touches all the animals on the farm when Hen gives Pig an egg. **TIP** Adults should give children a hug whenever the word "kind" is said. (Animals/Farms/Kindness)

————. *I Kissed the Baby!* Cambridge, MA: Candlewick Press. 2004.

Bold, black-and-white illustrations with splashes of yellow add excitement as all the animals ask one another about their experience meeting the baby! Although available now only in board-book format, this simple sing-song story conveys the fun and excitement of having a new baby around. (Animals/Babies/Daily Life)

————. *I Like It When . . .* New York: Houghton Mifflin, 2005.

Little penguin likes to share all his favorite things with a very special person, his mother. Bold, primary-colored, two-page illustrations makes this a fun book to share with groups. (Birds/Mothers)

————. *A Kiss Like This*. Somerville, MA: Candlewick Press, 2012.

This book, filled with a series of animal parents sharing all kinds of kisses with their children, will encourage listeners to give a kiss to their own special person. **TIP** Encourage the adults and children to share different kisses, like those a fish, a giraffe, or an owl might give. (Animals/Feelings/Mothers)

Murray, Alison. *One Two That's My Shoe!* New York: Disney Hyperion Books, 2011.

A mischievous puppy adds a new twist to the nursery rhyme "1, 2, Buckle My Shoe," and fun ensues. This whimsical story begs to be read again and again, not only for its silliness but also for practice counting and showing the number three ways: numerical, word, and image. (Counting/Dogs/Stories in Rhyme)

Oxenbury, Helen. 1993. *It's My Birthday!* Cambridge, MA: Candlewick Press.

A little boy asks his animal friends to help him gather the ingredients for his birthday cake. **TIP** *It's My Birthday!* is a possible flannel-board story, or use props pulled from a bag or box. The storyteller can mime mixing the cake. (Animals/Birthdays/Daily Life/Flannel Board/Food/Friends)

————. *Tickle, Tickle*. New York: Aladdin Books, 1987.

Illustrations of multicultural children are large and clear in bright colors in this oversized board book with rhyming text. (Babies/Games/Sounds)

Patricelli, Leslie. *Yummy, YUCKY*. Cambridge, MA: Candlewick Press, 2003.

Using only these two words, Patricelli presents a story of opposites—things that are yummy and things that are yucky. **TIP** Use facial expressions to visualize what the words "yummy" and "yucky" mean. Encourage the participants to do this also with the adults looking at the children. (Concepts/Food/Opposites)

Peterson, Mary, and Jennifer Rofé. *Piggies in the Pumpkin Patch.* **Watertown, MA: Charlesbridge, 2010.**

Pigs have a wonderful time playing in the pumpkin patch and other spots on the farm, encountering other animals along the way. (Adventure/Concepts/Farms/Pigs)

Polacco, Patricia. *Mommies Say Shh!* **New York: Philomel Books, 2005.**

Using the simplest of text and a variety of animal noises, this read-aloud story is fun to share. (Animals/Mothers/Sounds)

Prap, Lila. *Animals Speak.* **New York: North-South Books, 2006.**

Does a cow always say, "Moo"? This text is a guide to animal "languages" around the world. Enjoy seeking and hearing how animals "speak" in other lands, including such languages as German, Spanish, Swahili, Thai, and Farsi. Each sound is offered in English and at least three other languages, with each sound identified by the country's name and flag. Each is also spelled out in its original alphabet and the English equivalent. A pronunciation guide appears in the front and back of the book. (Animals/Sounds)

Raffi. *Five Little Ducks.* **New York: Crown, 1989.**

Mother Duck sets off to find her little ducklings after they disappear one by one. (Counting/Ducks/Exploring/Numbers/Songs)

Rice, Eve. *Sam Who Never Forgets.* **New York: Greenwillow Books, 1977.**

What happens when the animals at the zoo realize the elephant has not been fed? Did Sam the zookeeper forget? Returned to print in 1987, this story once again has the listener wondering along with the poor elephant if dinner will ever arrive. (Animals/Elephants/Food/Zoo)

Rockwell, Anne, and Harlow Rockwell. *The First Snowfall.* **New York: Macmillan, 1987.**

From the very first snowflake, we join a little girl as she enjoys the sights and sounds of her snow-covered world. (Clothes/Snow/Weather/Winter)

Rohann, Eric. *A Kitten's Tale.* **New York: Alfred A. Knopf, 2008.**

Winter snow is on its way, and the three little kittens are worried, but the fourth little kitten can't wait! (Animals/Cats/Play/Seasons/Snow/Winter)

Rosen, Michael. *We're Going on a Bear Hunt.* **London: Mantra, 1989.**

This follow-the-leader story may be used with children 12 to 24 months old as a participation story. Helen Oxenbury's illustrations enhance the story but with large groups they may be difficult to see. **TIP** Before starting *We're Going on a Bear Hunt*, ask everyone to clap their hands to its rhythm and do actions to get past each obstacle. Vary the length of the story by limiting the places the readers "travel" through, such as just the grass, mud, river, or cave, to find the bear or by reading the entire text. (Adventures/Animals/Bears/Games/Participation)

Savage, Stephen. *Little Tug.* **New York: Roaring Book Press, 2012.**

Little Tug may not be the biggest ship in the harbor, but he still has an important job to do. (Things That Go)

Sayre, April Pulley. *If You're Hoppy*. **New York: Greenwillow Books, 2011.**

The traditional song "If You're Happy and You Know It . . ." gets a new twist. Various animals hop, growl, and flap and are sloppy, slimy, scaly, and mean in this brightly illustrated and funny book. (Animals/Movement/Music/Songs/Stories in Rhyme)

Schertle, Alice. *All You Need for a Snowman*. **San Diego: Harcourt, 2002.**

This story lists everything needed to build a snowman. **TIP** During *All You Need for a Snowman*, have listeners roll their hands, each around the other, to make "snowballs." Tie the story to an activity, such as dancing to "The Waltz of the Snowflakes" from *The Nutcracker* or toss tulle circles (available at most fabric or craft stores) in the air and try to catch the "snowflakes." (Play/Snow/Winter)

Scott, Ann Herbert. *On Mother's Lap*. **New York: Clarion Books, 1992.**

Mother's lap can hold everything a little Eskimo boy would want, but he is not sure there's room for baby. This simple text with the soothing and repeating line "Back and forth, back and forth they rocked" invites the participants to rock back and forth along with their children. **TIP** Encourage children to sit with the adults, preferably on their laps, and rock back and forth. (Babies/Families/Mothers)

Seuss, Dr. *My Many Colored Days*. **New York: Random House, 1996.**

This rhyming story uses colors to describe a day by associating its mood or feeling with a color. The story can also be presented as a flannel-board story. (Colors/Feelings/Stories in Rhyme)

Shaw, Nancy. *Sheep in a Jeep*. **Boston: Houghton Mifflin, 1986.**

This is a funny, rollicking, rhyming story of sheep driving a jeep. Word sounds are great for reading aloud. (Sheep/Stories in Rhyme/Things That Go)

Siddals, Mary McKenna. *Millions of Snowflakes*. **New York: Clarion Books, 1998.**

A child counts snowflakes as they fall. This is a small book with a playful and rhyming text. (Flannel Board/Snow/Stories in Rhyme/Weather/Winter)

Simmons, Jane. *Come Along, Daisy!* **New York: Little, Brown, 1997.**

Duckling Daisy gets so involved in discovering her surroundings that she momentarily loses her mother. Artwork is in bright colors, and the page size makes this large enough to share with a group. The story can be shortened, as desired, by turning from the page where Daisy discovers herself alone to the page where she hears rustling on the riverbank. **TIP** Have participants repeat the line "Come along, Daisy!" as it is read. (Adventure/Ducks/Exploring/Mothers)

Smee, Nicola. *Clip-Clop*. **London: Boxer Books, 2006.**

Mr. Horse is very happy to give Cat, Dog, Pig, and Duck a ride but warns them to hold on tight when asked to "Go faster!" **TIP** Participants can clap to the "clip-clop" phrase, or adults can bounce the child on their laps/knees. Have adults give the children a big hug on "Whoa!" (Animals/Farms/Friends/Horses/Play)

Stoeke, Janet. 1994. *A Hat for Minerva Louise.* **New York: Dutton.**

> This is a charming story about everyone's favorite hen. To stay out longer in the snow, Minerva Louise looks for something to keep her warm. `TIP` When reading *A Hat for Minerva Louise*, use scarves to put on the children's heads as hats. Have different kinds of hats for the children to try on (these will need to be disinfected after using). Talk to the audience about what the picture shows Minerva Louise is really looking at, for example, a garden hose instead of a scarf. (Animals/Chickens/Clothes/Farms/Seasons/Winter)

Suen, Anastasia. *Red Light, Green Light.* **Orlando: Harcourt, 2005.**

> The imagination of a little boy gets all the trucks, cars, and helicopters moving, not only visually but with various sound effects. `TIP` Use hand signals to show "stop" and "go." (Cars/Stories in Rhyme/Things That Go/Trucks)

Suteyev, V. *The Chick and the Duckling.* **New York: Macmillan, 1972.**

> Chick wants to do everything Duckling does with some interesting results. The original story is translated from the Russian by Mirra Ginsburg. (Adventure/Animals/Chickens/Ducks)

Tafuri, Nancy. *The Big Storm: A Very Soggy Counting Book.* **New York: Simon and Schuster Books for Young Readers, 2009.**

> As a rainstorm arrives, the animals of the forest run to a hill hollow to stay dry. Come the morning, they discover someone else was using it to stay dry as well. (Animals/Counting/Numbers/Rain/Water/Weather)

———. *Blue Goose.* **New York: Simon and Schuster Books for Young Readers, 2008.**

> A black-and-white farm is so dull! What would be better than to liven it up using lots of colors? When Farmer Gray goes out, Blue Goose, Red Goose, Yellow Goose, and White Goose get busy painting the farm. `TIP` Have everyone help mix the colors together by circling their arms in front of themselves like they are stirring something in a bowl. (Animals/Colors/Farms)

———. *The Busy Little Squirrel.* **New York: Simon and Schuster Books for Young Readers, 2006.**

> Squirrel is so busy getting ready for winter that there is no time to play, hop, or nibble when asked to join in with his friends' activities. Introduce the American Sign Language sign for each animal. For more information, see the Language section and its corresponding resources in chapter 5 (Animals/Fall/Seasons/Sign Language/Work)

———. *Five Little Chicks.* **New York: Simon and Schuster Books for Young Readers, 2006.**

> Looking for breakfast, the chicks learn from Mother Hen. (Animals/Chickens/Farms)

———. *Have You Seen My Duckling?* **New York: Greenwillow Books, 1984.**

> While Mother Duck is looking for her little one, he is off exploring the world. Children will enjoy spotting him in the illustrations while Mother Duck is looking elsewhere. (Adventure/Ducks/Exploring/Mothers/Water)

————. *Mama's Little Bears.* New York: Scholastic Press, 2002.

This is a simple story of three little bears exploring the woods "on their own" with Mama always in the background, adding a sense of security. The cubs find the answers to their questions of what is over, under, in, and so on. The large size of this book makes it easy to share with groups. TIP While reading *Mama's Little Bears,* pause to give the children time to locate objects in the pictures and perhaps answer the questions that the little bears ask. You can also ask them if they see Mama and point her out in each of the pictures. (Adventure/Animals/Bears/Families/Mothers/Question-and-Answer Stories)

————. *This Is the Farmer.* New York: HarperCollins, 1994.

A chain of events that begins with a farmer's kiss proves to be a lively romp. Children will enjoy looking for the mouse found on most pages. (Animals/ Animals, Farms/Farms/Mice)

————. *Whose Chick Are You?* New York: HarperCollins, 2007.

Whom does the newborn hatchling belong to? The farm animals know it is not theirs, but then whose? The answer is right in the picture, and so are the parents, if one looks closely. TIP Use animal sounds to bring the participants' attention back to the story. (Animals/Babies/Families/Farms/Sounds)

Thomas, Jan. *Can You Make a Scary Face?* New York: Simon and Schuster, 2009.

This interactive story, told by a funny green bug, encourages the participants to make their own scary faces, act out ways they would react to various situations like a bug in their shirt, and, finally, help the bug scare the great big frog. Boldly colored illustrations outlined in black make this book easy to share with groups. TIP Have participants make their own scary faces and get up and move to the storyline (chicken dance anyone?). (Animals/Bugs/Feelings/Frogs)

————. *Pumpkin Trouble.* New York: Harper, 2011.

Turning a pumpkin into a jack-o-lantern can be a scary adventure, as Duck, Pig, and Mouse find out. (Animals/Ducks/Farms/Holidays/Mice/Pigs)

Thompson, Lauren. *Mouse's First Fall.* New York: Simon and Schuster, 2006.

Bright fall colors illustrate this simple story of Mouse and Minka sharing a windy autumn day. (Animals/Fall/Friends/Mice/Play/Seasons)

————. *Mouse's First Snow.* New York: Simon and Schuster, 2005.

Little Mouse and Poppa discover all the fun things one can do in the white winter snow. (Animals/Mice/Seasons/Snow/Winter)

————. *Mouse's First Spring.* New York: Simon and Schuster, 2005.

Little Mouse and Mama head outside to see if spring has arrived. (Animals/ Mice/Seasons/Spring)

Tidholm, Anna-Clara. *Knock! Knock!* San Francisco: Mackenzie Smiles, 2009.

Surprises await the reader as each colored door is opened one after the other. TIP Before each page is turned, thus opening a door, everyone has to "knock" on the floor or make the "knock" sound. (Colors/Sounds)

Van Rynbach, Iris. *The Five Little Pumpkins.* **Honesdale, PA: Boyds Mills Press, 1995.**

This traditional finger rhyme is illustrated with large, easy-to-see illustrations. (Holidays/Seasons/Stories in Rhyme)

Vere, Ed. *Chick.* **New York: Henry Holt, 2010.**

This pop-up book of a chick's very first day in the world is simply told with bright, primary-color illustrations. From the crack of the egg to pecking, pooping, and sleeping, this wide-eyed chick will keep the audience's attention focused on the story. **TIP** Participants can join in on making the sound effects. (Animals/Chickens/Movable Books)

Waddell, Martin. *Owl Babies.* **Cambridge, MA: Candlewick Press, 1992.**

Baby owls Sarah, Percy, and Bill try to be brave when Mother Owl goes out one night. Sticking together and talking to one another help until Mother Owl comes home. Through it all, each personality shines, from the logical Sarah to the nervous Percy, and there is no question that Mother Owl is very important to Bill. **TIP** Use care when reading this story about separation. In addition to using three different voices for the three baby owls, you can use facial expressions to help soften the impact of Mother Owl being gone. (Birds/Feelings/Mothers/Owls)

Wellington, Monica. *Mr. Cookie Baker.* **New York: Dutton Children's Books, 2006.**

The reader follows Mr. Cookie Baker through his day, from getting things ready to bake till he closes the store. The text is simple and the colors are bright. Cookie recipes are included in the back. **TIP** Have participants do the motions that go along with stirring, rolling, and otherwise preparing the cookie dough. (Food/Movement)

Whippo, Walt. *Little White Duck.* **New York: Little, Brown, 2000.**

This popular children's song, illustrated by Joan Paley with bright colors, begs to be shared. The book is a good size for sharing with groups. The score, by Bernard Zaritsky, is included. This is a definite hit with a group. **TIP** Encourage those who know this song to sing *Little White Duck* along with you. (Animals/Ducks/Music/Songs)

Willems, Mo. *Cat the Cat, Who Is That?* **New York: HarperCollins, 2010.**

Cat the Cat introduces everyone to her friends. (Animals/Cats/Friends)

Williams, Sue. *I Went Walking.* **San Diego: Harcourt Brace Jovanovich, 1990.**

Out for a walk, a boy identifies the different colored animals that he sees. Great for identifying not only the animals but the colors as well. This would work well as a flannel-board story. (Adventure/Animals/Animals, Farms/Outside/Question-and-Answer Stories/Response Books/Stories in Rhyme)

——. *Let's Go Visiting.* **San Diego: Harcourt Brace, 1998.**

Off on a day of visiting the animals on the farm, a child counts and gives the color of each one he sees. Available in a big-book format, it can also be told as a flannel-board story. (Animals/Animals, Farm/Counting/Numbers/Response Books/Stories in Rhyme)

Williams, Vera B. *"More More More," Said the Baby.* New York: Greenwillow Books, 1990.

Father, Grandmother, and Mother all give their own baby some loving attention. Each of the three stories can be used on its own. (Babies/Families)

Wilson, Karma. *Bear Snores On.* New York: Margaret K. McElderry Books, 2002.

One cold night, the animals decide to stay in Bear's den and have a party. After all, Bear is sound asleep and nothing can wake him up, but something does. Bear wakes up to discover his friends had a party without him, and he becomes very upset. The animals make things right by having another party. **TIP** Have the group make noise, and then with a "Shhhhh" say, "Bear snores on." (Animals/Bears/Friends/Seasons/Winter)

———. *The Cow Loves Cookies.* New York: Margaret K. McElderry Books, 2010.

Why does the cow love cookies when all the other farm animals eat their usual food? The fun, rhyming text follows the farmer as he feeds his animals and answers the question. **TIP** Rub tummy when "the cow loves cookies" is read aloud. (Cows/Farms/Food)

Wojtowycz, David. *Can You Moo?* New York: Cartwheel, 2003.

In this brightly illustrated story, each little animal makes its own sound. **TIP** An invitation to join in gives the participants a chance to make animal sounds. (Animals/Sounds)

Wolf, Sallie. *Truck Stuck.* Watertown, MA: Charlesbridge, 2008.

No one can figure out how to remove a big truck stuck under a bridge. Rhyming text describes the various trucks caught in the traffic jam and what's going on. Everyone celebrates when things are resolved. (Stories in Rhyme/Things That Go/Trucks)

Wood, Audrey. *Blue Sky.* New York: Blue Sky Press, 2012.

Using simple words and artistic illustrations, Wood celebrates the changing sky throughout the day, from "blue sky" to "cloud sky" to "rain sky" to "star sky." Looking up has never been so interesting! (Clouds/Daily Life/Night/Rain/Weather)

Wood, Don and Audrey. *The Little Mouse, the Red Ripe Strawberry, and the Big Hungry Bear.* New York: Child's Play (International), 1984.

The narrator/reader tells Little Mouse that the big hungry bear will find the strawberry no matter what. Artwork is clear, bright, colorful, and large enough for groups to see. All ages will delight in Little Mouse's ideas for hiding the berry. (It's a good story to show how picture books can be fun for adults too.) (Bears/Food/Mice)

———. *Piggies.* New York: Harcourt Brace Jovanovich, 1991.

This rollicking tale unfolds as piggies dance across a child's fingertips. **TIP** The adults can give the children "tickles" during the reading of this story to add to the fun. (Bedtime/Body/Games/Pigs)

Ziefert, Harriet, and Simms Taback. *Who Said Moo?* New York: Blue Apple Books, 2009.

This simple story starts when Rooster hears "Moo" in answer to his "Cock-a-doodle do" one morning. He asks each animal he meets, "Was it you?" Half-page flaps are easy to use and clearly give each animal's sound when turned. Delightful, bright, colored illustrations will keep the little ones' attention.
(Animals/Farms/Lift-the-Flap Books/Sounds)

Theme Index for Books

To simplify planning and to save the presenter time, the books from the previous bibliography are here organized into themes, or subjects. These are by no means the only titles available for each topic; new titles are always being released, and older titles have a way of being rediscovered. When you find a title that works for you, just add it to the list. This way you will have a relatively easy time when setting up the program and have easy access to the titles that work for you.

ADVENTURE
Across the Stream by Mirra Ginsburg
The Chick and the Duckling by V. Suteyev
Come Along, Daisy! by Jane Simmons
Have You Seen My Duckling? by Nancy Tafuri
I Went Walking by Sue Williams
In the Tall, Tall Grass by Denise Fleming
Mama's Little Bears by Nancy Tafuri
Oh, A-Hunting We Will Go by John Langstaff
Piggies in the Pumpkin Patch by Mary Peterson and Jennifer Rofé
We're Going on a Bear Hunt by Michael Rosen
Whose Mouse Are You? by Robert Kraus

ANIMALS
The ABC Bunny by Wanda Gag
Across the Stream by Mirra Ginsburg
Animals Speak by Lila Prap
Ask Mr. Bear by Marjorie Flack
Baby Says "Moo!" by JoAnn Early Macken
Barnyard Banter by Denise Fleming
Bear Snores On by Karma Wilson
The Big Storm by Nancy Tafuri
Blue Goose by Nancy Tafuri

Book! Book! Book! by Deborah Bruss
The Bridge Is Up by Babs Bell
Brown Bear, Brown Bear, What Do You See? by Bill Martin Jr.
The Busy Little Squirrel by Nancy Tafuri
Can You Make a Scary Face? by Jan Thomas
Can You Moo? by David Wojtowycz
Cat the Cat, Who Is That? by Mo Willems
Chick by Ed Vere
The Chick and the Duckling by V. Suteyev
Chicky Chick Chook Chook by Cathy MacLennan
Chuck's Truck by Peggy Perry Anderson
Clip-Clop by Nicola Smee
Dancing Feet! by Lindsey Craig
Dog Wants to Play by Christine McDonnell
Dogs by Emily Gravett
Down on the Farm by Merrily Kutner
Duck and Goose Find a Pumpkin by Tad Hills
Duck in the Truck by Jez Alborough
Five Little Chicks by Nancy Tafuri
From Head to Toe by Eric Carle
The Golden Egg Book by Margaret Wise Brown
A Good Day by Kevin Henkes
Good Morning, Chick by Mirra Ginsburg
Good Night, Good Night by Sandra Boynton
A Hat for Minerva Louise by Janet Stoeke
Hello, Day! by Anita Lobel
Home for a Bunny by Margaret Wise Brown
Honk! by Chris Demarest
How Kind! by Mary Murphy
I Can Help by David Costello
I Kissed the Baby! by Mary Murphy
I Like Books by Anthony Browne
I Like Me! by Nancy Carlson
I Love Animals by Flora McDonnell
I Went Walking by Sue Williams
If You're Hoppy by April Sayre
In the Small, Small Pond by Denise Fleming
In the Tall, Tall Grass by Denise Fleming
Is That an Elephant Over There? by Rebecca Elgar
It's My Birthday! by Helen Oxenbury
Jump, Frog, Jump! by Robert Kalan

A Kiss Like This by Mary Murphy

Kitten's Autumn by Eugenie Fernandes

Kitten's Spring by Eugenie Fernandes

A Kitten's Tale by Eric Rohann

Kitty Cat, Kitty Cat, Are You Waking Up? by Bill Martin Jr.

Let's Go Visiting by Sue Williams

Little Gorilla by Ruth Bornstein

The Little Red Hen by Paul Galdone

Little White Duck, by Walt Whippo

Little White Rabbit by Kevin Henkes

Maggie's Ball by Lindsay Barrett George

Maisy Dresses Up by Lucy Cousins

Maisy Drives the Bus by Lucy Cousins

Maisy's Morning on the Farm by Lucy Cousins

Mama's Little Bears by Nancy Tafuri

Meeow and the Big Box by Sebastien Braun

Mommies Say Shh! by Patricia Polacco

Mouse's First Fall by Lauren Thompson

Mouse's First Snow by Lauren Thompson

Mouse's First Spring by Lauren Thompson

My Heart Is Like a Zoo by Michael Hall

A New House for Mouse by Petr Horáček

Oh! by Kevin Henkes

Oh, A-Hunting We Will Go by John Langstaff

Old Bear by Kevin Henkes

Old MacDonald Had a Farm by Frances Cony

On Our Way Home by Sebastien Braun

One More Hug for Madison by Caroline Church

Over in the Meadow by John Langstaff

The Owl and the Pussycat by Edward Lear

Peek-a-Boo by Francesca Ferri

Peek-a-Moo! by Marie Torres Cimarusti

Pete the Cat: I Love My White Shoes by Eric Litwin

Pumpkin Trouble by Jan Thomas

Sam Who Never Forgets by Eve Rice

Says Who? by David Carter

Sleepy, Oh So Sleepy by Denise Fleming

Splash! by Ann Jonas

Spring Is Here by Will Hillenbrand

Stretch by Doreen Cronin and Scott Menchin

Ten Red Apples by Virginia Miller

This Is the Farmer by Nancy Tafuri

Treasure by Suzanne Bloom

Tuck Me In! by Dean Hacohen and Sherry Scharschmidt

The Very Quiet Cricket by Eric Carle

We're Going on a Bear Hunt by Michael Rosen

What Shall We Do with the Boo-Hoo Baby? by Cressida Cowell

Where Is the Green Sheep? by Mem Fox

Who Said Moo? by Harriet Ziefert and Simms Taback

Whose Chick Are You? by Nancy Tafuri

Whose Nose and Toes? by John Butler

The Wide-Mouthed Frog by Keith Faulkner

ANIMALS, FARM

Good Morning, Chick by Mirra Ginsburg

Barnyard Banter by Denise Fleming

Farmyard Beat by Lindsey Craig

Honk! by Chris Demarest

I Love Animals by Flora McDonnell

I Went Walking by Sue Williams

Let's Go Visiting by Sue Williams

Old MacDonald Had a Farm by Frances Cony

This Is the Farmer by Nancy Tafuri

ANIMALS, JUNGLE

Is That an Elephant Over There? by Rebecca Elgar

Little Gorilla by Ruth Bornstein

Splash! by Flora McDonnell

APPLES

A New House for Mouse by Petr Horáček

Ten Red Apples by Virginia Miller

BABIES

All of Baby Nose to Toes by Victoria Adler

Baby Faces by Margaret Miller

Baby Loves by Michael Lawrence

I Kissed the Baby! by Mary Murphy

Mama Cat Has Three Kittens by Denise Fleming

"More More More," Said the Baby by Vera B. Williams

On Mother's Lap by Ann Herbert Scott

Peekaboo Morning by Rachel Isadora

Pots and Pans by Patricia Hubbell

Ten Little Fingers and Ten Little Toes by Mem Fox

Tickle, Tickle by Helen Oxenbury

Uh-oh! by Rachel Isadora

What Shall We Do with the Boo-Hoo Baby? by Cressida Cowell

What's on My Head? by Margaret Miller

Where Is Baby's Bellybutton? by Karen Katz

Whose Chick Are You? by Nancy Tafuri

Whose Mouse Are You? by Robert Kraus

BATHTIME—*SEE* WATER

BEARS

Ask Mr. Bear by Marjorie Flack

Bear Snores On by Karma Wilson

Just Like Daddy by Frank Asch

Little Mouse, the Red Ripe Strawberry, and the Big Hungry Bear
 by Don and Audrey Wood

Mama's Little Bears by Nancy Tafuri

Old Bear by Kevin Henkes

On Our Way Home by Sebastien Braun

Ten Red Apples by Virginia Miller

Treasure by Suzanne Bloom

We're Going on a Bear Hunt by Michael Rosen

BEDTIME

Farmyard Beat by Lindsey Craig

Good Night, Good Night by Sandra Boynton

Goodnight Moon by Margaret Wise Brown

Grandfather Twilight by Barbara Berger

I'm Not Sleepy! by Jonathan Allen

On Our Way Home by Sebastien Braun

One More Hug for Madison by Caroline Church

Piggies by Don and Audrey Wood

Sleepy, Oh So Sleepy by Denise Fleming

Ten, Nine, Eight by Molly Bang

Time for Bed by Mem Fox

Tuck Me In! by Dean Hacohen and Sherry Scharschmidt

BIRDS

Birds by Kevin Henkes
A Good Day by Kevin Henkes
I Like It When . . . by Mary Murphy
I'm Not Sleepy! by Jonathan Allen
Little Robin Redbreast by Shari Halpern
The Owl and the Pussycat by Edward Lear
Owl Babies by Martin Waddell
Treasure by Suzanne Bloom
Wow! Said the Owl by Tim Hopgood

BIRTHDAYS

Ask Mr. Bear by Marjorie Flack
It's My Birthday! by Helen Oxenbury
Little Gorilla by Ruth Bornstein

BODY

All of Baby Nose to Toes by Victoria Adler
Baby Faces by Margaret Miller
Here Are My Hands by Bill Martin Jr.
Piggies by Don and Audrey Wood
Ten Little Fingers and Ten Little Toes by Mem Fox
What's on My Head? by Margaret Miller

BOOKS

Book! Book! Book! by Deborah Bruss
I Like Books by Anthony Browne

BUGS

Beetle Bop by Denise Fleming
Can You Make a Scary Face? by Jan Thomas
Caterpillar's Wish by Mary Murphy
Chicky Chicky Chook Chook by Cathy MacLennan
I Love Bugs! by Emma Dodd
In the Tall, Tall Grass by Denise Fleming
Ten Little Caterpillars by Bill Martin Jr.
The Very Quiet Cricket by Eric Carle

BUSES

The Bus for Us by Suzanne Bloom

Maisy Drives the Bus by Lucy Cousins

CARS

Red Light, Green Light by Anastasia Suen

CATERPILLARS

Caterpillar's Wish by Mary Murphy

Ten Little Caterpillars by Bill Martin Jr.

CATS

Cat the Cat, Who Is That? by Mo Willems

Chicky Chicky Chook Chook by Cathy MacLennan

Just Like Jasper! by Nick Butterworth

Kitten's Autumn by Eugenie Fernandes

Kitten's First Full Moon by Kevin Henkes

Kitten's Spring by Eugenie Fernandes

A Kitten's Tale by Eric Rohann

Kitty Cat, Kitty Cat, Are You Waking Up? by Bill Martin Jr.

Little Robin Redbreast by Shari Halpern

Mama Cat Has Three Kittens by Denise Fleming

Meeow and the Big Box by Sebastien Braun

The Owl and the Pussycat by Edward Lear

Pete the Cat: I Love My White Shoes by Eric Litwin

CHICKENS

Across the Stream by Mirra Ginsburg

Big Fat Hen by Keith Baker

Chick by Ed Vere

The Chick and the Duckling by V. Suteyev

Chicky Chicky Chook Chook by Cathy MacLennan

Five Little Chicks by Nancy Tafuri

Good Morning, Chick by Mirra Ginsburg

A Hat for Minerva Louise by Janet Stoeke

The Little Red Hen by Paul Galdone

CLOTHES

The First Snowfall by Anne and Harlow Rockwell
A Hat for Minerva Louise by Janet Stoeke
Maisy Dresses Up by Lucy Cousins
Under My Hood I Have a Hat by Karla Kuskin

CLOUDS

Blue Sky by Audrey Wood
Little Cloud by Eric Carle

COLORS

Blue Goose by Nancy Tafuri
Brown Bear, Brown Bear, What Do You See? by Bill Martin Jr.
Freight Train by Donald Crews
Go Away, Big Green Monster! by Ed Emberley
Knock! Knock! by Anna-Clara Tidholm
Lunch by Denise Fleming
My Heart Is Like a Zoo by Michael Hall
My Many Colored Days by Dr. Seuss
Pete the Cat: I Love My White Shoes by Eric Litwin
Rain by Robert Kalan
Where Is the Green Sheep? by Mem Fox
Wow! Said the Owl by Tim Hopgood

CONCEPTS

Blue Sea by Robert Kalan
Dogs by Emily Gravett
Duckie's Splash by Frances Barry
Little White Rabbit by Kevin Henkes
Perfect Square by Michael Hall
Pete the Cat: I Love My White Shoes by Eric Litwin
Piggies in the Pumpkin Patch by Mary Peterson and Jennifer Rofé
Where Is Baby's Bellybutton? by Karen Katz
Where Is the Green Sheep? by Mem Fox
Yummy, YUCKY by Leslie Patricelli

CONSTRUCTION

Tap, Tap, Bang, Bang by Emma Garcia
Tip, Tip, Dig, Dig by Emma Garcia

COUNTING

Big Fat Hen by Keith Baker

The Big Storm by Nancy Tafuri

Five Little Ducks by Raffi

Let's Go Visiting by Sue Williams

My Heart Is Like a Zoo by Michael Hall

One Two That's My Shoe! by Alison Murray

Over in the Meadow by John Langstaff

Splash! by Ann Jonas

Ten, Nine, Eight by Molly Bang

Ten Little Caterpillars by Bill Martin Jr.

Ten Red Apples by Virginia Miller

COWS

The Cow Loves Cookies by Karma Wilson

DAILY LIFE

Baby Faces by Margaret Miller

Baby Loves by Michael Lawrence

Blue Sky by Audrey Wood

I Can Do It Too! by Karen Baicker

I Kissed the Baby! by Mary Murphy

It's My Birthday! by Helen Oxenbury

Kitty Cat, Kitty Cat, Are You Waking Up? by Bill Martin Jr.

Peekaboo Morning by Rachel Isadora

Ten Little Fingers and Ten Little Toes by Mem Fox

Uh-oh! by Rachel Isadora

DOGS

Dog Wants to Play by Christine McDonnell

Dogs by Emily Gravett

A Good Day by Kevin Henkes

Maggie's Ball by Lindsay Barrett George

One Two That's My Shoe! by Alison Murray

Where's Spot? by Eric Hill

DUCKS

Across the Stream by Mirra Ginsburg

The Chick and the Duckling by V. Suteyev

Come Along, Daisy! by Jane Simmons

Duck and Goose Find a Pumpkin by Tad Hills

Duck in the Truck by Jez Alborough
Duckie's Splash by Frances Barry
Five Little Ducks by Raffi
The Golden Egg Book by Margaret Wise Brown
Have You Seen My Duckling? by Nancy Tafuri
Little White Duck by Walt Whippo
Pumpkin Trouble by Jan Thomas

ELEPHANTS

Dancing Feet! by Lindsey Craig
Is That an Elephant Over There? by Rebecca Elgar
Sam Who Never Forgets by Eve Rice
Splash! by Flora McDonnell

EXERCISE

From Head to Toe by Eric Carle

EXPLORING

Come Along, Daisy! by Jane Simmons
Five Little Ducks by Raffi
Have You Seen My Duckling? by Nancy Tafuri

FALL

The Busy Little Squirrel by Nancy Tafuri
Duck and Goose Find a Pumpkin by Tad Hills
Kitten's Autumn by Eugenie Fernandes
Maisy Dresses Up by Lucy Cousins
Mouse's First Fall by Lauren Thompson
Ten Red Apples by Virginia Miller

FAMILIES

Baby Loves by Michael Lawrence
Honk! by Chris Demarest
I Can Do It Too! by Karen Baicker
Just Like Daddy by Frank Asch
Mama Cat Has Three Kittens by Denise Fleming
Mama's Little Bears by Nancy Tafuri
"More More More," Said the Baby by Vera B. Williams
On Mother's Lap by Ann Herbert Scott
Snowballs by Lois Ehlert

Time for Bed by Mem Fox
Time to Play! by Nigel Gray
Titch by Pat Hutchins
Uh-oh! by Rachel Isadora
Whose Chick Are You? by Nancy Tafuri
Whose Mouse Are You? by Robert Kraus

FARMS

Barnyard Banter by Denise Fleming
Blue Goose by Nancy Tafuri
Book! Book! Book! by Deborah Bruss
Chicky Chicky Chook Chook by Cathy MacLennan
Chuck's Truck by Peggy Perry Anderson
Clip-Clop by Nicola Smee
The Cow Loves Cookies by Karma Wilson
Dog Wants to Play by Christine McDonnell
Down on the Farm by Merrily Kutner
Farmyard Beat by Lindsey Craig
Five Little Chicks by Nancy Tafuri
Good Morning, Chick by Mirra Ginsburg
A Hat for Minerva Louise by Janet Stoeke
Hello, Day! by Anita Lobel
Honk! by Chris Demarest
How Kind! by Mary Murphy
I Love Animals by Flora McDonnell
Kitten's Autumn by Eugenie Fernandes
Kitten's Spring by Eugenie Fernandes
Maisy's Morning on the Farm by Lucy Cousins
Old MacDonald Had a Farm by Frances Cony
Peek-a-Boo by Francesca Ferri
Peek-a-Moo! by Marie Torres Cimarusti
Piggies in the Pumpkin Patch by Mary Peterson and Jennifer Rofé
Pumpkin Trouble by Jan Thomas
This Is the Farmer by Nancy Tafuri
Where Is the Green Sheep? by Mem Fox
Who Said Moo? by Harriet Ziefert and Simms Taback
Whose Chick Are You? by Nancy Tafuri

FATHERS

Just Like Daddy by Frank Asch

FEELINGS

Can You Make a Scary Face? by Jan Thomas
A Good Day by Kevin Henkes
A Kiss Like This by Mary Murphy
My Heart Is Like a Zoo by Michael Hall
My Many Colored Days by Dr. Seuss
Owl Babies by Martin Waddell
Perfect Square by Michael Hall

FISH

Blue Sea by Robert Kalan
Hooray for Fish! by Lucy Cousins

FLANNEL BOARD

Ask Mr. Bear by Marjorie Flack
The Bridge Is Up by Babs Bell
Brown Bear, Brown Bear, What Do You See? by Bill Martin Jr.
Freight Train by Donald Crews
It's My Birthday! by Helen Oxenbury
Lunch by Denise Fleming
Millions of Snowflakes by Mary McKenna Siddals
Under My Hood I Have a Hat by Karla Kuskin

FOOD

The Cow Loves Cookies by Karma Wilson
It's My Birthday! by Helen Oxenbury
Kitten's Autumn by Eugenie Fernandes
The Little Mouse, the Red Ripe Strawberry, and the Big Hungry Bear
    by Don and Audrey Wood
Lunch by Denise Fleming
Mr. Cookie Baker by Monica Wellington
Sam Who Never Forgets by Eve Rice
The Wide-Mouthed Frog by Keith Faulkner
Yummy, YUCKY by Leslie Patricelli

FRIENDS

Bear Snores On by Karma Wilson
Cat the Cat, Who Is That? by Mo Willems
Clip-Clop by Nicola Smee
Dog Wants to Play by Christine McDonnell
The Golden Egg Book by Margaret Wise Brown
Home for a Bunny by Margaret Wise Brown

I Can Help by David Costello
I Like Me! by Nancy Carlson
It's My Birthday! by Helen Oxenbury
Maggie's Ball by Lindsay Barrett George
Mouse's First Fall by Lauren Thompson
Spring Is Here by Will Hillenbrand
Treasure by Suzanne Bloom

FROGS

Can You Make a Scary Face? by Jan Thomas
Jump, Frog, Jump! by Robert Kalan
The Wide-Mouthed Frog by Keith Faulkner

GAMES

Dog Wants to Play by Christine McDonnell
Is That an Elephant Over There? by Rebecca Elgar
Peek-a-Boo by Francesca Ferri
Peekaboo Morning by Rachel Isadora
Peek-a-Moo! by Marie Torres Cimarusti
Piggies by Don and Audrey Wood
Pots and Pans by Patricia Hubbell
Says Who? by David Carter
Tickle, Tickle by Helen Oxenbury
We're Going on a Bear Hunt by Michael Rosen
Where Is Baby's Bellybutton? by Karen Katz

GARDENS

The Carrot Seed by Ruth Krauss
Titch by Pat Hutchins

GIVING

Giving by Shirley Hughes

GROWING UP

Little Gorilla by Ruth Bornstein
Titch by Pat Hutchins

HELPING

I Can Help by David Costello
The Little Red Hen by Paul Galdone
What Shall We Do with the Boo-Hoo Baby? by Cressida Cowell

HOLIDAYS

Five Little Pumpkins by Iris Van Rynbach
Pumpkin Trouble by Jan Thomas

HORSES

Clip-Clop by Nicola Smee

HOUSES

A New House for Mouse by Petr Horáček

IMAGINATION

Little White Rabbit by Kevin Henkes
Meeow and the Big Box by Sebastien Braun

INTERACTIVE BOOKS

Go Away, Big Green Monster! by Ed Emberley
Peek-a-Moo! by Marie Torres Cimarusti

KINDNESS

How Kind! by Mary Murphy

LIFT-THE-FLAP BOOKS

Peek-a-Boo by Francesca Ferri
Peek-a-Moo! by Marie Torres Cimarusti
Time to Play! by Nigel Gray
Tuck Me In! by Dean Hacohen and Sherry Scharschmidt
Where Is Baby's Bellybutton? by Karen Katz
Where's Spot? by Eric Hill
Who Said Moo? by Harriet Ziefert and Simms Taback

MANNERS

Lunch by Denise Fleming

MESSES

Lunch by Denise Fleming
Pete the Cat: I Love My White Shoes by Eric Litwin
Pots and Pans by Patricia Hubbell

MICE

The Little Mouse, the Red Ripe Strawberry, and the Big Hungry Bear
    by Don and Audrey Wood

Lunch by Denise Fleming
Maisy Dresses Up by Lucy Cousins
Maisy Drives the Bus by Lucy Cousins
Maisy's Morning on the Farm by Lucy Cousins
Mouse's First Fall by Lauren Thompson
Mouse's First Snow by Lauren Thompson
Mouse's First Spring by Lauren Thompson
A New House for Mouse by Petr Horáček
One More Hug for Madison by Caroline Church
Pumpkin Trouble by Jan Thomas
This Is the Farmer by Nancy Tafuri
Whose Mouse Are You? by Robert Kraus

MONKEYS
I Like Books by Anthony Browne

MOON
Kitten's First Full Moon by Kevin Henkes

MOTHERS
Ask Mr. Bear by Marjorie Flack
Come Along, Daisy! by Jane Simmons
Have You Seen My Duckling? by Nancy Tafuri
Honk! by Chris Demarest
I Like It When . . . by Mary Murphy
A Kiss Like This by Mary Murphy
Mama Cat Has Three Kittens by Denise Fleming
Mama's Little Bears by Nancy Tafuri
Mommies Say Shh! by Patricia Polacco
On Mother's Lap by Ann Herbert Scott
Owl Babies by Martin Waddell

MOVABLE BOOKS
Chick by Ed Vere
Honk! by Chris Demarest
If You're Happy and You Know It, Clap Your Hands! by David Carter
Is That an Elephant Over There? by Rebecca Elgar
Old MacDonald Had a Farm by Frances Cony
Says Who? by David Carter
Where's Spot? by Eric Hill
The Wide-Mouthed Frog by Keith Faulkner

MOVEMENT

Clap Your Hands by Lorinda Bryan Cauley
Dancing Feet! by Lindsey Craig
Farmyard Beat by Lindsey Craig
From Head to Toe by Eric Carle
If You're Hoppy by April Sayre
Mr. Cookie Baker by Monica Wellington
Stretch by Doreen Cronin and Scott Menchin

MULTICULTURAL STORIES

Peekaboo Morning by Rachel Isadora
Ten Little Fingers and Ten Little Toes by Mem Fox
Uh-oh! by Rachel Isadora

MUSIC

If You're Happy and You Know It, Clap Your Hands! by David Carter
If You're Hoppy by April Sayre
Little White Duck. Lyrics by Walt Whippo
Meeow and the Pots and Pans by Sebastien Braun
Pete the Cat: I Love My White Shoes by Eric Litwin
Pots and Pans by Patricia Hubbell

NIGHT

Blue Sky by Audrey Wood
Kitten's First Full Moon by Kevin Henkes
One More Hug for Madison by Caroline Church

NUMBERS

Big Fat Hen by Keith Baker
The Big Storm by Nancy Tafuri
Five Little Ducks by Raffi
Let's Go Visiting by Sue Williams
My Heart Is Like a Zoo by Michael Hall
Over in the Meadow by John Langstaff
Splash! by Ann Jonas
Ten, Nine, Eight by Molly Bang
Ten Red Apples by Virginia Miller

OCEAN

Hooray for Fish! by Lucy Cousins

OPPOSITES

Dogs by Emily Gravett

Yummy, YUCKY by Leslie Patricelli

OUTSIDE

I Went Walking by Sue Williams

In the Small, Small Pond by Denise Fleming

In the Tall, Tall Grass by Denise Fleming

Ten Little Caterpillars by Bill Martin Jr.

OWLS

I'm Not Sleepy! by Jonathan Allen

The Owl and the Pussycat by Edward Lear

Owl Babies by Martin Waddell

Wow! Said the Owl by Tim Hopgood

PARTICIPATION

Brown Bear, Brown Bear, What Do You See? by Bill Martin Jr.

Clap Your Hands by Lorinda Bryan Cauley

Down on the Farm by Merrily Kutner

From Head to Toe by Eric Carle

Jump, Frog, Jump! by Robert Kalan

Knock at the Door and Other Baby Action Rhymes by Chorao Kay

Pete the Cat: I Love My White Shoes by Eric Litwin

We're Going on a Bear Hunt by Michael Rosen

PARTIES

Maisy Dresses Up by Lucy Cousins

PHOTOGRAPHS

What's on My Head? by Margaret Miller

PIGS

I Like Me! by Nancy Carlson

Piggies by Don and Audrey Wood

Piggies in the Pumpkin Patch by Mary Peterson and Jennifer Rofé

Pumpkin Trouble by Jan Thomas

PLAY

All You Need for a Snowman by Alice Schertle

Clap Your Hands by Lorinda Bryan Cauley

Clip-Clop by Nicola Smee
Jump, Frog, Jump! by Robert Kalan
A Kitten's Tale by Eric Rohann
Maggie's Ball by Lindsay Barrett George
Meeow and the Pots and Pans by Sebastien Braun
Mouse's First Fall by Lauren Thompson
Oh! by Kevin Henkes
Pots and Pans by Patricia Hubbell
Splash! by Flora McDonnell
Time to Play! by Nigel Gray
Treasure by Suzanne Bloom
Under My Hood I Have a Hat by Karla Kuskin

POETRY

Big Fat Hen by Keith Baker
Knock at the Door and Other Baby Action Rhymes by Chorao Kay
Little Robin Redbreast by Shari Halpern
Mary Had a Little Lamb by Sarah Josepha Hale
The Owl and the Pussycat by Edward Lear

POP-UP BOOKS—*SEE* MOVABLE BOOKS

QUESTION-AND-ANSWER STORIES

Brown Bear, Brown Bear, What Do You See? by Bill Martin Jr.
Dancing Feet! by Lindsey Craig
Duck and Goose Find a Pumpkin by Tad Hills
I Went Walking by Sue Williams
Is That an Elephant Over There? by Rebecca Elgar
Mama's Little Bears by Nancy Tafuri
Whose Nose and Toes? by John Butler
Where's Spot? by Eric Hill

RABBITS

The ABC Bunny by Wanda Gag
The Golden Egg Book by Margaret Wise Brown
Goodnight Moon by Margaret Wise Brown
Home for a Bunny by Margaret Wise Brown
Little White Rabbit by Kevin Henkes

RAIN

Big Storm by Nancy Tafuri

Blue Sky by Audrey Wood

Chicky Chicky Chook Chook by Cathy MacLennan

Little Cloud by Eric Carle

Rain by Robert Kalan

Raindrop, Plop! by Wendy Lewison

RESPONSE BOOKS

Barnyard Banter by Denise Fleming

Brown Bear, Brown Bear, What Do You See? by Bill Martin Jr.

I Went Walking by Sue Williams

If You're Happy and You Know It, Clap Your Hands! by David Carter

Is That an Elephant Over There? by Rebecca Elgar

Jump, Frog, Jump! by Robert Kalan

Let's Go Visiting by Sue Williams

Says Who? by David Carter

Where's Spot? by Eric Hill

SEASONS

Bear Snores On by Karma Wilson

The Busy Little Squirrel by Nancy Tafuri

Caterpillar's Wish by Mary Murphy

Duck and Goose Find a Pumpkin by Tad Hills

Five Little Pumpkins by Iris Van Rynbach

A Hat for Minerva Louise by Janet Stoeke

In the Small, Small Pond by Denise Fleming

A Kitten's Tale by Eric Rohann

Maisy Dresses Up by Lucy Cousins

Mouse's First Fall by Lauren Thompson

Mouse's First Snow by Lauren Thompson

Mouse's First Spring by Lauren Thompson

Oh! by Kevin Henkes

Old Bear by Kevin Henkes

Rain by Robert Kalan

Spring Is Here by Will Hillenbrand

Ten Red Apples by Virginia Miller

Under My Hood I Have a Hat by Karla Kuskin

SEASONS, SPECIFIC—*SEE* FALL/SPRING/WINTER

SHAPES

Little Cloud by Eric Carle

My Heart Is Like a Zoo by Michael Hall
Perfect Square by Michael Hall

SHARING
Giving by Shirley Hughes

SHEEP
Mary Had a Little Lamb by Sarah Josepha Hale
Sheep in a Jeep by Nancy Shaw
Where Is the Green Sheep? by Mem Fox

SIGN LANGUAGE
Brown Bear, Brown Bear, What Do You See? by Bill Martin Jr.
The Busy Little Squirrel by Nancy Tafuri
Kitten's Autumn by Eugenie Fernandes
Kitten's Spring by Eugenie Fernandes

SIZE
Blue Sea by Robert Kalan
Little Gorilla by Ruth Bornstein

SNOW
All You Need for a Snowman by Alice Schertle
The First Snowfall by Anne and Harlow Rockwell
A Kitten's Tale by Eric Rohann
Millions of Snowflakes by Mary McKenna Siddals
Mouse's First Snow by Lauren Thompson
Oh! by Kevin Henkes
Snowballs by Lois Ehlert

SONGS
Five Little Ducks by Raffi
If You're Happy and You Know It, Clap Your Hands! by David Carter
If You're Hoppy by April Sayre
Little White Duck by Walt Whippo
Mary Had a Little Lamb by Sarah Josepha Hale
Oh, A-Hunting We Will Go by John Langstaff
Old MacDonald Had a Farm by Frances Cony
Over in the Meadow by John Langstaff
Pete the Cat: I Love My White Shoes by Eric Litwin

SOUNDS

Animals Speak by Lila Prap

Baby Says "Moo!" by JoAnn Early Macken

Barnyard Banter by Denise Fleming

Book! Book! Book! by Deborah Bruss

Can You Moo? by David Wojtowycz

Hello, Day! by Anita Lobel

Honk! by Chris Demarest

Kitten's Autumn by Eugenie Fernandes

Kitten's Spring by Eugenie Fernandes

Knock! Knock! by Anna-Clara Tidholm

Meeow and the Pots and Pans by Sebastien Braun

Mommies Say Shh! by Patricia Polacco

Peek-a-Moo! by Marie Torres Cimarusti

Pots and Pans by Patricia Hubbell

Says Who? by David Carter

Stretch by Doreen Cronin and Scott Menchin

Tap, Tap, Bang, Bang by Emma Garcia

Tickle, Tickle by Helen Oxenbury

Tip, Tip, Dig, Dig by Emma Garcia

Trains Go by Steve Light

The Very Quiet Cricket by Eric Carle

Who Said Moo? by Harriet Ziefert and Simms Taback

Whose Chick Are You? by Nancy Tafuri

SPRING

Caterpillar's Wish by Mary Murphy

Kitten's Spring by Eugenie Fernandes

Mouse's First Spring by Lauren Thompson

Spring Is Here by Will Hillenbrand

STORIES IN RHYME

The ABC Bunny by Wanda Gag

All of Baby Nose to Toes by Victoria Adler

Barnyard Banter by Denise Fleming

Beetle Bop by Denise Fleming

Big Fat Hen by Keith Baker

Brown Bear, Brown Bear, What Do You See? by Bill Martin Jr.

Chicky Chicky Chook Chook by Cathy MacLennan

Chuck's Truck by Peggy Perry Anderson

Chugga-Chugga Choo-Choo by Kevin Lewis

Clap Your Hands by Lorinda Bryan Cauley

Dog Wants to Play by Christine McDonnell

Down on the Farm by Merrily Kutner

Duck in the Truck by Jez Alborough

Farmyard Beat by Lindsey Craig

Five Little Pumpkins by Iris Van Rynbach

Good Night, Good Night by Sandra Boynton

Goodnight Moon by Margaret Wise Brown

Here Are My Hands by Bill Martin Jr.

Hooray for Fish! by Lucy Cousins

I Love Bugs! by Emma Dodd

I Went Walking by Sue Williams

If You're Happy and You Know It, Clap Your Hands! by David Carter

If You're Hoppy by April Sayre

In the Small, Small Pond by Denise Fleming

In the Tall, Tall Grass by Denise Fleming

Kitten's Spring by Eugenie Fernandes

Kitty Cat, Kitty Cat, Are You Waking Up? by Bill Martin Jr.

Let's Go Visiting by Sue Williams

Little Robin Redbreast by Shari Halpern

Mary Had a Little Lamb by Sarah Josepha Hale

Millions of Snowflakes by Mary McKenna Siddals

My Many Colored Days by Dr. Seuss

Oh, A-Hunting We Will Go by John Langstaff

One Two That's My Shoe! by Alison Murray

Over in the Meadow by John Langstaff

The Owl and the Pussycat by Edward Lear

Raindrop, Plop! by Wendy Lewison

Red Light, Green Light by Anastasia Suen

Sheep in a Jeep by Nancy Shaw

Snowballs by Lois Ehlert

Ten, Nine, Eight by Molly Bang

Ten Little Caterpillars by Bill Martin Jr.

Time for Bed by Mem Fox

Time to Play! by Nigel Gray

Truck Stuck by Sallie Wolf

THINGS THAT GO

The Bridge Is Up by Babs Bell

The Bus for Us by Suzanne Bloom

Chuck's Truck by Peggy Perry Anderson
Chugga-Chugga Choo-Choo by Kevin Lewis
Duck in the Truck by Jez Alborough
Freight Train by Donald Crews
Little Tug by Stephen Savage
Maisy Drives the Bus by Lucy Cousins
Meeow and the Big Box by Sebastien Braun
Red Light, Green Light by Anastasia Suen
Sheep in a Jeep by Nancy Shaw
Tip, Tip, Dig, Dig by Emma Garcia
Trains Go by Steve Light
Truck Stuck by Sallie Wolf

TOOLS

Tap, Tap, Bang, Bang by Emma Garcia

TOYS

Chugga-Chugga Choo-Choo by Kevin Lewis
Just Like Jasper! by Nick Butterworth
Maggie's Ball by Lindsay Barrett George
Titch by Pat Hutchins

TRAINS

Chugga-Chugga Choo-Choo by Kevin Lewis
Freight Train by Donald Crews
Trains Go by Steve Light

TRUCKS

Chuck's Truck by Peggy Perry Anderson
Duck in the Truck by Jez Alborough
Red Light, Green Light by Anastasia Suen
Tip, Tip, Dig, Dig by Emma Garcia
Truck Stuck by Sallie Wolf

WATER

Across the Stream by Mirra Ginsburg
The Big Storm by Nancy Tafuri
Blue Sea by Robert Kalan
Have You Seen My Duckling? by Nancy Tafuri
In the Small, Small Pond by Denise Fleming
Jump, Frog, Jump! by Robert Kalan

Splash! by Ann Jonas
Splash! by Flora McDonnell

WEATHER

The Big Storm by Nancy Tafuri
Blue Sky by Audrey Wood
Chicky Chicky Chook Chook by Cathy MacLennan
The First Snowfall by Anne and Harlow Rockwell
Little Cloud by Eric Carle
Millions of Snowflakes by Mary McKenna Siddals
Rain by Robert Kalan
Raindrop, Plop! by Wendy Lewison

WINTER

All You Need for a Snowman by Alice Schertle
Bear Snores On by Karma Wilson
The First Snowfall by Anne and Harlow Rockwell
A Hat for Minerva Louise by Janet Stoeke
A Kitten's Tale by Eric Rohann
Millions of Snowflakes by Mary McKenna Siddals
Mouse's First Snow by Lauren Thompson
Oh! by Kevin Henkes
Snowballs by Lois Ehlert
Under My Hood I Have a Hat by Karla Kuskin

WORK

The Busy Little Squirrel by Nancy Tafuri
The Little Red Hen by Paul Galdone

ZOO

My Heart Is Like a Zoo by Michael Hall
Sam Who Never Forgets by Eve Rice

Nursery Rhymes and Fingerplays

Introduction

Nursery rhymes and fingerplays should be an intrinsic part of childhood, and they can be found in cultures around the world. They are one of the first language-building experiences for most children. Rhymes help children develop the skills of listening, being able to comprehend directions, and knowing how to act on them. Adults who did not have exposure to them as children may find them silly and sometimes be embarrassed when doing them. Rhymes, however, are an important part of language development. Children learn by listening and doing. By actively engaging the child, the adult not only helps the child learn about language but also shares in the experience with the child.

Use a core collection of familiar rhymes for each program, and print them on a handout to go home with the participants so they can learn them and/or repeat them on their own. This will lessen the pressure on adults to remember everything that takes place during the program and encourage them to continue the language experiences at home. Because repetition of rhymes is common in storytime programs, the participants will become familiar with the material and thus gain confidence in their own abilities to speak and act out the rhymes on their own. As the participants become more familiar with the rhymes, they will also be less hesitant to try unfamiliar rhymes if only a few new ones are introduced at a time.

How does one teach a rhyme or fingerplay? First of all, treat the material as new for the entire group, especially at programs where there are different cultures and languages present. Speak clearly, and use simple terms as you demonstrate the actions. I have found the following three methods to work well:

- The presenter says the desired rhyme/fingerplay in its entirety, demonstrating the actions that go with it at the same time. It is then repeated by the whole group.
- The presenter says one line at a time, demonstrating the action that goes with it. The entire group then repeats the line with the presenter. After the whole rhyme is presented this way, the entire group does the whole rhyme/fingerplay straight through together.
- Use an audio recording, such as a CD, to support the presenter. This way the presenter can act along with the group to learn the rhyme. *The Baby Record* by Bob McGrath and Katharine Smithrim is a good example of one to use.

The Internet offers another way for rhymes, songs, and actions to be learned. Libraries, performers who focus on children's music, consultants, and other institutions offer rhymes, songs, and more through websites and YouTube. The following list offers a selection of those available:

- Burnaby Public Library, British Columbia, Canada. "Embracing Diversity: Sharing Our Songs and Rhymes" http://bpl.bc.ca/kids/embracing-diversity. Videos of 30 songs and rhymes in 15 languages.

Additional songs and rhymes are available on the Embracing Diversity Vimeo channel at http://vimeo.com/channels/embracingdiversity.

- Chappaqua Library, Chappaqua, New York. "Multilingual Mother Goose." http://vimeopro.com/newcastlemediacenter/nccmc/video/40470140. This is a video of one Multilingual Mother Goose program that was taped for cable television.
- Colorado Libraries for Early Literacy (CLEL). "StoryBlocks." www.storyblocks.org/. A project of CLEL and Rocky Mountain Public Broadcasting Services, this collection includes 30- to 60-second videos of songs, rhymes, and fingerplays appropriate for early childhood. Each clip includes early literacy tips.
- Dr. Jean. "Songs for Young Children and the Grown-Ups Who Love Them." http://drjean.org/. Dr. Jean Feldman, educator, author, and consultant in the field of early childhood, has created this wonderful site for learning rhymes and songs. Dr. Jean uses YouTube to demonstrate many traditional and original rhymes and songs.
- King County Library System, Washington. "Tell Me a Story." http://wiki.kcls.org/tellmeastory/index.php/Main_Page. This storytime companion offers a plethora of rhymes, songs, stories, and program ideas. The "Rhymes and Songs" section supplies the words and actions to hundreds of rhymes and songs. If you want more help, the librarians themselves demonstrate with the help of YouTube.
- Nancy Stewart, Seattle, Washington. "Children's Music, Concerts, Recordings, and Free Songs" by Nancy Stewart. http://nancymusic.com/. This website is a treasure trove of original songs with words, sheet music, directions, American Sign Language signs, and expanded activities. The materials include non-English rhymes and songs and are print and audio in nature. Nancy has created an original song every month since 2002 that can be downloaded free of charge. She also organizes them by category, year and month, and alphabetically and includes various playlists. This is sure to become a favorite link!
- Sing with Our Kids. "Free Resources for Early Learning through Community Singing." http://singwithourkids.com/. This website offers free songs, music, lyrics, information, and resources for early learning though community singing. Based on a community project, this free Internet resource for early learning went online September 1, 2012. Content will be added as the project progresses. Resources include a song library, video library, community toolbox, grandparents' corner, tips and tricks from experts, and early learning and music information.

Rhymes are often put to tunes and therefore may be defined also as songs. In addition to the list of resources for rhymes, fingerplays, and songs at the end of this chapter, be sure to look through the other resources as well.

Rhymes with this icon are performed by the author at **alaeditions.org/webextras**

Nursery Rhyme, Fingerplay, and Song Scripts

ÁBRANLAS, CIÉRRENLAS

Ábranlas, ciérrenlas.

Ábranlas, ciérrenlas.

Pla, pla, pla, pla, pla.

Ábranlas, ciérrenlas.

Ábranlas, ciérrenlas.

Pónganlas acá.

OPEN, SHUT THEM

Open, shut them.	*Open, close hands.*
Open, shut them.	*Open, close hands.*
Give a little clap.	*Clap hands.*
Open, shut them.	*Open, close hands.*
Open, shut them.	*Open, close hands.*
Put them in your lap.	*Fold hands in lap.*

ACKA BACKA

Acka backa soda cracker,

Acka backa boo!

> *Rock, swing, or bounce child.*

Acka backa soda cracker,

I love you!

> *Pick up and give child a hug.*

Acka backa soda cracker,

Acka backa boo!

> *Rock, swing, or bounce child.*

Acka backa soda cracker,

Up goes you!

> *Lift child up into the air.*

This can be a bouncing rhyme with child in adult lap or have group form a circle, moving first to the left and then to the right.

ALL AROUND THE MULBERRY BUSH

All around the mulberry bush,

The monkey chased the weasel.

The monkey thought 'twas all in fun—

POP! goes the weasel.

> *"Mulberry bush" can be changed to "cobbler's bench."*

APPLE TREE   See *Way Up High in the Apple Tree*

BAA, BAA, BLACK SHEEP

Baa, baa, black sheep, have you any wool?

Yes sir, yes sir, three bags full.

One for my master and one for my dame,

And one for the little boy who lives down the lane.

This works well as a flannel-board presentation.

BABY'S NAP

This is a baby ready for a nap.

Hold up index finger.

Lay him down in his mother's lap.

Place index finger in palm of hand.

Cover him up so he won't peep.

Fold other fingers over the index finger to cover.

Rock him 'til he's fast asleep.

Rock hands to and fro.

BEEHIVE

Here is the little beehive.

Hold up fist.

Where are the bees?

Hidden away where nobody sees.

Soon they come creeping out of the hive.

One, two, three, four, five.

Open fist slowly and then tickle child on five.

BALL FOR BABY

Here's a ball for baby,

Touch fingertips, forming ball.

Big and soft and round.

Here is baby's hammer,

Pound one fist on the other.

Oh, how he can pound.

Here is baby's music,

Clap hands.

Clapping, clapping so.

Here are baby's soldiers,

Hold ten fingers erect.

Standing in a row.

Here is baby's trumpet,

Place one fist in front of the other at mouth.

Toot, toot-toot, toot-toot, toot.

Here's the way that baby

Plays at peek-a-boo.

Spread fingers in front of eyes.

Here's a big umbrella

*Hold index finger of right hand erect; place palm of left hand on top of finger.
Youngest can put hands over heads.*

To keep the baby dry.

Here is baby's cradle,

Cross arms.

Rock-a-baby bye.

Rock back and forth.

BEND AND STRETCH

Bend and stretch, reach for the stars.

There goes Jupiter, here comes Mars.

Bend and stretch, reach for the sky.

Stand on tip-e-toe, oh! So high!

Suit actions to words.

BINGO

There was a farmer had a dog and Bingo was his name-o.

B-I-N-G-O

B-I-N-G-O

B-I-N-G-O

And Bingo was his name-o.

Do this as a clapping song; walk in a circle holding child, and move toward center one step with each letter. You can also do this in front of a mirror.

Idea from *Babies Make Music* by Lynn Kleiner (Van Nuys, CA: Alfred Publishing, 2000)

CHOO-CHOO TRAIN

This is a choo-choo train,

Bend arms at elbows.

Puffing down the track.

Rotate arms in rhythm.

Now it's going forward,

Now it's going back.

Step forward, and then step back.

Now the bell is ringing,

Pretend to pull bell cord with closed fist or gently tap child's nose.

Now the whistle blows.

Hold fist near mouth and nose or blow on child's head.

What a lot of noise it makes,

Cover ears.

Everywhere it goes.

Stretch out arms.

Since children have difficulty holding up fingers, you could do this as a flannel-board story.

CINCO CALABACITAS

Cinco calabacitas sentadas en un portón:

Cross hands and use one hand, five fingers for five pumpkins.

La primera dijo,

Hold up finger.

"Se está haciendo tarde."

La segunda dijo,

Hold up second finger.

"Hay brujas en el aire."

La tercera dijo,

Hold up third finger.

"No le hace."

La cuarta dijo,

Hold up fourth finger.

"¡Corramos, corramos!"

La quinta dijo,

Hold up thumb.

"Es una noche de espanto."

Uuuu, hizo el viento

Wave arms.

Y se apagaron las luces.

Clap.

Las cinco calabacitas

¡Corrieron a esconderse!

Run fingers behind back.

FIVE LITTLE PUMPKINS

Five little pumpkins sitting on a gate:

The first one said,

"My, it's getting late."

The second one said,

"There are witches in the air."

The third one said,

"But we don't care."

The fourth one said,

"Let's run, let's run!"

The fifth one said,

"It's Halloween fun."

"WOOOOOOOOO," went the wind,

And out went the lights.

These five little pumpkins

Ran fast out of sight!

CLAP YOUR HANDS

Clap your hands one, two, three.

> *Clap hands on one, two, and three.*

Clap your hands, just like me!

> *Clap on last three words.*
> *You can do other verses using "Roll your hands," "Wave your hands," "Nod your head," etc.*

COBBLER, COBBLER

Cobbler, cobbler, mend my shoe.

Give it one stitch, give it two,

Give it three, give it four,

And if it needs it, give it more.

> *Pat shoe or foot; have child pat adult's shoe or foot.*

CRISS-CROSS APPLESAUCE

Criss-cross applesauce

> *Draw an X on child's back with finger.*

Spiders running up your back

> *Walk fingers up child's back.*

Cool breeze

> *Blow gently on child's neck and back of head.*

Tight squeeze

> *Give child a big hug.*

Now you've got the shivers!

> *Tickle child gently all over.*

DANCE TO YOUR DADDY

Dance to your daddy, my little laddy,

Dance to your daddy, my little lamb.

You shall have a fishy in a little dishy,

You shall have a fishy when the boat comes in.

DOS PAJARITOS | TWO LITTLE BIRDS

See also *Two Little Blackbirds*

Dos pajaritos muy sentados	Two little birds
Extend two index fingers.	
En una cerca muy alta:	Sitting on a fence:
Vuela Panchito, vuela Pedrito.	Panchito flys away, Pedrito flys away.
Fly hands behind back.	
Vuelve Panchito, vuelve Pedrito.	Panchito returns, Pedrito returns.
Return hands to front with index fingers still extended.	

DOWN AT THE STATION

Down at the station, early in the morning,

See the little puffer-bellies all in a row;

See the station master pull the little handle—

Chug, chug, toot, toot, off we go!

DRUMS

Boom! Boom! Boom!

Goes the big bass drum.

Tat-a-tat-tat goes the little one.

And down the street in line we come

To the boom, boom, boom

Of the big bass drum

And the tat-a-tat-tat of the little one.

> *Pound one fist on the palm of the other hand in time with the big and little drum noises.*

THE EENCY, WEENCY SPIDER

The eency, weency spider went up the waterspout.

Down came the rain and washed the spider out!

Out came the sun and dried up all the rain.

And the eency, weency spider went up the spout again!

THE ENGINE

Here is an engine

That runs on the track.

It whistles—"Toot Toot"

And then it runs back.

> *Use left arm for track and right hand for engine that runs up and down.*

FATHER AND MOTHER AND UNCLE JOHN   See *Mother and Father and Uncle John*

FEE-FI-FO-FUM

Fee-fi-fo-fum—

> *Point to fingers, one by one.*

See my fingers,

> *Wiggle fingers.*

See my thumbs.

> *Wiggle thumbs.*

Fee-fi-fo-fum—Good-bye fingers, Good-bye thumbs.

> *Wiggle fingers and thumbs, and then hide them behind back.*

FISHIES

Reprinted with permission from *Little Songs for Little Me*, by Nancy Stewart (© 1992)

For fish patterns, see http://nancymusic.com/Fishiesplay.htm.

There are so many fishies in the deep blue sea.

What color fishy do you see?

Red, red, this one's red. This little fishy is red.

Have cut out five fish shapes in different colored felt; change color to match song.

There are so many fishies in the deep blue sea.

Can you count the fishies with me? . . . 1, 2, 3, 4, 5

FIVE LITTLE PUMPKINS

See also *Cinco Calabacitas*

Five little pumpkins sitting on a gate:

Hold up five fingers.

The first one said, "My, it's getting late."

Hold up one finger and then point to wrist.

The second one said, "There is magic in the air."

Hold up two fingers; wave hand in air.

The third one said, "I don't care!"

Hold up three fingers and shake head "no."

The fourth one said, "Let's run and run and run."

Hold up four fingers and pump arms as if running.

The fifth one said, "I'm ready for some fun."

Hold up five fingers and then point to self.

Ooooooh, went the wind,

Out went the light.

Clap hands.

And the five little pumpkins rolled out of sight.

Roll hands.

FIVE PLUMP PEAS

Five plump peas in a pea pod pressed.

Hold one fist up.

One grew, two grew, and so did all the rest.

Open fist one finger at a time.

They grew and they grew and they never stopped.

Put both hands together and then move them apart on each "grew."

They grew so big that the pea pod popped!

Clap hands on "popped."

FROM WIBBLETON TO WOBBLETON ▶

From Wibbleton to Wobbleton is fifteen miles,

From Wobbleton to Wibbleton is fifteen miles,

From Wibbleton to Wobbleton, from Wobbleton to Wibbleton,

From Wibbleton to Wobbleton is fifteen miles.

> *This rhyme is fun to clap to or to use as a bouncing rhyme.*

GACK-GOON

"Gack-goon," went the little green frog one day.

"Gack-goon," went the little green frog.

"Gack-goon," went the little green frog one day.

And his eyes went, "Gack-gack-goon."

> *Clap or open hands on "Gack-goon."*

THE GRAND OLD DUKE OF YORK

The grand old Duke of York,

He had ten thousand men.

He marched them up to the top of the hill,

And he marched them down again.

And when they were up, they were up,

And when they were down, they were down,

And when they were only halfway up,

They were neither up nor down.

> *This is a great marching rhyme; hop up on last line.*

GRANDMA'S GLASSES   See *These Are Grandma's Glasses*

GRAY SQUIRREL

Gray squirrel, gray squirrel,

Swish your bushy tail.

Gray squirrel, gray squirrel,

Swish your bushy tail.

> *With child on lap, swing knees side to side.*

Wrinkle up your little nose.

> *Tap child's nose.*

Hold a nut between your toes.

> *Tickle child's toes.*

Gray squirrel, gray squirrel,

Swish your bushy tail.

> *Swing knees side to side.*

THE GREAT BIG SPIDER ▶

The great, big spider went up the waterspout.

> *Standing, move arms and legs in a climbing motion.*

Down came the rain and washed the spider out.

> *Drop arms down and swing them back and forth.*

Out came the sun and dried up all the rain,

> *Raise arms in circle over head.*

And the great big spider went up the spout again.

> *Standing, move arms and legs in a climbing motion.*

HEAD AND SHOULDERS, KNEES AND TOES ▶

Head and shoulders, knees and toes.

Knees and toes. Knees and toes.

Head and shoulders, knees and toes.

Eyes, ears, mouth, and nose.

> *Touch appropriate part of own body or child's body.*

HERE COMES A MOUSE

From *Catch Me and Kiss Me and Say It Again* by Clyde Watson, © 1978.

Here comes a mouse, mousie, mousie, mouse.

> *Wiggle fingers by child.*

On tiny light feet and a soft pink nose, tickle, tickle, wherever he goes.

> *Tickle child.*

He'll run up your arm and under your chin,

> *Run fingers up child's arm to chin.*

Don't open your mouth, or the mouse will run in!

Mousie, mousie, mouse.

> *Child will almost always open mouth; tap chin, nose, or lips on last three words.*

HERE IS A BEEHIVE ▶

Here is a beehive.

> *Hold up a fist.*

Where are the bees?

> *Shrug shoulders.*

Hidden inside where nobody sees.

> *Point to fist.*

Soon they'll come out, out of the hive,

One, two, three, four, five.

> *Slowly unfold fingers and on five give a tickle.*

HERE IS A BUNNY

Here is a bunny with ears so funny,

Make fist with one hand and hold two fingers straight up.

And here's his hole in the ground.

Put other hand on waist, with arm bent at elbow.

When a noise he hears,

Cup hand to ear.

He picks up his ears,

And jumps in his hole in the ground.

Jump up in air or hop rabbit into hole.

HERE IS A CHOO-CHOO TRAIN
Reprinted with permission from Little Songs for Little Me by Nancy Stewart, © 1992

Here is a choo-choo train, chugging down the tracks.

Bend arms at elbows and rotate arms.

Now it's going faster, now the bell is ringing,

Pretend to ring bell.

Now the whistle blows.

Pretend to blow whistle.

What a lot of noise it makes, everywhere it goes!

Cover ears and shake head.

HERE IS BABY
See Baby's Nap

HERE IS THE ENGINE

Here is the engine on the track.

Here is the coal car, just in back.

Here is the boxcar to carry freight.

Here is the mail car. Don't be late!

Way back here at the end of the train

Rides the caboose through the sun and rain.

You can hold up fingers in order, starting with thumb, or do as a flannel-board story.

HERE WE GO 'ROUND THE MULBERRY BUSH   *See All around the Mulberry Bush*

HERE WE GO UP-UP-UP

Here we go up-up-up.

And here we go down-down-down.

And here we go back-and-forth and back-and-forth.

And here we go around and around and around.

> *Move child by lifting or with legs crossed and child sitting on foot.*

HERE'S A BALL

Here's a ball,

> *Form circle with two hands.*

And here's a ball.

> *Move hands apart.*

And a great big ball I see.

> *Form large circle with arms.*

Shall we count them?

Are you ready?

One, two, three!

> *Repeat shapes.*

HERE'S A CUP

Here's a cup, and here's a cup.

> *Make cup shape with hands or just hold up fists.*

And here's a pot of tea.

> *Cup hands together or pop up one thumb.*

Pour a cup and pour a cup,

> *Make pouring motion.*

And have a cup with me.

> *Make drinking motion.*

HEY, DIDDLE, DIDDLE

Hey, diddle, diddle, the cat and the fiddle,

The cow jumped over the moon.

The little dog laughed to see such fun,

And the dish ran away with the spoon.

HICKETY, PICKETY, MY BLACK HEN

Hickety, pickety, my black hen,

She lays eggs for gentlemen.

Gentlemen come every day

To see what my black hen doth lay.

HICKORY, DICKORY, DOCK ▶

Hickory, dickory, dock,

> *Clasp hands together and swing gently back and forth.*

The mouse ran up the clock.

> *Run fingers up so hands end up above head.*

The clock struck one,

> *Clap hands once.*

The mouse ran down,

> *Bring arms back down in front.*

Hickory, dickory, dock.

> *Clasp hands and swing gently back and forth.*
> *You can also run fingers up child's arm and touch nose on "one."*

HOW MUCH IS THAT DOGGIE IN THE WINDOW?

How much is that doggie in the window?

The one with the waggily tail.

How much is that doggie in the window?

I do hope that doggie's for sale!

Woof! Woof!

> *This is fun to do with rhythm instruments, such as shakers, or clap hands.*

HUMPTY DUMPTY ▶

Humpty Dumpty sat on a wall.

Humpty Dumpty had a great fall.

All the king's horses and all the king's men

Couldn't put Humpty together again.

> *Bounce child gently on lap or sit on floor with child on raised knees; part legs or straighten them to slide child down when Humpty falls.*

I HEAR THUNDER ▶

Sing to the tune of "Frère Jacques."

I hear thunder;

I hear thunder.

Pound hands gently on floor or lap.

Hark, don't you?

Cup one hand by ear to listen.

Hark, don't you?

Cup other hand by other ear to listen.

Pitter, patter raindrops,

Pitter, patter raindrops,

Wiggle fingers in falling motion in front of face.

I'm wet through;

Shake body.

So are you!

Point to child or give child a little tickle.

IF YOU'RE HAPPY AND YOU KNOW IT

If you're happy and you know it, clap your hands.

If you're happy and you know it, clap your hands.

If you're happy and you know it, then your face will surely show it.

Frame face with hands.

If you're happy and you know it, clap your hands.

Clap hands, tickle belly, pat head, etc.

IF YOU'RE WEARING RED TODAY

If you're wearing red today,

Red today, red today;

If you're wearing red today,

Please stand up!

Clap hands and have child stand alone or be supported when asked.
You can substitute any other color for "red" and do multiple verses using a variety of colors.

I'LL DRIVE A DUMP TRUCK ▶   Reprinted with permission from *Little Songs for Little Me* by Nancy Stewart, © 1992.

Hold up pictures of what you're singing about, such as truck, car, etc.

I'll drive a dump truck, dump truck, dump truck.

I'll drive a dump truck all day long.

Hold hands as if on a steering wheel or slap thighs in rhythm.
Repeat with school bus, airplane, fire truck, choo-choo train, tugboat, etc.

I'M A LITTLE TEAPOT

I'm a little teapot, short and stout.

Here is my handle;

> *Put one hand on hip.*

Here is my spout.

> *Put other hand up in the air.*

When I get all steamed up,

Hear me shout.

Tip me over and pour me out.

> *Bend over at waist to the side and then stand upright again.*

I'm a special teapot, it is true.

Here, let me show you what I can do.

I can change my handle and my spout.

> *Switch positions of arms.*

Tip me over and pour me out.

> *Bend to the side at waistline.*

IT'S RAINING, IT'S POURING

It's raining, it's pouring,

The old man is snoring.

Bumped his head,

And he went to bed,

And he didn't get up till the morning.

JACK AND JILL

Jack and Jill went up the hill

To fetch a pail of water.

Jack fell down and broke his crown,

And Jill came tumbling after.

JACK BE NIMBLE

Jack be nimble.

Jack be quick.

Jack jumped over the candlestick.

> *Bounce child on lap and then lift up on last line.*

JACK IN THE BOX

Jack in the box, you sit so still.

> *Kneel on floor with head covered by arms or hands.*

Won't you come out? Yes, I will!

> *Pop up on last phrase.*

JEREMIAH, BLOW THE FIRE

Jeremiah, blow the fire,

Puff, puff, puff.

First you blow it gently . . .

> *Blow softly in child's hair.*

Then you blow it rough!

> *Blow harder in child's hair and tickle.*

JOHNNY HAMMERS ONE HAMMER

Johnny hammers one hammer, one hammer, one hammer.

Johnny hammers with one hammer all day long.

> *Pat one hand on leg to beat.*

Johnny hammers with two hammers, two hammers, two hammers.

Johnny hammers with two hammers all day long.

> *Pump both hands up and down; add feet to repeat for three and four hammers.*

LEG OVER LEG

Leg over leg,

The dog went to Dover.

When he came to a stile . . .

Jump! He went over.

> *With child on lap, bounce or move child's legs back and forth; make dramatic pause before jump and lift child up.*

LITTLE BOY BLUE

Little boy blue, come blow your horn.

The sheep's in the meadow, the cow's in the corn.

Where is the boy who looks after the sheep?

He's under the haystack fast asleep.

Will you wake him?

No, not I, for if I do he's sure to cry.

> See *The Flannel Board Storytelling Book*, 2nd ed., by Sierra for great ideas.

LITTLE MISS MUFFET

Little Miss Muffet sat on a tuffet,

Eating her curds and whey.

Along came a spider and sat down beside her,

And frightened Miss Muffet away.

LITTLE TURTLE ▶

Vachel Lindsay, *The Golden Whales of California and Other Rhymes in the American Language*, Macmillan, 1920.

The youngest child may simply open and close hand for "mouth" motion.

There was a little turtle.

Make a fist with your thumb sticking out. Put your other hand over your thumb like a shell.

He lived in a box.

Cup your hands.

He swam in a puddle.

Make paddling motion with hands.

He climbed on the rocks.

Climb hands upward in front of body.

He snapped at a mosquito.

Make "mouth" motion—touch fingers to thumb—on last word.

He snapped at a flea.

Make "mouth" motion—touch fingers to thumb—on last word.

He snapped at a minnow.

Make "mouth" motion—touch fingers to thumb—on last word.

He snapped at me.

Make "mouth" motion—touch fingers to thumb—on last word by your nose.

He caught the mosquito.

Clap on last word.

He caught the flea.

Clap on last word.

He caught the minnow.

Clap on last word.

But he didn't catch me!

Point to self and shake head "NO!"

LONDON BRIDGE IS FALLING DOWN

London Bridge is falling down, falling down, falling down.

London Bridge is falling down, my fair ladies.

This can be done as a circle game with participants marching in a circle or as a bouncing rhyme with adults holding the children and "dropping" them (bend at the knees) when the bridge falls down.

LOTS OF CARS

Reprinted with permission from *Plant a Little Seed* by Nancy Stewart, © 1995.

There are lots of cars driving down the street.

> *Place hands as if on steering wheel, turning back and forth.*

Tell me what color do you see.

> *On flannel board, place felt car shape or use a picture.*

Big cars,

> *Spread arms wide apart.*

Little cars,

> *Bring hands close together.*

Beep, beep, beep.

> *Tap nose with hand three times.*

Repeat using different colored cars; for car patterns, go to http://nancymusic.com/SOM/2009/lots-of-cars.htm.

MARY, MARY, QUITE CONTRARY

Mary, Mary, quite contrary,

How does your garden grow?

With silver bells and cockle shells,

And pretty maids all in a row.

> *Present this as a flannel-board story.*

MARY HAD A LITTLE LAMB

Mary had a little lamb,

Little lamb, little lamb.

Mary had a little lamb,

Its fleece was white as snow.

He followed her to school one day,

School one day, school one day.

He followed her to school one day,

Which was against the rule.

It made the children laugh and play,

Laugh and play, laugh and play.

It made the children laugh and play,

To see a lamb at school.

THE MORE WE GET TOGETHER

The more we get together, together, together,

> *Clap hands together.*

The more we get together, the happier we'll be.

> *Clap hands together.*

For your friends are my friends, and my friends are your friends,

> *Point to group and then point to self.*

The more we get together, the happier we'll be.

> *Clap hands together.*

MOTHER AND FATHER AND UNCLE JOHN ▶

Mother and Father and Uncle John went to town one by one.

Mother fell off.

And Father fell off.

But Uncle John went on and on and on and on and on!

Bounce child on lap, tipping child to side on "off," and lots of bounces on last line.

MOTOR BOAT

Motor boat, motor boat, go so slow.

Motor boat, motor boat, go so fast.

Motor boat, motor boat, step on the gas!

Roll hands around each other at speed indicated.

MR. TURKEY AND MR. DUCK

Reprinted with permission from *Little Songs for Little Me* by Nancy Stewart, © 1992.

Start with hands behind back.

Mr. Turkey went out one day in bright sunshiny weather.

Move one hand to front.

He met Mister Duck along the way.

Bring other hand out.

They stopped to talk together.

Move hands up and down.

Gobble, gobble, gobble, quack, quack, quack.

Gobble, gobble, gobble, quack, quack, quack.

Alternate hands during sounds, moving one for the turkey, the other for the duck.

And then they both went back—QUACK!

Put hands behind back; bring "duck" hand out to sneak one last quack.

MY PONY MACARONI

I have a little pony.

Bounce.

His name is Macaroni.

He trots and trots and then he STOPS.

Pause.

My funny little pony,

Mac-a-RO-ni!

Bounce child on knees, give child a jiggle on "RO," and resume bounce.

MY WIGGLES

I wiggle my fingers.

I wiggle my toes.

I wiggle my shoulders.

I wiggle my nose.

Now the wiggles are out of me,

And I'm just as still as I can be.

> *Suit actions to words; adult can do actions to child.*

OLD MACDONALD HAD A FARM

Old MacDonald had a farm, e-i-e-i-o.

And on his farm he had a duck, e-i-e-i-o.

With a quack, quack here and a quack, quack there.

Here a quack, there a quack, everywhere a quack, quack.

Old MacDonald had a farm, e-i-e-i-o.

> *Repeat using other animals and sounds. Other ideas: use stuffed toy animals and pull out of a bag or stick puppets with animal shapes on them.*

ONE, TWO

Reprinted with permission from *"Song of the Month"* (http://nancymusic.com) by Nancy Stewart, © 2008.

> *Use with toddlers.*

One, two, one, two,

> *Hold up index fingers as you count.*

I have two eyes, so do you.

> *Point to your eyes and then child's eyes.*

One, two, one, two,

> *Hold up index fingers as you count.*

I have two ears, so do you.

> *Point to your ears and then child's.*

One, two, one, two,

> *Hold up index fingers as you count.*

I have two lips, so do you.

> *Point to your lips and then child's.*

One, two, one, two,

> *Hold up index fingers as you count.*

I have two hands, so do you.

> *Hold up hands and turn them front to back; then point to child's hands.*

So . . . do . . . you.

> *Clap once on each word.*

ONE, TWO, BUCKLE MY SHOE

One, two, buckle my shoe,

Three, four, shut the door,

Five, six, pick up sticks,

Seven, eight, lay them straight,

Nine, ten, a big, fat hen.

> *Do this as a bouncing rhyme.*

1, 2, 3, BABY'S ON MY KNEE

See Rooster Crows

1, 2, 3, 4, 5, I CAUGHT A FISH ALIVE

1, 2, 3, 4, 5,

> *Clap your hands together.*

I caught a fish alive!

> *Hug child.*

6, 7, 8, 9, 10,

> *Clap your hands together.*

I let him go again!

> *Tickle child.*

OPEN, SHUT THEM

Open, shut them. Open, shut them.

Give a little clap.

> *Open and close fists and then clap.*

Open, shut them. Open shut them.

Lay them in your lap.

> *Open and close fists and then put them in lap.*

Creep them, creep them,

Creep them, creep them,

Right up to your chin.

> *Walk fingers up chest.*

Open up your little mouth,

But do not let them in.

> *Hide hands behind back.*

PANCAKE

Mix a pancake, stir a pancake,

Pop it in a pan.

Fry a pancake, toss a pancake,

Catch it if you can!

> *Suit actions to words.*

PATTY CAKE, PATTY CAKE (OR PAT-A-CAKE)

Patty cake, patty cake, baker's man,

Bake me a cake as fast as you can.

> *Clap hands.*

Roll it,

> *Roll hands.*

And pat it,

> *Clap hands.*

And mark it with a "B,"

> *Draw letter "B" on child's hand, tummy, or back.*

And there'll be enough for baby and me.

> *Clap hands.*

PEASE PORRIDGE HOT

Pease porridge hot,

Pease porridge cold,

Some like it in the pot nine days old.

Some like it hot.

Some like it cold.

Some like it in the pot nine days old.

> *This is an easy bouncing rhyme or clapping game.*

PLANT A LITTLE SEED

Reprinted with permission from *Plant a Little Seed* by Nancy Stewart, © 1995.

Plant a little seed.

> *With one hand, make cup/pot shape; other hand moves down into pot in time with the music.*

Watch it grow.

> *Bring plant hand back up through pot as if growing.*

Soon we will have a vegetable.

> *Place one fist on top of the other, and then fist over fist "growing" upward.*

At end of song, hold up picture of vegetable or the real thing. Ask what it might be, and then name it.

POP! GOES THE WEASEL

All around the mulberry bush,

The monkey chased the weasel.

The monkey thought 'twas all in fun—

POP! goes the weasel.

A penny for a spool of thread,

A penny for a needle,

That's the way the money goes—

POP! goes the weasel.

> *Join hands and circle around; jump up on "Pop!"*

POPCORN

Popcorn, popcorn,

Put it in the pot.

> *Bounce child.*

Shake it, shake it.

> *Give child a jiggle around belly.*

Pop! Pop! Pop!

> *Give child strong bounces, raise arms, or lift child in the air with each "Pop!"*

PUSSY CAT, PUSSY CAT

Pussy cat, pussy cat, where have you been?

I've been to London to visit the queen.

Pussy cat, pussy cat, what did you do there?

I frightened a little mouse under her chair.

RAIN, RAIN, GO AWAY

Rain, rain, go away.

Come again some other day.

Little [*child's name*] wants to play.

Rain, rain, go away.

RAIN IS FALLING DOWN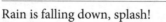

Rain is falling down, splash!

Rain is falling down, splash!

Pitter patter, pitter patter,

Rain is falling down, SPLASH!

> *Wiggle finger down in front of child or as tickle, making splashing motion at end of line. Make a big splash at the end. This is fun in the tub or pool.*

RAIN ON THE GREEN GRASS

Rain on the green grass,

Rain on the tree.

Rain on the house top,

But not on me.

> *Pound hands gently to make rain sounds for first three lines; point to self and shake head "No" on last line.*

REACH FOR THE CEILING

Reach for the ceiling,

Touch the floor,

Stand up again—

Let's do some more.

Touch your head,

Then your knee,

Up to your shoulders—

Like this, you see.

Reach for the ceiling,

Touch the floor,

That's all now—

There isn't any more.

Suit actions to words.

RIDE, BABY, RIDE

Ride, baby, ride.

Ch, ch, ch, ch, ch, ch.

Ride that horsey, ride.

Ch, ch, ch, ch, ch, ch.

Repeat.

Whoa . . .

Bounce child on knee by raising the heel of your foot or try walking around the room.
You can do this at any pace and as long as the child likes. To end, give child a hug on "Whoa."

RIDE A COCK HORSE

Ride a cock horse

To Banbury Cross,

To see a fine lady

Upon a white horse.

Bounce child on lap.

With rings on her fingers

Tickle child's fingers.

And bells on her toes,

Tickle child's toes.

She shall have music

Wherever she goes.

Bounce child on lap.

RIDING ON MY PONY

Riding on my pony, my pony, my pony.

Riding on my pony—trot, trot, trot.

> *Bounce child on knee.*

RING AROUND THE ROSIE

Ring around the rosie,

A pocket full of posies,

Ashes, ashes,

We all fall down!

> *If you want to get up again, try the following verse as an ending.*

Pulling up the daisies,

Pulling up the daisies,

Hush-a, hush-a,

We all stand up!

> *Or you can use this one.*

Cows are in the meadow,

Eating buttercups,

Thunder, lightning,

We all stand up!

> *Gently pound hands on floor; stand on last line.*

ROLY-POLY

Roly-poly, roly-poly,

Up—up—up!

Roly-poly, roly-poly,

Down—down—down!

Roly-poly, roly-poly,

Out—out—out!

Roly-poly, roly-poly,

In—in—in!

> *Roll hands on lines of roly-poly; do action described in others.*

ROOSTER CROWS (OR 1, 2, 3, BABY'S ON MY KNEE)

One, two, three,

Baby's on my knee.

Rooster crows,

And away she [or he] goes!

> *Bounce child on knee; on last line, lift child high in air or slide down legs.*

'ROUND AND 'ROUND THE GARDEN

'Round and 'round the garden goes the teddy bear.

Trace circle on child's hand, back, or tummy.

One step, two step, tickle her [or him] under there.

Move fingers up arm; tickle under chin or arm.

ROW, ROW, ROW YOUR BOAT

Row, row, row your boat,

Gently down the stream.

Merrily, merrily, merrily, merrily,

Life is but a dream.

Move hands and arms forward and backward in rowing motion.
Child may be on adult's lap or on floor between adult's legs, facing the adult or not.

RUB-A-DUB-DUB

Rub-a-dub-dub,

Three men in a tub.

Rub belly with circular motion.

And who do you think they be?

The butcher, the baker,

The candlestick maker.

Pat belly three times.

Throw them out—Knaves all three.

Tickle.

> This rhyme can be adapted by changing the last two lines to "And [children's names] / All went out to sea!"

SHOE THE OLD HORSE

Shoe the old horse.

Pat child's foot.

Shoe the old mare.

Pat child's other foot.

Let the little pony run, bare, bare, bare.

Pat child's bottom.

SING A SONG OF SIXPENCE

Sing a song of sixpence,

A pocket full of rye.

Four and twenty blackbirds,

Baked in a pie.

When the pie was open,

The birds began to sing.

Wasn't that a dainty dish

To set before the king?

SNOW IS FALLING DOWN

Snow is falling down, shhhhh.

Snow is falling down, shhhhh.

Snowing here, snowing there,

Snow is falling down, shhhhh.

Wiggle finger down in front of child or as tickle; make "shhhh" motion with finger across lips.

SOMETIMES I AM TALL

Sometimes I am tall.

Stand up straight.

Sometimes I am small.

Bend or crouch to floor.

Sometimes I am very, very tall.

Stand and stretch arms above head.

Sometimes I am very, very, small.

Bend down toward floor.

Sometimes tall, sometimes small—

Stretch high; bend low.

See how I am now!

Stand up normally.

STAR LIGHT, STAR BRIGHT

Star light, star bright,

First star I see tonight.

I wish I may, I wish I might,

Have the wish I wish tonight.

SUPPOSE

Do you suppose a giant

Reach toward ceiling.

Who is tall, tall, tall

Could ever be a brownie

Who is small, small, small?

Crouch down on floor.

But the brownie who is tiny

Will try, try, try

To reach up to the giant

Who is high, high, high.

Reach toward ceiling.

TALL AS A TREE ⏵

Tall as a tree,

Stretch arms up high over head.

Wide as a house,

Stretch arms out to either side.

Thin as a pin,

Put arms straight down at your side.

And small as a mouse.

Crouch down on floor.

TEDDY BEAR, TEDDY BEAR

Teddy Bear, Teddy Bear, turn around.

Teddy Bear, Teddy Bear, touch the ground.

Teddy Bear, Teddy Bear, show your shoe.

Teddy Bear, Teddy Bear, that will do.

Do actions and then clap on last three words.

Teddy Bear, Teddy Bear, go to bed.

Teddy Bear, Teddy Bear, rest your head.

Teddy Bear, Teddy Bear, turn out the light.

Teddy Bear, Teddy Bear, say good night.

Do actions and then wave on the last line.

TEN LITTLE FIREMEN

Ten little firemen sleeping in a row.

Hold child on lap.

Ding-dong! goes the bell.

Give child a gentle shake or tickle.

Down the pole they go.

Run fingers down child's back or slide child down legs.

THERE WAS A LITTLE MAN ⏵

There was a little man.

Point to child.

He had a little crumb.

Tickle child's cheek.

And over the mountain he did run.

Run fingers over child's head.

With a belly full of fat,

Jiggle child's belly.

And a big, tall hat,

Pat child's head.

And a pancake stuck to his bum, bum, bum.

Pat child's bottom.

THESE ARE BABY'S FINGERS

These are baby's fingers.

> *Wiggle the child's fingers.*

These are baby's toes.

> *Wiggle the child's toes.*

This is baby's bellybutton,

> *Point to the child's bellybutton.*

Around and around it goes!

> *Move finger in a circle over the child's bellybutton.*
> *You can substitute the child's name for "baby."*

THESE ARE GRANDMA'S GLASSES

These are Grandma's glasses.

> *Touch index fingers and thumbs together around eyes for glasses.*

This is Grandma's hat.

> *Point hands together above head.*

This is the way she folds her hands,

> *Fold hands.*

And lays them in her lap.

> *Put hands in lap.*
> *You can substitute other family members for Grandma.*

THIS IS MY GARDEN

This is my garden.

> *Hold out one hand, palm up.*

I'll rake it with care.

> *Use other hand to scratch palm.*

And then some flower seeds
I'll plant in there.

> *Plant seeds on palm.*

The sun will shine.

> *Raise arms above head in circle.*

The rain will fall.

> *Wiggle fingers downward.*

And soon my garden
Will grow straight and tall.

> *Stretch arms up slowly above head.*

THIS IS THE WAY THE LADIES RIDE

This is the way the ladies ride—prim, prim, prim.

Bounce child gently on knee.

This is the way the gentlemen ride—trim, trim, trim.

Bounce child slightly harder.

This is the way the farmer rides—trot, trot, trot.

Bounce child by lifting first on one knee and then on the other.

This is the way the hunter rides—a-gallop, a-gallop, a-gallop.

Bounce child quickly.

THIS LITTLE PIGGY

This little piggy went to market.

This little piggy stayed home.

This little piggy had roast beef.

This little piggy had none.

And this little piggy ran wee, wee, wee, wee, wee,

All the way home.

Traditionally, wiggle each finger or toe per line, or you can wiggle child's whole arm and leg, one for each line, ending with tickle on last line.

THREE GREEN AND SPECKLED FROGS

Reprinted with permission from
Little Songs for Little Me by Nancy Stewart, © 1992.

Three green and speckled frogs sat on a speckled log,

Hold up three fingers.

Eating the most delicious bugs—yum, yum!

Rub tummy.

One jumped into the pool where it was nice and cool,

Hold up one finger.

Then there were two green speckled frogs—gulp, gulp!

Hold up two fingers; repeat with two and then one, till no frogs left.

THREE LITTLE MONKEYS

Three little monkeys,

Hold up three fingers.

Jumping on the bed.

Jump fingers off palm of other hand.

One fell off and bumped his head.

Pat head gently.

Mama called the doctor,

And the doctor said,

Hold one hand to ear as if on phone.

"Put those monkeys right to bed."

Shake pointer finger.

TICK-TOCK

Tick-tock, tick-tock,

I'm a little cuckoo clock.

Tick-tock, tick-tock,

Now it's almost one o'clock—

Cuckoo!

Tick-tock, tick-tock,

I'm a little cuckoo clock.

Tick-tock, tick-tock,

Now it's almost two o'clock—

Cuckoo! Cuckoo!

Tick-tock, tick-tock,

I'm a little cuckoo clock.

Tick-tock, tick-tock,

Now it's almost three o'clock—

Cuckoo! Cuckoo! Cuckoo!

Rock child back and forth and lift child up or play peek-a-boo on each "Cuckoo."

TO MARKET, TO MARKET

To market, to market, to buy a fat pig,

Home again, home again, jiggity jig.

Bounce child up and down on knee.

To market, to market, to buy a fat hog,

Home again, home again, jiggity jog.

Keep bouncing child.

TOMMY THUMBS UP

Tommy Thumbs up and Tommy Thumbs down,

Tommy Thumbs dancing all around the town.

Dance them on your shoulders,

Dance them on your head,

Dance them on your knees,

And tuck them into bed.

Using thumbs, do actions, making fists on last line.

TROT, TROT TO BOSTON

Trot, trot to Boston,

Trot, trot to Lynn,

Look out little [child's name]—

You might fall in!

> *Child sits facing adult on lap. Bounce to rhyme, putting in child's name; open legs and, while holding firmly, let the child slip through opening.*

Trot, trot to Denver,

Trot, trot to Dover,

Look out little [child's name]—

You might fall over!

> *Tip child off to side.*

Trot, trot to Boston,

Trot, trot to town,

Look out little [child's name]—

You might fall down!

TWINKLE, TWINKLE, LITTLE STAR

Twinkle, twinkle, little star,

> *Raise hands in air and wiggle fingers.*

How I wonder what you are.

> *Scratch head or place index finger against cheek.*

Up above the world so high,

Like a diamond in the sky.

> *Wave hands above head.*

Twinkle, twinkle, little star,

How I wonder what you are.

> *Raise hands in air and wiggle fingers.*

TWO LITTLE BLACKBIRDS

See also *Dos Pajaritos*

Two little blackbirds sitting on a hill.

> *Hold both hands up in air.*

One named Jack; the other named Jill.

> *Hold up one hand and then the other.*

Fly away, Jack; fly away, Jill.

> *Move hands behind back.*

Come back, Jack; come back, Jill.

> *Bring hands back to the front of body. You can change the color of the birds, if desired.*

WARM HANDS WARM

Warm hands warm—

Do you know how?

If you want to warm your hands,

> *Rub hands together while saying above lines.*

Blow on them now.

> *Blow gently on your hands.*

WASH THE DISHES

Wash the dishes,

Wipe the dishes,

Ring the bell for tea.

> *Wipe hands down child's arms on first two lines and then touch nose for bell.*

Three good wishes,

Three good kisses,

I will give to thee.

One—two—three!

> *Wipe hands down child's arms on "wishes" and give kisses on the count.*

WAY UP HIGH IN THE APPLE TREE

Way up high in the apple tree,

> *Hold arms above head, fingers spread.*

Two little apples did I see.

> *Make two fists.*

So I shook that tree as hard as I could,

> *Shake and wiggle body.*

And d-o-w-n came the apples.

> *Lower arms.*

Umm! They were good!

> *Rub tummy.*

THE WHEELS ON THE BUS

The wheels on the bus go 'round and 'round,

'Round and 'round, 'round and 'round.

The wheels on the bus, go 'round and 'round,

All through the town.

Roll hands together on 'round and 'round. Continue with more verses using the following phrases.

The windows on the bus go up and down, . . . (etc.)

Lift arms up and down.

The doors on the bus go open and shut, . . . (etc.)

Clap hands together.

The horn on the bus goes beep, beep, beep, . . . (etc.)

Tap child's nose or pat belly.

The wipers on the bus go swish, swish, swish, . . . (etc.)

Wave hands in front of body using swishing motion. End by repeating the first verse, if desired.

WHEN DUCKS GET UP IN THE MORNING

Reprinted with permission from
Plant a Little Seed by Nancy Stewart, © 1995.

When ducks get up in the morning, they always say good day.

When ducks get up in the morning, they always say good day.

Quack, quack, quack, quack—that is what they say; they say

Quack, quack, quack, quack—that is what they say.

*Repeat using other animals. Slap thighs in rhythm or clap to keep rhythm.
You can also hold up a picture of an animal or stuffed animal.*

WHERE IS THUMBKIN?

Where is Thumbkin? Where is Thumbkin?

Put hands behind back.

"Here I am; here I am."

Bring hands to front; hold up one thumb and then the other.

"How are you today, sir?"

"Very well, I thank you."

Run away, run away.

Hide hands behind back or just make fists.

Where is Pointer? Where is Pointer?

"Here I am; here I am."

Bring hands to front; hold up one index finger and then the other.

"How are you today, sir?"

"Very well, I thank you."

Run away, run away.

Hide hands behind back or just make fists.

WHOOPS, JOHNNY! ▶

Johnny, Johnny, Johnny, Johnny,

Whoops, Johnny!

Whoops, Johnny, Johnny, Johnny, Johnny.

> *Use one index finger to tap each finger on opposite hand, starting at little finger. For the "Whoops!," slide down space between index finger and up thumb. Reverse action. You can use child's name in place of "Johnny."*

WIGGLE YOUR FINGERS ▶

Wiggle your fingers.

Wiggle your toes.

Wiggle your shoulders.

Now, wiggle your nose.

> *Wiggle appropriate body part.*

ZOOM DOWN THE FREEWAY

Zoom down the freeway,

Zoom down the freeway,

Zoom down the freeway,

FAST!

> *With child on knees, slide arms forward on "Zoom" and clap hands on "FAST."*

Up goes the drawbridge,

Up goes the drawbridge,

Up goes the drawbridge,

A ship is going past.

> *Raise knees so child goes up.*

Down goes the drawbridge,

Down goes the drawbridge,

Down goes the drawbridge,

The ship has passed at last.

> *Lower knees so child goes down.*

Zoom down the freeway,

Zoom down the freeway,

Zoom down the freeway,

FAST!

> *With child on knees, slide arms forward on "Zoom" and clap hands on "FAST."*
> *This action rhyme is best done with adult sitting on the floor, legs out straight in front, and child sitting on knees of adult.*

Programs

Theme Index for Programs

The following material is arranged by themes. Each theme consists of suggested stories, rhymes, fingerplays, and songs that can be incorporated into the program. If the material is appropriate for more than one theme, this is indicated in the heading. Keep in mind the brevity of this type of program, and select the material with which you feel most comfortable. The majority of the rhymes, fingerplays, and songs are of European origin and the language is English. For rhymes, fingerplays, and songs that are more multiethnic, please see the Resources for Rhymes, Fingerplays, and Songs section at the end of this chapter. For more information concerning songs and music, see chapter 5. You can use the material offered here as a starting place for you to create your own unique program, whether you use a theme or not. The previously listed rhymes, fingerplays, and songs do not all appear in the following theme program listing. Some of those included can be found in a collection of Mother Goose rhymes. They all work well with very young children.

ANIMALS/ANIMALS, FARM/FARMS
STORIES

The ABC Bunny by Wanda Gag

Across the Stream by Mirra Ginsburg

Ask Mr. Bear by Marjorie Flack

Barnyard Banter by Denise Fleming

Brown Bear, Brown Bear, What Do You See? by Bill Martin Jr.

The Chick and the Duckling by V. Suteyev

Farmyard Beat by Lindsey Craig

From Head to Toe by Eric Carle

The Golden Egg Book by Margaret Wise Brown

Good Night, Good Night by Sandra Boynton

Honk! by Chris Demarest

I Love Animals by Flora McDonnell

In the Small, Small Pond by Denise Fleming

In the Tall, Tall Grass by Denise Fleming

Oh, A-Hunting We Will Go by John Langstaff

Old MacDonald Had a Farm by Frances Cony

Over in the Meadow by John Langstaff
The Owl and the Pussycat by Edward Lear
Peek-a-Moo! by Marie Torres Cimarusti
Says Who? by David Carter
This Is the Farmer by Nancy Tafuri

RHYMES, FINGERPLAYS, AND SONGS

"Baa, Baa, Black Sheep"

"Bingo"

"Gray Squirrel"

"Here Is a Bunny"

"Little Boy Blue"

"Little Turtle"

"Mary Had a Little Lamb"

"Mr. Turkey and Mr. Duck"

"Old MacDonald Had a Farm"

"Plant a Little Seed"

"Rooster Crows"

"Shoe the Old Horse"

"This Is the Way the Ladies Ride"

"This Little Pig Had a Scrub-a-Dub–Dub"
    (from *The Baby Record* by McGrath and Smithrim)

"This Little Piggy"

"Three Little Ducks Went Out One Day"

"To Market, to Market"

"Two Little Blackbirds"

"Way Up High in the Apple Tree"

"When Ducks Get Up in the Morning"

ANIMALS, JUNGLE/ELEPHANTS/ZOO

STORIES

Is That an Elephant Over There? by Rebecca Elgar
Little Gorilla by Ruth Bornstein
Sam Who Never Forgets by Eve Rice
Splash! by Flora McDonnell

RHYMES, FINGERPLAYS, AND SONGS

"An Elephant Goes Like This and That"

"Here Is a Bunny"

"Here Is a Nest for a Robin"

"Hickory, Dickory, Dock"

"Leg Over Leg"

"Mama's Taking Us to the Zoo Tomorrow"

"Pussy Cat, Pussy Cat"

"This Little Piggy"

"Three Little Monkeys"

"Two Little Blackbirds"

BABIES—*SEE* FAMILIES

BATHTIME/WATER

STORIES

Across the Stream by Mirra Ginsburg

Blue Sea by Robert Kalan

Have You Seen My Duckling? by Nancy Tafuri

In the Small, Small Pond by Denise Fleming

Jump, Frog, Jump! by Robert Kalan

Splash! by Flora McDonnell

RHYMES, FINGERPLAYS, AND SONGS

"Catch Me and Kiss Me and Say It Again"

"Charlie over the Water"

"Fishies"

"Gack-Goon"

"The Great Big Spider"

"I'm a Little Teapot"

"Jack and Jill"

"1, 2, 3, 4, 5, I Caught a Fish Alive"

"Rain, Rain, Go Away"

"Rain Is Falling Down"

"Row, Row, Row Your Boat"

"Rub-a-Dub-Dub"

"Little Turtle"

"This Is the Way We Wash Our Face"

"Three Green and Speckled Frogs"

BEARS

STORIES

Ask Mr. Bear by Marjorie Flack

Just Like Daddy by Frank Asch

The Little Mouse, the Red Ripe Strawberry, and the Big Hungry Bear
        by Don and Audrey Wood

Mama's Little Bears by Nancy Tafuri

We're Going on a Bear Hunt by Michael Rosen

RHYMES, FINGERPLAYS, AND SONGS
"Bear Went over the Mountain"
"Going on a Bear Hunt"
"'Round and 'Round the Garden"
"Teddy Bear, Teddy Bear"

BEDTIME

STORIES

Farmyard Beat by Lindsey Craig

Good Night, Good Night by Sandra Boynton

Goodnight Moon by Margaret Wise Brown

Grandfather Twilight by Barbara Berger

Piggies by Don and Audrey Wood

Ten, Nine, Eight by Molly Bang

Time for Bed by Mem Fox

Tuck Me In! by Dean Hacohen

RHYMES, FINGERPLAYS, AND SONGS
"Baby's Nap"
"Jack Be Nimble"
"Star Light, Star Bright"
"Teddy Bear, Teddy Bear"
"There Were Five in the Bed"
"Three Little Monkeys"
"Twinkle, Twinkle, Little Star"

BIRDS

STORIES

Birds by Kevin Henkes

Duck and Goose Find a Pumpkin by Tad Hills

A Good Day by Kevin Henkes

I'm Not Sleepy! by Jonathan Allen

Little Robin Redbreast by Shari Halpern

The Owl and the Pussycat by Edward Lear

RHYMES, FINGERPLAYS, AND SONGS
"Dos Pajaritos (Two Little Birds)"
"Here Is a Nest for a Robin"
"Hickety, Pickety, My Black Hen"
"Little White Duck"
"Mr. Turkey and Mr. Duck"
"One, Two, Buckle My Shoe"
"Rooster Crows"

"Sing a Song of Sixpence"

"Tall as a Tree"

"Three Little Ducks Went Out One Day"

"Two Little Blackbirds"

"Way Up High in the Apple Tree"

BIRTHDAYS/GROWING UP

STORIES

Ask Mr. Bear by Marjorie Flack

It's My Birthday! by Helen Oxenbury

Little Gorilla by Ruth Bornstein

RHYMES, FINGERPLAYS, AND SONGS

"Happy Birthday to You"

"Head and Shoulders, Knees and Toes"

"Here's a Cup"

"If You're Happy and You Know It"

"I'm a Little Teapot"

"Mix a Pancake"

"The Muffin Man"

"Patty Cake, Patty Cake"

"Pease Porridge Hot"

"Sometimes I Am Tall"

"Suppose"

"Tall as a Tree"

"These Are Baby's Fingers"

BOATS—*SEE* THINGS THAT GO

BUGS—*SEE* GARDENS

CATS/DOGS

STORIES

Dog Wants to Play by Christine McDonnell

A Good Day by Kevin Henkes

Kitty Cat, Kitty Cat, Are You Waking Up? by Bill Martin Jr.

One Two That's My Shoe! by Alison Murray

Pete the Cat: I Love My White Shoes by Eric Litwin

Where's Spot? by Eric Hill

RHYMES, FINGERPLAYS, AND SONGS

"Bingo"

"Hey, Diddle, Diddle"

"How Much Is That Doggie in the Window"

"Here Comes a Mouse" (from *Catch Me and Kiss Me and Say It Again*
by Watson)

"Hickory, Dickory, Dock"

"Leg Over Leg"

"Pussy Cat, Pussy Cat"

CHICKENS/DUCKS

STORIES

Across the Stream by Mirra Ginsburg

Big Fat Hen by Keith Baker

The Chick and the Duckling by V. Suteyev

Come Along, Daisy! by Jane Simmons

Duckie's Splash by Frances Barry

Five Little Ducks by Raffi

The Golden Egg Book by Margaret Wise Brown

Have You Seen My Duckling? by Nancy Tafuri

RHYMES, FINGERPLAYS, AND SONGS

"Five Little Ducks Went Out One Day"

"Hickety, Pickety, My Black Hen"

"Mr. Turkey and Mr. Duck"

"One, Two, Buckle My Shoe"

"When Ducks Get Up in the Morning"

CLOUDS–*SEE* WEATHER

DOGS–*SEE* CATS

DUCKS–*SEE* CHICKENS

ELEPHANTS–*SEE* ANIMALS, JUNGLE

FAMILIES/BABIES/MOTHERS/FATHERS

STORIES

Ask Mr. Bear by Marjorie Flack

Baby Loves by Michael Lawrence

Come Along, Daisy! by Jane Simmons

Have You Seen My Duckling? by Nancy Tafuri

Honk! by Chris Demarest

Just Like Daddy by Frank Asch

A Kiss Like This by Mary Murphy

"More More More," Said the Baby by Vera B. Williams

On Mother's Lap by Ann Herbert Scott

Pots and Pans by Patricia Hubbell

Tickle, Tickle by Helen Oxenbury

Whose Mouse Are You? by Robert Kraus

RHYMES, FINGERPLAYS, AND SONGS

"Come'a Look'a See, Here's My Mama"

"Mother and Father and Uncle John"

"Patty Cake, Patty Cake"

"There Was a Little Man"

"These Are Baby's Fingers"

"These Are Grandma's Glasses"

"This Is My Father, This Is My Mother"

"Tommy Thumbs Up"

"Where Is Grandma? Where Is Grandma?"

FARMS—*SEE* ANIMALS/FARMS

FATHERS—*SEE* FAMILIES

FOOD/MESSES

STORIES

The Cow Loves Cookies by Karma Wilson

The Little Mouse, the Red Ripe Strawberry, and the Big Hungry Bear
    by Don and Audrey Wood

Lunch by Denise Fleming

Pots and Pans by Patricia Hubbell

Sam Who Never Forgets by Eve Rice

The Wide-Mouthed Frog by Keith Faulkner

RHYMES, FINGERPLAYS, AND SONGS

"Acka Backa"

"Criss-Cross Applesauce"

"Cup of Tea"

"Do You Know the Muffin Man?"

"Five Plump Peas"

"Georgie Porgie"

"Hot Cross Buns"

"Humpty Dumpty"

"I'm a Little Teapot"

"Pancake"

"Patty Cake, Patty Cake"

"Pease Porridge Hot"

"Sing a Song of Sixpence"

"There Was a Little Man"

"To Market, to Market"

"Tortillas Tortillas"

"Wash the Dishes"

"Way Up High in the Apple Tree"

GAMES–*SEE* TOYS

GARDENS/BUGS/OUTSIDE

STORIES

The Carrot Seed by Ruth Krauss

Chicky Chicky Chook Chook! by Cathy MacLennan

I Went Walking by Sue Williams

In the Small, Small Pond by Denise Fleming

In the Tall, Tall Grass by Denise Fleming

Ten Little Caterpillars by Bill Martin Jr.

Titch by Pat Hutchins

The Very Quiet Cricket by Eric Carle

RHYMES, FINGERPLAYS, AND SONGS

"All around the Mulberry Bush"

"Arabella Miller"

"Five Plump Peas"

"Gack-Goon"

"Gray Squirrel"

"The Great Big Spider"

"Here Is a Beehive"

"Little Turtle"

"Mary, Mary, Quite Contrary"

"Plant a Little Seed"

"'Round and 'Round the Garden"

"Slowly, Slowly, Very Slowly Creeps the Garden Snail"

"Tall as a Tree"

"There Was a Little Turtle"

"This Is My Garden"

"Three Green and Speckled Frogs"

"Way Up High in the Apple Tree"

GETTING DRESSED/HATS

STORIES

Maisy Dresses Up by Lucy Cousins

Under My Hood I Have a Hat by Karla Kuskin

What's on My Head? by Margaret Miller

RHYMES, FINGERPLAYS, AND SONGS

"All around the Mulberry Bush"

"Cobbler, Cobbler"

"Head and Shoulders, Knees and Toes"

"Here Are Baby's Fingers"

"If You're Wearing Red Today"

"Shoe the Old Horse"

"These Are Grandma's Glasses"

"Thumb in the Thumb Place"

"Tommy Thumbs Up"

"Warm Hands Warm"

HATS—*SEE* GETTING DRESSED

MESSES—*SEE ALSO* FOOD

STORIES

Lunch by Denise Fleming

Pete the Cat: I Love My White Shoes by Eric Litwin

Pots and Pans by Patricia Hubbell

RHYMES, FINGERPLAYS, AND SONGS

"Criss-Cross, Applesauce"

"Do You Know the Muffin Man?"

"Humpty Dumpty"

"Patty Cake, Patty Cake"

MICE

STORIES

The Little Mouse, the Red Ripe Strawberry, and the Big Hungry Bear
    by Don and Audrey Wood

Lunch by Denise Fleming

Mouse's First Fall by Lauren Thompson

A New House for Mouse by Petr Horáček

This Is the Farmer by Nancy Tafuri

Whose Mouse Are You? by Robert Kraus

RHYMES, FINGERPLAYS, AND SONGS
"Here Comes a Mouse" (from *Catch Me and Kiss Me and Say It Again* by Watson)
"Hickory, Dickory, Dock"
"Pussy Cat, Pussy Cat"
"Slowly, Slowly, Very Slowly Creeps the Garden Snail"
"Wiggle Your Fingers"

MONKEYS

STORIES
I Like Books! by Anthony Browne

RHYMES, FINGERPLAYS, AND SONGS
"All around the Mulberry Bush"
"Three Little Monkeys"
"Wiggle Your Fingers"

MOTHERS–*SEE* FAMILIES

OUTSIDE–*SEE* GARDENS

PIGS

STORIES
I Like Me! by Nancy Carlson
Piggies by Don and Audrey Wood
Piggies in the Pumpkin Patch by Mary Peterson

RHYMES, FINGERPLAYS, AND SONGS
"Five Little Pigs"
"This Little Pig Had a Scrub-a-Dub"
"This Little Piggy"
"To Market, to Market"

PLAY–*SEE* TOYS

RABBITS

STORIES
The ABC Bunny by Wanda Gag
The Golden Egg Book by Margaret Wise Brown
Goodnight Moon by Margaret Wise Brown
Home for a Bunny by Margaret Wise Brown

RHYMES, FINGERPLAYS, AND SONGS
"Here Is a Bunny"
"Here Is a Nest for a Robin"
"Wiggle Your Fingers"

RAIN–*SEE* WEATHER

SEASONS–*SEE* WEATHER

SHEEP
STORIES
Mary Had a Little Lamb by Sarah Josepha Hale
Sheep in a Jeep by Nancy Shaw
Where Is the Green Sheep? by Mem Fox
RHYMES, FINGERPLAYS, AND SONGS
"Baa, Baa, Black Sheep"
"Little Boy Blue"
"Mary Had a Little Lamb"

THINGS THAT GO/BOATS/TRAINS
STORIES
The Bridge Is Up by Babs Bell
Chugga-Chugga Choo-Choo by Kevin Lewis
Freight Train by Donald Crews
Little Tug by Stephen Savage
Maisy Drives the Bus by Lucy Cousins
Sheep in a Jeep by Nancy Shaw
Trains Go by Steve Light
RHYMES, FINGERPLAYS, AND SONGS
"Airplanes Fly in the Sky"
"Choo-Choo Train"
"Dance to Your Daddy"
"Down at the Station"
"The Engine"
"Five Little Boats"
"The Grand Old Duke of York"
"Here Comes the Choo-Choo Train"
"Here Is a Choo-Choo Train"
"Here Is the Engine"

"I'll Drive a Dump Truck"

"Lots of Cars"

"Row, Row, Row Your Boat"

"This Is the Way the Ladies Ride"

"Trot, Trot to Boston"

"The Wheels on the Bus" (or Car, Truck, etc.)

"Zoom down the Freeway"

TOYS/PLAY/GAMES

STORIES

Chugga-Chugga Choo-Choo by Kevin Lewis

Clap Your Hands by Lorinda Bryan Cauley

Dog Wants to Play by Christine McDonnell

Is That an Elephant Over There? by Rebecca Elgar

Just Like Jasper! by Nick Butterworth

Maggie's Ball by Lindsay Barrett George

Peek-a-Moo! by Mari Torres Cimarusti

Piggies by Don and Audrey Wood

Pots and Pans by Patricia Hubbell

Says Who? by David Carter

Time to Play! by Nigel Gray

Titch by Pat Hutchins

RHYMES, FINGERPLAYS, AND SONGS

"All around the Mulberry Bush"

"All for Baby"

"Bump'n Downtown in My Little Red Wagon"

"Drums"

"Here Comes a Mouse" (from *Catch Me and Kiss Me and Say It Again* by Watson)

"Here We Go Up-Up-Up"

"Here's a Ball"

"Hickory, Dickory, Dock"

"Humpty Dumpty"

"Jack Be Nimble"

"Jack in the Box"

"Johnny Hammers One Hammer"

"Let Everyone Clap Hands Like Me"

"Ring around the Rosie"

"See My Pony, My Jet Black Pony"

"Teddy Bear, Teddy Bear"

"There Was a Little Turtle"

"This Is the Way the Ladies Ride"
"Three Little Monkeys"
"Two Little Blackbirds"
"Wiggle Your Fingers"

TRAINS—*SEE* THINGS THAT GO

WATER—*SEE* BATHTIME

WEATHER/CLOUDS/RAIN/SEASONS

STORIES

Blue Sky by Audrey Wood

Duck and Goose Find a Pumpkin by Tad Hills

Five Little Pumpkins by Iris Van Rynbach

In the Small, Small Pond by Denise Fleming

Little Cloud by Eric Carle

Rain by Robert Kalan

Raindrop, Plop! by Wendy Lewison

RHYMES, FINGERPLAYS, AND SONGS

"Dr. Foster"
"The Great Big Spider"
"I Hear Thunder"
"It's Raining, It's Pouring"
"Rain, Rain, Go Away"
"Rain Is Falling Down"
"Rain on the Green Grass"
"Snow Is Falling Down"
"Thumbs in the Thumb Place"
"Warm Hands Warm"
"Wheels on the Bus" (or Car, Truck, etc.)

Sample Program Outlines—A Baker's Dozen

The following program outlines are yours to use, either verbatim or adapted to match your personal style. The group's dynamics will also be a factor as to what materials you actually use. With active groups, more rhymes, songs, and other active literary experiences will be much more beneficial than trying to use all the books suggested. If naming your program is important to you, pick a general title that will leave you lots of room for program flexibility. "Story Stew," "Young Toddler Storytime," "Mother Goose," and "Rhyming Time" are only a few suggestions. The following "baker's dozen" programs are numbered simply for identification purposes; you can rename them however you like. Each program should run about 20 to 30 minutes.

PROGRAM 1

Opening stretch: "Sometimes I Am Tall"
Rhyme: "Open, Shut Them"
Rhyme: "Teddy Bear, Teddy Bear"
Book: *Brown Bear, Brown Bear, What Do You See?* by Bill Martin Jr.
Song: "The Wheels on the Bus"
Rhyme: "Here's a Ball"
Fingerplay: "These Are Baby's Fingers"
Rhyme: "Way Up High in the Apple Tree"
Rhyme: "Jack in the Box"
Book: *We're Going on a Bear Hunt* by Michael Rosen
Closing song: "The More We Get Together"

PROGRAM 2

Opening song: "The More We Get Together"
Rhyme: "Patty Cake, Patty Cake"
Rhyme: "Hickory, Dickory, Dock"
Song: "Row, Row, Row Your Boat"
Book: *Brown Bear, Brown Bear, What Do You See?* by Bill Martin Jr.
Rhyme: "Teddy Bear, Teddy Bear"
Song: "The Bear Went over the Mountain"
Rhyme: "Open, Shut Them"
Tickle: "'Round and 'Round the Garden"
Book: *The Little Mouse, the Red Ripe Strawberry, and the Big Hungry Bear*
      by Don and Audrey Wood
Flannel-board rhyme: "Two Little Blackbirds"
Fingerplay/song: "Mr. Turkey and Mr. Duck"
Closing song: "The More We Get Together"

PROGRAM 3

Opening rhyme: "Open, Shut Them"
Rhyme: "Patty Cake, Patty Cake"
Fingerplay: "Hickory, Dickory, Dock"
Book: *Is That an Elephant Over There?* by Rebecca Elgar
Rhyme: "An Elephant Goes Like This and That"
Song: "Three Little Monkeys"
Book: *Sam Who Never Forgets* by Eve Rice
Rhyme: "Humpty Dumpty"
Song: "Old MacDonald Had a Farm" (using flannel board)
Book: *Piggies* by Don and Audrey Wood
Closing song: "The More We Get Together"

PROGRAM 4

Opening song: "The More We Get Together"
Knee bounce: "Father and Mother and Uncle John"
Book: *Chicky Chicky Chook Chook* by Cathy MacLennan
Lap (or standing) game: "Here We Go Up-Up-Up"
Stretch: "Rain Is Falling Down"
Book: *Brown Bear, Brown Bear, What Do You See?* by Bill Martin Jr.
Lap game: "Leg Over Leg"
Book: *Freight Train* by Donald Crews
Song: "The Wheels on the Bus"
Fingerplay: "Three Little Monkeys"
Closing game: "Ring around the Rosie"

PROGRAM 5

Opening song: "The More We Get Together"
Fingerplay: "Clap Your Hands"
Book: *If You're Happy and You Know It Clap Your Hands* by David Carter
Lap (or standing) game: "Here We Go Up-Up-Up"
Stretch: "Jack in the Box"
Rhyme: "Cobbler, Cobbler"
Book: *Maggie's Ball* by Lindsay Barrett George
Tickle: "Criss-Cross Applesauce"
Book: *Clip-Clop* by Nicola Smee
Flannel-board or puppet rhyme: "Two Little Blackbirds"
Closing song: "The More We Get Together"

PROGRAM 6

Opening song: "The More We Get Together"

Fingerplay: "Rain Is Falling Down"

Book: *Brown Bear, Brown Bear, What Do You See?* by Bill Martin Jr.

Rhyme: "1, 2, 3, 4, 5, I Caught a Fish Alive"

Lap game: "Leg Over Leg"

Book: *Blue Sea* by Robert Kalan

Finger puppet or flannel-board rhyme: "Two Little Blackbirds"

Bounce: "My Pony Macaroni"

Lap (or standing) game: "Hickory, Dickory, Dock"

Song: "I Hear Thunder"

Book: *The Big Storm* by Nancy Tafuri

Tickle: "Criss-Cross Applesauce"

Rhyme/bounce: "Humpty Dumpty"

Closing song: "The More We Get Together"

PROGRAM 7

Opening Song: "The More We Get Together"

Fingerplay: "Open, Shut Them"

Lap game: "Head and Shoulders, Knees and Toes"

Book: *The Carrot Seed* by Ruth Krauss (presented as is, as a flannel-board story, or in big-book format)

Fingerplay: "Way Up High in the Apple Tree"

Rhyme/song: "The Great Big Spider"

Rhyme: "Tall as a Tree"

Book: *The Little Mouse, the Red Ripe Strawberry, and the Big Hungry Bear* by Don and Audrey Wood

Song: "The Wheels on the Bus"

Bounce: "Humpty Dumpty"

Rhyme: "'Round and 'Round the Garden"

Book: *Where's Spot?* by Eric Hill

Fingerplay: "Tommy Thumbs Up"

Bounce: "Bump'n Downtown in My Little Red Wagon"

Closing song: "If You're Happy and You Know It"

PROGRAM 8

Opening song: "The More We Get Together"

Fingerplay: "Open, Shut Them"

Fingerplay: "Roly-Poly"

Action song: "Head and Shoulders, Knees and Toes"

Book: *Where Is the Green Sheep?* by Mem Fox

Fingerplay: "There Was a Little Man"

Song/game: "Mr. Turkey and Mr. Duck"

Tickle: "'Round and 'Round the Garden"
Fingerplay: "1, 2, 3, 4, 5, I Caught a Fish Alive"
Book: *Down on the Farm* by Merrily Kutner
Song: "Row, Row, Row Your Boat"
Rhyme/game: "Here Is My Garden"
Book: *Titch* by Pat Hutchins
Song: "Plant a Little Seed" (using visuals)
Fingerplay: "Five Plump Peas"
Closing song: "The More We Get Together"

PROGRAM 9

Opening song: "The More We Get Together"
Fingerplay: "Head and Shoulders, Knees and Toes"
Fingerplay: "Tommy Thumbs Up"
Book: *Brown Bear, Brown Bear, What Do You See?* by Bill Martin Jr.
Song: "Row, Row, Row Your Boat"
Rhyme: "Hickory, Dickory, Dock"
Song: "Old MacDonald Had a Farm" (using stuffed toys pulled from cloth bag)
Rhyme/game: "The Great Big Spider"
Rhyme (standing): "Tall as a Tree"
Rhyme: "Jack in the Box"
Book: *Mary Had a Little Lamb* by Sarah Josepha Hale
Tickle: "'Round and 'Round the Garden"
Rhyme: "Here Is a Bunny"
Bounce: "This Is the Way the Ladies Ride"
Tickle: "Criss-Cross Applesauce"
Closing song: "The More We Get Together"

PROGRAM 10

Opening stretch: "Suppose"
Rhyme: "Wiggle Your Fingers"
Song: "Bump'n Downtown in My Little Red Wagon"
Rhyme: "1, 2, 3, 4, 5, I Caught a Fish Alive"
Book: *Brown Bear, Brown Bear, What Do You See?* by Bill Martin Jr.
Bounce: "To Market, to Market"
Song: "Wheels on the Bus"
Tickle: "Here Comes a Mouse" (from *Catch Me and Kiss Me and Say It Again* by Watson; using a mouse puppet)
Rhyme: "Tall as a Tree"
Rhyme: "Jack in the Box"
Story: *Just Like Jasper!* by Nick Butterworth

Rhyme: "Humpty Dumpty"

Rhyme/song: "The Great Big Spider"

Rhyme: "Cobbler, Cobbler"

Book: *On Mother's Lap* by Ann Herbert Scott

Closing song: "The More We Get Together"

PROGRAM 11

Opening song: "Welcome, Welcome!"

Greeting and guidelines

Clapping rhyme (to the tune of "Row, Row, Row Your Boat"):

> *Clap, clap, clap your hands.*
> *Clap them now with me.*
> *Clap your hands, let me see,*
> *Clap them now with me!*
> *Tap, tap, tap your knees. . . .*
> *Shake, shake, shake your feet. . . .*
> *Touch, touch, touch your nose. . . .*

Action rhyme: "Open, Shut Them"

Read-aloud: *Peek-a-Moo!* by Marie Torres Cimarusti

Standing action rhyme: "The Great Big Spider"

Action rhyme (to the tune of "Frère Jacques"):

> *Peek-a-boo, peek–a-boo,*
> *I see you, I see you.*
> *I see your button nose,*
> *I see your tiny toes,*
> *I see you.*
> *Peek-a-boo!*

Read-aloud: *All Fall Down* by Helen Oxenbury (Little Simon, 1999)

Rhyme: "Roly-Poly"

Dance: "Hokey Pokey!"

Rhyme: "Way Up High in the Apple Tree"

Song: "Row, Row, Row Your Boat"

Action rhyme: "1, 2, 3, 4, 5, I Caught a Fish Alive"

Closing song or rhyme

PROGRAM 12

Opening song: "Welcome, Welcome, Everyone"

Rhyme: "Wiggle Your Fingers"

Rhyme: "Open, Shut Them"

Game: "Head and Shoulders, Knees and Toes"

Read-aloud: *Baby Says "Moo!"* by JoAnn Early Macken

Rhyme: "I'm a Little Teapot"

Action rhyme: "The Great Big Spider"

Action song: "We Are Marching to the Drum" (using drum instrument)

Music time: Using rhythm instruments and CD of your choice for shaking to the rhythm of a nursery rhyme, such as "Do You Know the Muffin Man?" or "Twinkle, Twinkle, Little Star"; singing (to the tune of "Good Night Ladies") to put bells (or other instruments away): "Good-bye bells, good-bye bells, good-bye bells, we'll play another day."

Song: "If You're Happy and You Know It"

Closing song: "Skinnamarink" (from *The Elephant Show* by Sharon, Lois, and Bram, Drive Entertainment, 1994)

PROGRAM 13 (WITH SUGGESTED SCRIPT)

Opening announcements:

- "I don't expect your children to sit still, but let's keep them safe."
- "Really focus on the children during this program; make sure cell phones are off."
- "Big people take part!"

"Let's get started!"

- "Welcome, Welcome Everyone"

"It's early, so let's do some stretches! Can you do them too?"

- "Open, Shut Them"
- "Would you like to do more?" (using sign language for "more")
- "Open, Shut Them"

"For this one, you can give your child bounces, hugs, and a toss in the air!"

- "Acka Backa" (two times)

"Are you ready for some patty cake?"

- "Patty Cake, Patty Cake" (two times)

"Let's go for a bus ride!"

- "The Wheels on the Bus"

"Would you like to read a book? This is one of my favorites!"

- *Brown Bear, Brown Bear, What Do You See?* by Bill Martin Jr.

"Do you remember which way we lean with this one? Be careful and don't bump heads!"

- "Mother and Father and Uncle John" (two times)

"Where's your head? Can you put your hands on your head? Where're your shoulders? (etc.)"

- "Head and Shoulders, Knees and Toes" (two times)

"Since your child is sitting in front of you . . ."

- "Criss-Cross Applesauce"

"You want to read a book about monsters?" (using sign language for "book")
"I'll need your help! Can you say, 'Shoo shoo shoo'"?

- *Go Away, Big Green Monster!* by Ed Emberley

"Let's go for a ride!"

- "This Is the Way the Ladies Ride" (two times)

"This next one is a simple hand tickle."

- "'Round and 'Round the Garden" (two times)

"What do we have? This is a very special song."

- "Did You Ever See a Pumpkin?"

"Let's stretch up high!"

- "Way Up High in the Apple Tree"
- "Did you eat all the apples? Let's climb back up and get more!"
- Repeat "Way Up High in the Apple Tree"

"Okay, let's go for a rowboat ride, with your child in your lap!"

- "Row, Row, Row Your Boat"
- "Let's go faster!"
- "Too fast! Let's slow it down!"
- Repeat "Row, Row, Row Your Boat"

"Let's catch a fish! Your children are the fish, so clap around them and hug them!"

- "1, 2, 3, 4, 5, I Caught a Fish Alive"

"Let's all stand up so we can shake our sillies out!"

- "Shake Your Sillies Out" (from *More Singable Songs* by Raffi, Rounder, 1996)

"Let's get ready for some spiders!"

- "The Great Big Spider" (two times)

"Let's stretch!"
- "Tall as a Tree"

"Everyone down on the floor. Where is your shoe?"
- "Cobbler, Cobbler" (two times)

"Does it look like it's going to rain?"
- "Rain Is Falling Down"
- "You can make bigger splashes than that!"
- Repeat "Rain Is Falling Down"

"Would you like to help me with a song?"
- "If You're Happy and You Know It"
- (A tail! Do you have a tail? No? Let's just wiggle our bottoms then! Wings? etc.)

Closing song: "The More We Get Together"
Closing comments, handout

Resources

Resources for Books and Programming

Print Resources for Storytime Books and Programming

Association for Library Service to Children and Public Library Association. *Every Child Ready to Read*. 2nd ed. Kit. Chicago: American Library Association, 2011.

Blakemore, Caroline J., and Barbara Weston Ramirez. *Baby Read-Aloud Basics: Fun and Interactive Ways to Help Your Little One Discover the World of Words*. New York: American Management Association, 2006.

Butler, Dorothy. *Babies Need Books*. Revised ed. Portsmouth, NH: Heinemann, 1998.

Ernst, Linda L. *Baby Rhyming Time*. New York: Neal-Schuman, 2008.

———. *Lapsit Services for the Very Young II*. New York: Neal-Schuman, 2001.

Ghoting, Saroj Nadkarni, and Pamela Martin-Diaz. *Early Literacy Storytimes @ Your Library*. Chicago: American Library Association, 2006.

Marino, Jane. *Babies in the Library!* Lanham, MD: Scarecrow Press, 2003.

Marino, Jane, and Dorothy F. Houlihan. *Mother Goose Time: Library Programs for Babies and Their Caregivers*. New York: H. W. Wilson, 1992.

Odean, Kathleen. *Great Books for Babies and Toddlers: More Than 500 Recommended Books for Your Child's First Three Years.* New York: Ballantine Books, 2003.

Raines, Shirley, Karen Miller, and Leah Curry-Rood. *Story S-t-r-e-t-c-h-e-r-s for Infants, Toddlers, and Twos: Experiences, Activities, and Games for Popular Children's Books.* Beltsville, MD: Gryphon House, 2002.

Straub, Susan. *Reading with Babies, Toddlers and Twos.* Naperville, IL: Sourcebooks, 2006.

Sources for "Big Books"

Amazon. http://www.amazon.com/.

Bound-to-Stay-Bound. http://www.btsb.com/.

Childcraft. http://www.childcraft.com/.

Lakeshore Learning Store. http://www.lakeshorelearning.com/.

Scholastic (in the Teachers Store). http://shop.scholastic.com/.

E-resources for Storytime Books and Programming

Association for Library Service to Children (ALSC). http://www.ala.org/alsc/. This national organization for children's librarians in the United States offers bibliographies and early literacy information and activities.

Koester, Amy. *The Show Me Librarian* (blog). http://showmelibrarian.blogspot.com/. This blog, created in 2012, is devoted to children's librarianship. The blogger shares her own program successes and learning moments with other librarians, who in turn share theirs. The goal is to assist other librarians in their work. The blog reflects only the blogger's opinion while helping to share the contributions of the community of children's librarians.

Lambert, Sylvia Leigh. *Goose Time Pathfinder: Library Programs with Books and Babies.* Last updated July 9, 2003. http://www.unc.edu/~sllamber/pathfinder/mothergooseindex.html. This pathfinder is aimed at those who serve children in the public library field and are interested in starting and/or developing programs for very young children. Areas covered include books, fingerplays, props/puppets, recordings, educational resources, and potential partners.

McDowell, Kate. *Babies' Lap Time: How-To and Why Guide.* Last updated August 2006. http://katemcdowell.com/laptime/. This collection of programming resources includes structural suggestions for creating programs, themes, and tips.

Many libraries and library systems also have suggested bibliographies for very young children on their websites. Check out the following sources.

Hennepin County Library, Minnesota. "Birth to Six." http://www.hclib.org/BirthTo6. Besides program offerings and booklists, this website provides *Birth to Six News* (a newsletter), "Tech Together" (technology experiences for children), "Raising Readers" (early literacy websites), a Spanish version ("En Español"), tips on how to make the most of your library, and parenting/child-care resources, as well as Read to Me videos (http://hclib.org/Birthto6/readtome/index.cfm) that explain the importance of reading to children.

Kent District Library, Michigan. "Play-Grow-Read!" http://www.kdl.org/kids/go/pgr_main. This Parents and Kids section offers books, different literacy activities, tips for reading with your children in languages other than English, storytime videos, and the *Early Lit Bits* newsletter.

King County Library System, Washington. "Booklists: Ages Birth to Five." http://www.kcls.org/kids/whattoread/booklists/birth_to_five.cfm. This page offers a number of age categories to choose from; clicking on one will bring up the relevant booklist.

———. "Tell Me a Story." http://wiki.kcls.org/tellmeastory/index.php/Main_Page. From this page, you can access lists of titles used in children's librarians' actual storytimes.

Multnomah County Library, Oregon. "Early Literacy: Birth to Six." http://www.multcolib.org/birthtosix. This website offers information on early literacy, brain development, and more.

Prince George's County Memorial Library System, Maryland. "Reading Ever After." http://www.pgcmls.info/REA. This resource offers early literacy information, booklists, and things to do to promote reading readiness.

San Francisco Public Library, California. "Early Literacy." http://sfpl.org/index.php?pg=2000152501. This site offers bibliographies to share with babies, toddlers, and preschoolers. Click on the desired age group listed on the right-hand side of the page.

Resources for Rhymes, Fingerplays, and Songs

Print Resources

Ada, Alma Flor, and F. Isabel Campoy (selectors). *¡Muu, Moo!: Rimas de animales, Animal Nursery Rhymes*. English versions by Rosalma Zubizarreta. Illustrated by Vivi Escriva. New York: Rayo, 2010.

————. *¡Pío, Peep! Rimas tradicionales en español, Traditional Spanish Nursery Rhymes.* English adaptations by Alice Schertle. Illustrated by Vivi Escriva. New York: HarperCollins, 2003.

Cobb, Jane. *I'm a Little Teapot! Presenting Preschool Storytime.* Vancouver, BC: Black Sheep Press, 1996.

————. *What'll I Do with the Baby-O? Nursery Rhymes, Songs, and Stories for Babies.* Book with CD. Vancouver, BC: Black Sheep Press, 2007.

Collins, Heather. *Out Came the Sun: A Day in Nursery Rhymes.* Toronto, ON: Kids Can Press, 2007.

Diamant-Cohen, Betsy. *Early Literacy Programming en Español.* New York: Neal-Schuman, 2010.

Ernst, Linda. *Baby Rhyming Time.* Book with CD. New York: Neal-Schuman, 2008.

Feierabend, John M. *The Book of Bounces: Wonderful Songs and Rhymes Passed Down from Generation to Generation for Infants and Toddlers.* Chicago: First Steps, 2000.

————. *The Book of Wiggles and Tickles: Wonderful Songs and Rhymes Passed Down from Generation to Generation for Infants and Toddlers.* Chicago: First Steps, 2000.

Flint Public Library. *Ring a Ring O' Roses: Stories, Games and Finger Plays for Preschool Children.* 12th ed. Flint, MI: Flint Public Library, 2008.

Maddigan, Beth. *The Big Book of Stories, Songs and Sing Alongs: Programs for Babies, Toddlers and Families.* Westport, CT: Libraries Unlimited, 2003.

Marino, Jane. *Babies in the Library!* Lanham, MD: Scarecrow Press, 2003.

Marino, Jane, and Dorothy F. Houlihan. *Mother Goose Time: Library Programs for Babies and Their Caregivers.* New York: H. W. Wilson, 1992.

Roberts, Sheena (compiler). *Playsongs: Action Songs and Rhymes for Babies and Toddlers.* London: Playsongs Publications, 2006.

Schiller, Pam, Rafael Lara-Aecio, and Beverly J. Irby. *The Bilingual Book of Rhymes, Songs, Stories and Fingerplays/El libro bilingüe de rimas, canciones, cuentos y juegos.* Beltsville, MD: Gryphon House, 2004.

Silberg, Jackie. *The Complete Book of Rhymes, Songs, Poems, Fingerplays and Chants: Over 700 Selections.* Beltsville, MD: Gryphon House, 2006.

Scott, Barbara A. *1,000 Fingerplays and Action Rhymes: A Sourcebook and DVD.* New York: Neal-Schuman, 2010.

Treviño, Rose Zertuche. *Read Me a Rhyme in Spanish and English/Léame una rima en español e inglés.* Chicago: American Library Association, 2009.

Watson, Clyde. *Catch Me and Kiss Me and Say It Again.* New York: Philomel, 1978.

Wu, Faye-Lynn. *Chinese and English Nursery Rhymes.* Tokyo: Tuttle Publishing, 2010.

Yolen, Jane, ed. *This Little Piggy and Other Rhymes to Sing and Play.* Book with CD. Cambridge, MA: Candlewick Press, 2005.

Audio Resources

Cobb, Jane. *What'll I Do with the Baby-O?* Book with CD (English, Spanish, sampling of other languages such as German, Mandarin, French, and Dutch). Vancouver, BC: Black Sheep Press, 2006.

Ernst, Linda L. *Baby Rhyming Time.* Book with CD. New York: Neal-Schuman, 2008.

Jaeger, Sally, and Erika Webster. *Here Comes Mr. Bear!* CD. Aurora, ON: Merriweather Records, 2009.

McGrath, Bob, and Katharine Smithrim. *The Baby Record.* CD. Teaneck, NJ: Bob's Kids Music, 2000.

———. *Songs and Games for Toddlers.* CD. Teaneck, NJ: Bob's Kids Music, 2000.

Reid-Naiman, Kathy. *Sally Go Round the Sun.* CD. Aurora, ON: Merriweather Records, 2007.

———. *Tickles and Tunes: Tickles, Songs and Bounces for Children 6 Months to 6 Years Old.* CD. Aurora, ON: Merriweather Records, 1997.

Stewart, Nancy. *Little Songs for Little Me.* Activity Book and CD. Mercer Island, WA: Friends Street Music, 1992.

Sunseri, MaryLee. *Baby-O!* CD. Pacific Grove, CA: Piper Grove Music, 2003.

———. *Mother Goose Melodies: Four and Twenty Olde Songs for Young Children.* CD. Pacific Grove, CA: Piper Grove Music, 2003.

Yolen, Jane, ed. *This Little Piggy and Other Rhymes to Sing and Play.* Book with CD. Cambridge, MA: Candlewick Press, 2005.

E-resources

The Best Kids Booksite. http://thebestkidsbooksite.com/. This site has many English rhymes and fingerplays that you can browse through by topic and translate into other languages. You will need to check the translations for accuracy since word-for-word translations do not always work.

Colorado Libraries for Early Literacy (CLEL). "Storyblocks." http://storyblocks.org/. Working in partnership with Rocky Mountain Public Broadcasting Services, CLEL offers a collection of 30- to 60-second videos "to model to parents, caregivers, and library staff some songs, rhymes, and fingerplays appropriate for early childhood. English and Spanish rhymes are both represented."

King County Library System, Washington. "Tell Me a Story." http://wiki.kcls.org/tellmeastory/index.php/Main_Page. This page includes a link to words and visual online demonstrations of hundreds of rhymes and songs.

Enhancements

5

You have selected books, rhymes, and poems that will be a wonderful introduction to the world of language for the very young child. Once your basic program outline is set up, you may want to enhance or add to it with a variety of language experiences for the children in addition to what they absorb through their sense of hearing. This is important because children use all their senses and have multiple ways of learning. The following sections show how to use music, puppets, flannel-board stories, and movement to reinforce the language experience for the participants in various ways—visually, tactilely, and physically. Entire books cover these topics, if you desire to immerse yourself in a specific field; this text will start you on your way. See the Resources section at the end of this chapter for additional sources of inspiration.

The Creative Activities section contains ideas for take-home activities and for group activities to include in your program. These activities help to make learning language skills fun and are examples of how easy it is for the adult to help the child learn communication skills through everyday living. Creating displays will allow you to introduce services and materials of which participants may be unaware. Handouts can help them re-create language experiences outside the program boundaries and encourage them to continue language-skills learning experiences with the children on their own. Displays and handouts are also good ways to incorporate adult education into the program. See this book's appendix for sample handouts, which are also available at alaeditions.org/webextras; these handouts may be used "as is" or modified to suit your program needs.

IN THIS CHAPTER

✓ Music

✓ Flannel Boards

✓ Puppets

✓ Creative Activities

✓ Language

✓ Movement

✓ Props

✓ Play

✓ Displays

✓ Handouts

✓ Resources

Music

Children love to make and to listen to music. Of course, adults will often hear only the spoon banging on the tray, a bird chirping in a tree, or a little one babbling happily. The child is surrounded by music beginning in the womb, with the heartbeat and other sounds of the mother's body being the constant music. Songs, chants, and rhymes are ways we can enhance the child's world through the sense of hearing. Even the hearing-impaired child feels rhythm through sound vibrations. Traditional songs and rhymes span generations and can give a sense of continuity and community. They can bring back memories and create new ones. While singing, people often elongate the syllables of words so that the sounds that make them up can be heard clearly. Music takes words not used in everyday conversations and introduces them into a child's vocabulary. Think about how many different words a simple song like "Twinkle, Twinkle, Little Star" presents to children: twinkle, little, star, wonder, where, up, above, world, high, diamond, sky—you can keep going on your own—and this is simply looking at the first verse of a multiverse traditional song, one that uses the tune from a Mozart melody and is based on an 1806 poem! The thing about music is that it brings people together, and children need adults who actively participate with them in their world.

You can use music many different ways throughout your program. It can be background music while people are arriving or for various activities, such as free dance, game playing, and the like. Played afterward it can encourage conversations instead of silence between strangers. Music can also create an atmosphere that encourages interaction between each adult and child as well as among the adults themselves. These time periods are perfect opportunities to introduce various children's performers and music to the group. You can "frame" the program by starting every program with a welcome song and a closing song, an approach that gives children a routine that they recognize. Music can also be used as a transition tool to move from one element of the program to another. Use a song to help the children let go of shakers by singing and waving good-bye to them. For example, sing the following song using the tune to "Good Night Ladies" as you put shakers into a container:

> *Good-bye shakers,*
> *Good-bye shakers,*
> *Good-bye shakers,*
> *We'll play another day.*

It is amazing how this helps the children release the items. Songs are often stories in themselves, and many have been made into books, such as these popular songs: *If You're Happy and You Know It, Clap Your Hands! A Pop-Up Book* by David Carter; *Five Little Ducks* by Raffi; *Little White Duck* by Walt Whippo; and *Oh, A-Hunting We Will Go* by John Langstaff. Children's songs and music often derive from fingerplays, which can be helpful when trying to remember the words.

Many adults are self-conscious or severely critical of their singing ability. Chanting is a form of music that may be more comfortable to them. No matter what the adults may think, their children are nonjudgmental and simply amazed by their vocal ability. Once adults grasp this concept, they become more comfortable vocalizing. Encourage adults to actively sing, chant, and vocalize in the privacy of their homes, where their children will listen to them with amazement.

As the presenter, you can also use music to refocus the group, bringing their attention back to the program at hand. Sometimes a distraction is so large that closing the book and singing "The Wheels on the Bus" can encourage the participants to refocus on the presenter. Use whatever familiar song the group knows to help restore the rhythm of the program. Soft music can also calm some situations, such as a fussy or distracted child, especially when the accompanying adult sings along. Music is fun for everyone because it gets participants involved, by singing along, doing actions or movements, listening, or simply enjoying the mood created. Music for very young children tends to be repetitive with a recognizable beat. If the program includes participants of various ages, such familiar songs can get everyone engaged no matter their ability.

Rhythm Instruments

Keep rhythm instruments for this age group simple in design. It is very important to keep safety in mind. Do not allow broken instruments or those which have small pieces even to be brought into the area. Shakers, drums, and bells are the best instruments for children 12 to 24 months old. You can purchase these commercially from early-childhood curriculum stores, music stores, or toy stores, or you can furnish homemade instruments. No matter whether they are purchased or handmade, keep child safety foremost in mind; remember to clean them regularly and inspect them for wear before every program.

Shakers

You can purchase shakers in many colors and sizes, so remember the size of the hand that will be holding them. Be aware that some shakers are made of thin plastic that will crack and break. Not only will you have a mess to clean up; the sharp edges may cut someone.

Shakers are simple to make using various approaches. Colored plastic eggs make bright and easy-to-hold shakers. Open the egg and place noise-making material inside half of the egg. Rice and dried beans are common choices for filler. The type and amount you put into the egg will affect the sound. Using a hot glue gun, run a thin line of glue on the inside rim of the egg, put the two halves together, and hold to let it set. Cover the seam with colored electrical tape, which you can find in most hardware stores. Tape tends to attract dirt and lose its stickiness, so these shakers may require closer maintenance.

Another method of making shakers is to use prescription bottles with child-proof lids. Select bottles that can be held comfortably without muffling the sound. Use ones that have no labels and make sure they are clean, with absolutely no residue. Fill halfway with the same material as you would use for the egg, and replace the top securely. Decorate with signal dots or stickers, which you can find at most office supply, card craft, or curriculum stores.

To make larger shakers, use pie pans or paper plates. The challenge with these materials is to make sure that there are no sharp edges to cause injury and that the seal around the pans is tight enough to prevent the noise-making material from spilling out. Take two aluminum pie pans or two paper plates, place noise-making material in one, and then glue the second one upside down on top of it. You can also punch holes around the edge of the pans/plates and "sew" them shut with yarn. Once again, make sure there are adults to supervise when using this kind of shaker.

You can purchase commercially made shakers in music stores, early-childhood curriculum stores, and online. These can be expensive, but they tend to be more durable.

Store shakers in a box, basket, or bag, decorated any way you want. The storage containers will also make it easier to pass out and retrieve the shakers. Mesh laundry bags, which come in many colors and can hang from a hook, are one choice for shaker storage between programs. Pillowcases with bright, colorful designs are another alternative.

Drums

Give a child a spoon and the drumming will begin! Children will tap, bang, and drum on surfaces of all kinds. Any item in hand can become a drumstick, be it a wooden spoon, doll, or the child's hand. Children love to drum!

Purchasing drums for large groups may be cost prohibitive, and using one drum for a group of children may not work very well. You can, however, provide individual drums for a group using different household items. Plastic bowls, pots and pans, plastic dish pans, empty oatmeal containers (particularly the Quaker Oats container), and so on make perfect drums when turned upside down and banged on with wooden spoons. The ever-ready coffee can also makes a wonderful drum. Remove any outer wrapper, and then wash and dry the can thoroughly. Most coffee cans today are plastic and have an easy-grip handle that the child can grasp. Glue the lid onto the container and decorate the outside, if desired. If using wooden spoons as drumsticks, check to ensure there are no rough edges or splinters. Plastic serving spoons are another alternative, and then, of course, there is always the child's hand. If you do hand out drumsticks, remind the adults that this activity is one they need to do in conjunction with their children for safety reasons.

One other drum available is the floor. Drumsticks or rhythm sticks tapped on the floor is another way to keep rhythm. Participants can use these sticks to sound out syllables of words while reciting a rhyme or singing a song.

Bells

The sound of bells jingling can brighten up anyone's day. The pleasure derived from shaking bells shows brightly on little children's faces and in the wiggles of their bodies. When using bells, inspect them to make sure all of them are safely fastened with no rough edges. School supply stores, toy stores, and music stores handle these items. Bells generally come attached to a ridged form, shaped as a ring, stick, star, and so forth, that helps the child hold on to the bell. Shaking bells can add music to activities such as jumping up and down, marching in a circle, and exercising other large-motor skills. Giving directions during this activity will also help build children's vocabulary through the use of such words as "shake," "high," "low," "fast," and "slow."

Media

Technology has changed so dramatically that incorporating music into the program is getting simpler. CD players are more compact, streamlined, and affordable. Music is available on CDs and as downloads to an iPod or MP3 player. Whatever you use, here are a few tips for using sound equipment during a program:

- Make sure the equipment is set up in a safe area where the children cannot upset it or come in contact with wiring.
- Have the music ready to go when you need it. Write down the track number or have your media player set so you do not have to fumble around. If you are using multiple pieces throughout your program, list their track locations or numbers so there will be as little break in the program routine as possible. Technology that enables the creation of playlists of the desired songs also allows for smoother transitions.

- Check the volume *before* turning on the machine. Unbeknownst to you, little fingers may have played with the volume control.
- Actively involve the group in the music, rather than having them just listen to it. Adults can hold their children and rock them in time to the music. Encourage group movement through marching, swaying, or simply clapping along with the beat or have them even sing along. By starting and stopping the music, you can also create a game of start and stop, dance and freeze, with very young children.
- Unless you plan to devote the entire program to music, keep this section brief or disperse the music portions throughout the whole program.
- Using recorded music does provide a more dynamic music presentation, but beware of sound tracks on which the language disappears under the musical score. One advantage of using your own voice is that it tends to have more clarity and uses a simple melody that the participants can easily follow. The advantage to using recorded music is that you have backup for yourself, if you need the support. An example of this kind of recording is *Little Songs for Little Me* by Nancy Stewart. This solo voice singing the melody line with a simple guitar background enables the words to be clearly heard and understood. Some performers provide recordings that include first the lyrics with a music track and then a separate music track alone.

Visuals

The use of visual aids is one way to draw participants into the musical experience in different ways.

Many popular children's songs have been made into beautiful picture books. One example is *Over in the Meadow* by John Langstaff, which has been available for years and is still loved by children. Raffi has put many of his songs into the picture-book format, *Five Little Ducks*, for instance. Pop-up books, such as *If You're Happy and You Know It, Clap Your Hands!* by David Carter add an extra surprise to the presentation.

When working with non-English-speaking groups, visual aids enable the participants not only to learn the music but also to identify and name the subject of the song. Picture cards are a simple visual technique. You can create these using 8.5-by-11-inch sheets of paper on which you add pictures that reflect the song by copying, tracing, or gluing pictures on the paper. Nowadays you can find many pictures to download from online websites and clip-art software. Use stiff paper or tag board to hold the picture card for easy viewing. Slip these cards into plastic page protectors or laminate them to increase their durability and to make them sturdier for repeated manipulation.

Other visual aids include puppets and stuffed animals. These can be stored in a bag or box. The presenter can then pull out the puppet/stuffed animal at the appropriate time. A song that illustrates this kind of presentation is "When Ducks Get Up in the Morning" from *Plant a Little Seed* by Nancy Stewart (copyright 1995; reprinted with permission). The words are as follows:

When ducks get up in the morning, they always say good day.
When ducks get up in the morning, they always say good day.
Quack, quack, quack, quack—that is what they say; they say
Quack, quack, quack, quack—that is what they say!

Showing a picture of a duck or a puppet/stuffed toy duck, saying the word "duck," and making the sound that ducks "speak" helps solidify the connection between the animal identified and its English name. Of course, you can substitute other animals in place of the duck. Children can comprehend much sooner than they can verbalize, so pictures or other representations of the animals will help them identify the things in their world.

Music is often part of another activity. You can play it in the background as a story is read aloud to add "atmosphere." For free dance or movement time, music is a vital component, with its tempos, volume, and, at times, lyrics setting the pace. Programs like this are excellent ways to introduce children to music from other countries.

Recommended Recordings and DVDs

The following are tried-and-true recordings and performers and recommended foundation recordings and songs used successfully in programs with the very young. Information includes the performer, recording title, and a brief annotation with recommended songs to try first. Many of them contain material that can be done as fingerplays too. Since music, fingerplays, and rhymes are so closely connected, see chapter 4 for more information and resources.

There is a wealth of suitable music to explore, with new material constantly being introduced, often first appearing in the early childhood field. Many wonderful older recordings are no longer available due to various reasons, such as being in an obsolete format, for example, vinyl records or cassette tapes. It is much more practical to use CDs or to download songs from the Internet. These treasures are not always lost to us, however, because often they are available from sites such as Amazon.com, iTunes, and so forth, and also from the performers' websites. Many children's performers have websites that make their audio and/ or their printed material available either for purchase or downloading. See the Resources section at the end of the chapter for these and other websites.

Performers often have numerous collections of children's music to offer. The following list is meant only as a starting point to begin your exploration into the field of children's music. The Internet, Yahoo, iTunes, and so on, also feature performers from around the world for discovery and enjoyment. Investigate performers in your region for local children's music possibilities. The entries include websites when possible for access to more information about lyrics, tunes, and performers.

Babypants, Caspar (http://babypantsmusic.com/). *Here I Am!* **CD. Seattle, WA: Aurora Elephant Music, 2009.**

Christ Ballew, the lead singer and songwriter for the Presidents of the United States of America, has moved into the field of children's music, creating songs for the listening and wiggling pleasure of very young children and their caregivers.

Berkner, Laurie (http://www.laurieberkner.com/). *Whaddaya Think of That?* **CD. New York: Two Tomatoes, 2000.**

"These Are My Glasses" is a wonderful song to begin the program; for suggested hand gestures to use with it go to http://www.laurieberkner.com/music/song-lyrics/127-these-are-my-glasses.html; "We Are the Dinosaurs," with simple lyrics, has a great marching tempo that alternates with smooth flowing music; and "I'm a Little Snowflake" is good for stretching up and down while singing, or you can give the children tulle rounds (found at most fabric stores, or cut five-inch squares from tulle) that can be tossed up into the air while singing the song.

Chappelle, Eric (http://www.aventurinemusic.com/about-eric-chappelle.html). *Music for Creative Dance: Contrast and Continuum,* **Volume III. CD. Seattle, WA: Ravenna Ventures, 1998.**

Part of the Music for Creative Dance series, this volume offers twenty different contrast and continuum musical pieces for movement and instrument play. The styles range from Native American to Celtic, fiesta to fiddles. Creative dance ideas by Anne Green Gilbert are also included.

Feierabend, John M., and Luann Saunders. *'Round and 'Round the Garden: Music in My First Year.* **CD. Chicago: GIA Publications, 2000.**

Including more than sixty songs performed by one voice, guitar, and string bass, this recording offers a variety of bounces, wiggles, circle games, clapping rhymes, and lullabies that emphasize adult-child interaction.

Gill, Jim (http://www.jimgill.com/). *Jim Gill Sings the Sneezing Song and Other Contagious Tunes.* **CD. Chicago: Jim Gill Music, 1993.**

"Silly Dance Contest" involves moving and freezing in place, and "Alabama Mississippi" is a rhythmic song with which you can use shakers and scarves.

Hegner, Priscilla, and Rose Grasselli. *Diaper Gym: Fun Activities for Babies on the Move.* **CD. Long Branch, NJ: Kimbo Educational, 1985.**

The activities provide directions for two age groups, six weeks to seven months and eight months to one year, and include massage, mirror play stretches, and other games that match actions to the music. "Butterfly Kisses" and "Blow Me a Kiss" make great good-bye songs; "Peek-A-Boo" is fun to use with scarves; and "How Big Is Baby?" is good for stretching.

Jaeger, Sally (http://www.sallyjaeger.ca/index.html), and Erika Webster. *Here Comes Mr. Bear!* **CD. Aurora, ON: Merriweather Records, 2009.**

This CD features sixty-six tracks of hello songs, bounces, fingerplays, gallops, and more. Jaeger and Webster present simple, easy-to-follow tunes to rhymes old and new.

Jenkins, Ella (http://ellajenkins.com/). *Early, Early Childhood Songs.* **CD. Washington, DC: Smithsonian Folkways, 1990.**

Ella Jenkins, with a group of three- and four-year-olds, sings some of the most familiar English-language children's songs with simple accompaniment.

Lawrence-Kuehn, David. *Baby Dance: A Toddler's Jump on the Classics.* **CD. New York: Erato, 1994.**

This introduction to classical music encourages the adult to interact with the child verbally, physically, and emotionally.

McGrath, Bob (http://www.bobmcgrath.com/), and Katharine Smithrim. *The Baby Record.* **Cassette. CD. Racine, WI: Golden, 1990. The Grange, Toronto, ON: Bob's Kids Music, 2000.**

This recording arranges classic nursery rhymes and activity songs with directions by type: bouncing, action, finger- and toeplays, instruments, songs, and lullabies. This is a first choice for learning traditional English language rhymes and songs.

Monet, Lisa (http://www.lisamonetmusic.com/). *Circle Time: Songs and Rhymes for the Very Young.* **CD. Redway, CA: Music for Little People; distributed by Kid Rhino, 1994.**

Monet sings thirty favorite songs, accompanied by a folk guitar, to supply backup for presenters, if needed.

Palmer, Hap (http://www.happalmer.com/). *Early Childhood Classics: Old Favorites with a New Twist.* **CD. Topanga, CA: Hap-Pal Music, 2000.**

Tracks 1–15 are vocal renditions, and tracks 16–30 are instrumental versions.

Raffi (https://www.raffinews.com/). *Singable Songs for the Very Young.* **CD. Universal City, CA: Shoreline/MCA, 1976;** *More Singable Songs for the Very Young.* **CD. Universal City, CA: Shoreline/MCA, Rounder, 1996.**

Raffi presents popular, traditional English and French children's songs—helpful for those who are unfamiliar with the tunes.

Reid-Naiman, Kathy (http://208.106.133.235/Home.aspx?ID=9), with Ken
  Whiteley. *More Tickles and Tunes*. CD. Aurora, ON: Merriweather
  Records, 1997.

  Featuring primarily traditional songs, this recording also includes additional
  lyrics for some familiar songs and several original pieces. Lyric sheets with
  directions make it easy to follow along. "A Smooth Road" is a wonderful
  bouncing rhyme, and "Nelly Go 'Cross the Ocean" will get everyone moving,
  with the children enjoying being swung around.

Roberts, Sheena (compiler). *Playsongs: Action Songs and Rhymes for Babies and
  Toddlers*. Book and CD. London: Playsongs Publications, 2001.

  This includes new and traditional English-language songs, rhymes, and
  games for adults and children to enjoy, including "Spots, Spots, Spots," an
  original tickle song by Cynthia Raza, which, once learned, the participants
  will never want to stop.

Sharon, Lois, and Bram (http://www.casablancakids.com/abcs/casablanca_slb
  _splash.html). *Mainly Mother Goose*. CD. Toronto, ON: Casablanca Kids,
  2008, originally released in 1984.

  These popular children's musicians bring life to Mother Goose nursery rhymes.

Stewart, Georgiana. *Baby Face*. Cassette. Long Branch, NJ: Kimbo Educational,
  1983.

  These vintage songs add fun to exercise and games for adults and children to
  play together. "Baby's Hokey Pokey," an arm and leg exercise, is so much fun
  everyone will want to do it over and over again, and "Baby Face" helps add
  music to the game of peek-a-boo.

Stewart, Nancy (http://nancymusic.com/). *Little Songs for Little Me: Activity
  Songs for Ones and Twos*. Activity Kit and CD. Mercer Island, WA:
  Friends Street Music, 1992.

  More than just an easy-to-follow music CD, this kit includes lyric sheets,
  directions, suggestions on how to use the songs, flannel figures, and a flannel
  board! "Mr. Turkey and Mr. Duck" has a surprise ending that always elicits
  giggles, and "One Little Baby" has a simple tune and fun actions that climax
  with a peek-a-boo everyone enjoys.

———. *Plant a Little Seed: Songs for Growing Children*. CD. Mercer Island, WA:
  Friends Street Music, 1995.

  "When Ducks Get Up in the Morning" allows the presenter to sing the song
  while using visual elements such as picture cards or a bag full of stuffed
  animals; "Lots of Cars" is a fun song to use as a flannel-board song; and
  "Dinosaurs in Cars" delights little ones with not only being about dinosaurs
  but also including great sound effects like roars and "Ker-chunk!"

Sunseri, MaryLee (http://www.maryleemusic.com/). *Baby-O! Activity Songs for Babies*. **CD. Pacific Grove, CA: Piper Grove Music, 2005.**

This CD offers three individual sets of baby activity songs for lapsit programs and playtime.

———. *Mother Goose Melodies: Four and Twenty Olde Songs for Young Children.* **CD. Pacific Grove, CA: Piper Grove Music, 2003.**

This CD features twenty-four traditional Mother Goose songs with clear vocals accompanied by guitar, recorder, dulcimer, and lap harp.

———. *1-2-3 Sing with Me*. **CD. Pacific Grove, CA: Piper Grove Music, 2001.**

These traditional songs for children from birth through age three are easy to sing along with.

———. *Wee Chant: Chants, Songs and Lullabies from Around the World*. **CD. Pacific Grove, CA: Piper Grove Music, 2001.**

This is a collection of songs with repeating words and simple melodies that even those who "can't sing" will be able to manage successfully.

Tickle Tune Typhoon (http://tickletunetyphoon.com/). *Circle Around*. **CD. Seattle, WA: Tickle Tune Typhoon, 1984.**

"Clap Your Hands" is a simple song with actions even the youngest ones can do.

———. *Patty-Cakes and Peek-a-Boos: Activity Songs, Dances and Lullabies for Infants and Toddlers*. **CD. Seattle, WA: Tickle Tune Typhoon, 1994.**

This CD of classic children's music with vocals and full instrumentation includes lyrics. "Cuddle Up and Sing" is perfect for reinforcing that intimate bond between adult and child as the two cuddle and rock together, and "Clap Your Hands Melody" combines a fun activity song with the classic rhyme "Open, Shut Them."

Toddlers Sing Playtime. **CD. Redway, CA: Music for Little People, 1999.**

These interactive songs for little ones encourage movement and fun.

Flannel Boards

Flannel boards, felt boards, and magnetic boards are all useful when doing a program with the 12-to-24-month age group. With large groups, this kind of story presentation provides better visibility and attracts the audience's attention. It is best to keep the number of pieces to a minimum, to outline the pieces rather than include lots of detail, and to use bold colors. Boards vary in size, and you should try them out to find which one best suits your style of storytelling. The board itself can vary in size from 9-by-12 inches to the size of an artist's portfolio. You can use a pizza box (clean, of course), with felt covering the lid and story pieces stored inside. You may find shoe boxes or gift boxes more to your liking. I have found the smaller size to be easier to keep out of little hands; it is also less distracting when not in use. The larger ones, of course, allow for more and larger pieces, but, remember, you will want to put the board aside when the story is finished. When using an easel with a flannel board, make sure it is stabilized for safety. The thing to keep in mind is that the smaller the board, the smaller the pieces.

There are alternatives to using a flannel board for your presentation. You can use a mitt format, with a glove made of special Velcro-friendly material, or a garden glove or rubber glove with Velcro on the fingertips. *The Flannel Board Storytelling Book* (Sierra, 1997) includes directions for making different kinds of flannel boards, including a mitt, which moves with your hand so that all may see the presentation. You can also purchase or make an apron that has a nap conducive to "sticking." Materials that work best for flannel-board pieces include flannel, felt, and interfacing. You can also use paper and craft foam with double-stick tape or felt tape placed on the back. Double-stick tape or any kind of tape that can be looped sticky side out tends to lose its stickiness over time and use and will need to be replaced. See Flannel-Board Fun in the appendix for information on how to make small, individual flannel boards for your group.

It takes time and effort to create flannel-board pieces. You can use different materials besides felt or flannel. Paper is one of the alternatives. You can copy or even enlarge paper patterns or use software clip art and then color and glue them onto the material. Laminating the pieces improves durability. Laminating machines have become more accessible and compact. Check with the schools in your area or curriculum stores that may allow you to laminate gratis or for a small fee. Be aware of the type of printer you are using. Some printers use a wax material that produces sharp pictures, but these will melt and smudge if you use a hot laminating machine. Alternatively, you can place paper pieces between two sheets of clear contact paper.

Once you have made the pieces, you need to be able to store them for easy access and protection. Trying to find missing pieces is not the best way to prepare for a program. You can use file folders with closed sides, which come in a variety of sizes, to store the pieces. Each rhyme/story set can have its own labeled file to keep the pieces together. You can also use ziplock plastic bags for storage, but since these are slippery, they may not stand upright, so box storage may work better, or you can place the materials in hanging files in a file cabinet. Another method is to store the pieces in clear-plastic page protectors that are then placed in a loose-leaf binder. Be aware that this storage method does limit the size of your pieces. The binder can also include an index of the rhymes/songs stored there.

Many rhymes and songs are easy to adapt for flannel boards, allowing for variations in presenting each rhyme or song. The following list suggests stories from the annotated bibliography found in chapter 4 that you can present as flannel-board stories; it also includes a rhyme and a song from chapter 4 that you can do with a flannel board. If this style of storytelling becomes a favorite, you can add to the list as many titles as you wish!

- *Ask Mr. Bear* by Marjorie Flack
- *Blue Sea* by Robert Kalan
- *The Bridge Is Up* by Babs Bell
- *Brown Bear, Brown Bear, What Do You See?* by Bill Martin Jr.
- *The Carrot Seed* by Ruth Krauss
- *Five Little Pumpkins* by Iris Van Rynbach
- *Freight Train* by Donald Crews
- *Go Away, Big Green Monster!* by Ed Emberley
- "Here Is the Engine" (rhyme)
- *I Went Walking* by Sue Williams
- *Let's Go Visiting* by SueWilliams
- *Lunch* by Denise Fleming
- *Millions of Snowflakes* by Mary McKenna Siddals
- *My Many Colored Days* by Dr. Seuss
- *Oh, A-Hunting We Will Go* by John Langstaff
- "Old MacDonald Had a Farm" (traditional song)
- *Over in the Meadow* by John Langstaff
- *Under My Hood I Have a Hat* by Karla Kuskin

Puppets

Many a child's face lights up with delight at the sight of a puppet. There is an immediate connection between the child and this creation. Most of the time the reaction is a positive one, but on occasion the child can be frightened or upset by the appearance of a puppet. When using puppets with this age group, the presenter needs to keep in mind a number of things.

First of all, the child will likely grab for the puppet or try to reach it. Usually this is because the children want to make sure the adults they are with see it, too. I have seen puppets being walked all over the room by children who want to share the puppet with the other participants or want to keep it for themselves. Quite often the adult will try to "return" the puppet. The resulting tug-of-war between adult and child can develop into a big distraction. Let the adult know it is all right for the child to have the puppet by simply stating so and continuing with your program. If you need it back, ask the child for it or try asking the child to put the puppet "to bed" or "in its room" by placing it in a box, basket, or other location (like your arms). Keeping puppets out of reach is the best preventative measure, unless you want the children to interact directly with them. If you use a host puppet to greet the participants, putting it down on a chair or low table invites the children to come and meet it. Placing it or other demonstration puppets you may use up and away as "observers" of the program minimizes distractions.

Second, keep in mind your comfort level with the size of puppet chosen. If you use an oversized puppet as a demonstration tool, you must be competent in manipulating it. Smaller puppets, such as finger puppets, can "disappear" into a container or your pocket when you are finished with them. However, small size does not always ensure that everything will work smoothly. I use two small blackbird finger puppets for the rhyme "Two Little Blackbirds." Once one "flew" out into the group, and it had to be caught before the program could continue. Whatever size you use, make sure you practice with the puppet prior to the program.

Third, be wary of incorporating too many puppets into your program. It can be tempting to liven up your programs by including a variety of puppets with many songs, stories, and rhymes. The challenge is having them available when you need them while also having a place to hold them when not in use. Too many puppets may give the children too many things to focus on at one time. Beware of overstimulating the children or giving them "too much of a good thing." Perhaps you can use the same puppet with all songs, rhymes, and stories throughout the program, or it might work better if you always have one mascot puppet for the program and use it every time. You can then introduce others as "guests" at subsequent programs.. Children like the familiar and will grow accustomed and comfortable with a puppet that is used repeatedly.

The fourth thing to remember is to watch the children's reactions to the puppet and take your cue from them. Let the children approach the puppet, if that is your intention. Not every child wants the host puppet to be "up close and personal"; some may prefer more distance between themselves and the puppet. Children can also be wary of puppets until they recognize them as "friends," so take the introduction slowly, and it can lead to a wonderful relationship between child and puppet-friend.

Finally, make sure your puppet will hold together. It is very upsetting to a child to hug a host puppet and have its head come off. Commercially made puppets are often sturdy enough, as are many handmade ones, but test them first. Many books contain patterns and ideas for making puppets yourself; see the Resources section at the end of this chapter for suggested titles. If you make puppets to use for these programs, remember that children this age still tend to put things in their mouths. Make sure eyes and so forth are firmly attached.

How can puppets be used in programming for the very young? Quite often a puppet is used as a storytime host or to demonstrate activities. The puppet stands in as the presenter's "child" to demonstrate fingerplays and action rhymes. You can also use puppets to act out rhymes, fingerplays, songs, or even stories. If actual puppets are unavailable, you can use stuffed toys. For example, the ever-popular Bill Martin Jr. story *Brown Bear, Brown Bear, What Do You See?* can be brought to life in a variety of ways. Create a stick-puppet theater of animal cutouts on straws, or use a stuffed toy to represent each animal character. As you recite or read the story, hold up the corresponding animal. In this manner, the participants will hear a familiar story being presented in a variety of ways, and you, the presenter, will be able to keep the story fresh by varying the presentation while staying true to the story.

Puppets are sold through distributors such as Folkmanis, early-childhood curriculum companies, and toy stores. Library supply stories, such as Demco and Highsmith, also handle puppets. To make your own puppets, check out the early-childhood education books, puppetry books, and websites in the Resources section. Craft fairs and bazaars can also be a source for puppets.

Creative Activities

Why Do Activities?

Remember, it is the learning *process* of the activity that is important, not the end result. Open-ended activities that allow for creativity, dialogue, and exploration are best. Encourage the adult to actively participate with the child in the activity, being careful to facilitate rather than direct the child as to what to do. Young children need to take time to examine and process what they are doing in order to learn. Have the adults take their cues from the children as to the pace and focus of the activity. The children may respond with a body action, pointing or clapping, or their voices. At this stage of development, children learn through all their senses. They are learning to associate meaning with the sounds they hear around them, becoming aware that these sounds/words are used to identify, direct, and communicate. Encourage the adult to engage with the child, talking about what is happening, using positive statements and body language. Activities help to build language skills, as the adult can talk to the child about what is being done, felt, smelled, seen, and heard, reinforcing what the child is experiencing and helping the adult and child both be actively engaged in the activity. The adult may also be learning a new skill, such as reading aloud, or new rhymes or activities, and, through participation, how to become a role model for the child.

Keep in mind the "fun" element when selecting activities. This will encourage the participants to re-create the experience again and again. Be mindful of safety issues. For example, children of this age are still putting everything in their mouths, so you will need to ensure that any materials used are nontoxic, easily cleaned, and large enough to prevent choking.

When to Do Activities

You can use activities within the program and/or suggest their use to adults as follow-ups to do at home. You can use an activity as a "warm-up" as people arrive and then put it away at the start of the program. If using an activity during the program, plan its duration and how you will transition in and out in advance. An activity scheduled at the conclusion of the program can give the child-adult pair time to practice and extend the language-learning experience. This also gives the presenter an opportunity to mingle, offering encouragement, suggestions, and explanations to individual couples. You can include activity ideas in a handout along with the stories, rhymes, songs, and so on, for that program/series.

Observation and feedback by the presenter and given to the adult during or directly after this activity adds another way to help the adults understand the importance and fun of sharing books with the very young. A simple statement can mean more than you realize. The following are some suggested statements that might get you started:

- "I like the way you are letting [child's name] practice turning the pages—he is getting better at it!"
- "Sharing a book as you cuddle together can be such a pleasant encounter. Emotions can impact a child's learning experience, and you are making this a good one!"
- "[Child's name] certainly likes to look at that page. You are doing a good job of letting her set a pace you can both enjoy."
- "Pointing out things you see on the page and naming them is certainly going to build your child's vocabulary knowledge."

Types of Activities

Arts and Crafts

When doing arts and crafts projects with this age group, it is important to remember the following points:

- It is the *process* that is important, not the end result.
- The children are the creators, and the adults need to allow the children to do the activity and not do it for them. Supplying enough materials for the adults to create their own projects helps. Children like to do what they see the adults doing.
- Allow for room to move around. Children at this age use large-motor skills rather than fine-motor skills. Large pieces of paper, chunky crayons, and easy-to-hold materials are all necessary for the children to feel successful in the creation process and to help avoid frustration.
- Messes are inevitable. Remind the adults that it is all about how the children are learning about their world. Hands need to "dig in"; old clothes, drop cloths, and a sense of play are important. Making a mess may not be desired due to facility restrictions (e.g., new carpet in the room) or scheduling of staff or facilities that limits involved cleanup time. You can adapt some arts and crafts activities to minimize messes. For example, a portable finger-painting bag, often called a "squish bag," encases the paint in a ziplock freezer bag. See the following Painting section for directions on how to make these bags.
- All materials should be nontoxic. Children of this age are still putting things in their mouths. There are recipes for paint, playdough, glue, and so forth, that are all safe. See the Resources section at the end of this chapter for sources. Check out the Art Activity Recipes handout in the appendix for some basic recipes as well.
- There needs to be a caring, involved adult with the child during every activity. Encourage the adult to talk to the child about what he or she is doing, respond verbally to the child, and provide the opportunity for the child to respond. Keep the exchange positive in nature, not critical. Remind the adult that, just as in a reading experience, the child needs time to respond and to proceed at his or her own pace.
- Create an environment that is comfortable for the children—low tables or folding tables laid flat on the floor. You can cover the tables completely with craft or butcher paper (usually found in long rolls at school or craft supply stores) taped in place. Make sure the children can reach the tabletops. If the floor is hard and smooth enough, simply tape the paper to the floor to prevent its moving around.

Ready-to-use arts and crafts activities to take home are most appreciated by adult participants. For example, supply adults with a handful of homemade playdough in a ziplock bag along with the recipe, or give them a paper apple shape labeled with the lyrics to "Way Up High in the Apple Tree" that they can place on their refrigerators.

Painting

Children will more than likely use their hands rather than paintbrushes. Many times, their surface for painting will include the highchair tray, the floor or walls, and themselves. You can use water as a good "paint" outside during warm weather; let the children paint the building walls, the sidewalk, rocks, and so on.

For the youngest ones, put a small amount of applesauce, pureed carrots, or other colored food on the highchair trays and let the children create. If this is too messy for you, create a "squish bag" from a plastic ziplock freezer bag with something inside of it that can be used as finger paint, such as instant pudding made with half the amount of liquid (substitute water for milk), whipped cream, or any mushy food. Vanilla pudding and whipped cream can change color through the addition of food coloring, while chocolate pudding makes great "mud." Fill the squish bag with a small amount of "paint" (2 tablespoons to ¼ cup depending on bag size), being careful not to overfill. The bag should lie flat without showing any of the surface under it. Press out the air gently and zip the bag tightly closed. For durability, reinforce the edges on all four sides with tape. Masking tape, packing tape, or duct tape works best. Use tape wide enough to fold over the edges. You now have a portable, nonmessy, finger-painting bag. Children can move the "finger paint" around inside the bag and create patterns by pressing their fingers or hands on the bag's surface, giving them an experience that is both visual and tactile. Safety tip: remember to keep the bag out of the child's mouth.

If you decide to provide brushes, you can put the paint into pie pans for easy access. There are many kinds of brushes available, but also consider using other items that can serve as painting tools: sponges (perhaps cut into shapes), daubers (available at arts and crafts supply stores), the wheels of toy trucks, feathers, rollers, and so on. To contain the mess, consider putting paper in the bottom of a disposable baking pan. The edges are high enough to keep the paint contained while still allowing for easy access.

Paper and Coloring

Think beyond coloring sheets with preprinted pictures. Provide various types of paper or catalogs to let children practice turning pages and learn the different textures paper can have. Crunch the paper into balls and let the children toss or roll the balls back and forth. Provide black or other dark-colored paper and let the children draw on it with chunky white chalk. Since the children's fine-motor skills are still developing, be aware that they will use large motions and need plenty of room to draw and play.

Collages are a wonderful medium for children to create their own master-pieces. To limit the mess, use glue sticks, or you can simplify a project needing glue by using stickers instead. Cut or tear paper into pieces and then glue the paper onto something else. Provide various pictures from magazines and let the children select the ones they want to use.

Clear contact paper provides a sticky surface for a "canvas" with little mess. Tape the contact paper sticky side up onto a surface, such as a refrigerator door, the floor, a tabletop, the lower portion of a wall, or even a good-sized piece of cardboard. Give the children things to stick onto the paper, such as feathers, pom-poms, and the like. A popular project is to let the children decorate the contact paper's sticky side and then press the sticky side of another clear piece on top, with the material sandwiched in between the two sheets. Safety tip: gluing or sticking requires an adult be with the child to ensure safety and to assist the child before frustration sets in, since glue situations often can become too sticky.

Playdough

Playdough is available commercially, but you can also make it from scratch (see the Art Activity Recipes handout in the appendix). Homemade playdough is not very difficult or time-consuming to make, and if kept in the refrigerator, it will last quite a while. Playing with it at different temperatures provides lots of opportunities for language learning through descriptions of soft, hard, cold, warm, and the like. Use food coloring to make different-colored doughs, and give the children two different colors so they can create a third color of dough. Add vanilla, cinnamon, or other scents to engage their sense of smell. Be aware that this may tempt the children to taste the dough, so this approach should be reserved for older children or for inclusion on a handout, though edible play-dough is a good option if the children are still putting things in their mouths. Children can stick things into the playdough, such as fake flowers, toy animals, straws, and so on. You can also provide cookie cutters, stamping tools, and popsicle sticks for the children to play with in the dough.

Puzzles

Commercially made puzzles are durable and safe for children, and they are an investment that you can use again and again. Look for ones that have large pieces, knobs for little hands to hold on to, and smooth edges. You can also cre-ate your own puzzles by gluing pictures to sturdy cardboard or foam core—the thicker material makes it easier for the children to pick up the pieces—or simply draw or encourage the children to create a picture on the cardboard. Cut the puzzle into no more than four pieces and do not make the cuts too complicated.

The children can tackle more complicated puzzles as they grow. An even simpler method for making puzzles is to provide different shapes—squares, rectangles, triangles, circles, and so forth—and let the children create a picture from them. A square and triangle can make a house; an orange circle with some small black triangles will make a pumpkin.

Language

Board Books

Providing board books for the children to look through and letting them select one to share with their adults is a wonderful language activity. Make sure the books are in good condition, not ripped, dirty, or chewed on. It might be best to keep a collection of board books separate from your circulating collection. Some adults may want to wipe the books off with a disinfectant wipe, so have some available. Place the books in a pile so the children can investigate and make their own choices. Another variation is to give everyone the same title so they can read along with the presenter. You can obtain books for this purpose by using part of the collection budget and/or through grants or a generous donation (see chapter 3 for information on grants and partnerships).

Flannel Boards (Individual)

Individual flannel boards are useful for encouraging participants to retell a story on their own. Small boards are available for purchase through such companies as Lakeshore Learning, or you can make your own. This is a good project for volunteers. Use a personal-sized pizza box or sturdy cardboard cut to fit inside a plastic ziplock bag (quart or gallon size) as a base. Cut solid-color felt or flannel to fit the outside top of the box or cardboard. Glue the fabric in place (glue sticks work fine for this) and put tape around the edges to prevent curling. You can store the flannel-board pieces inside the boxes or zipped into the bags along with the cardboard bases. Distribute these to the participants for use during activity time. (See also the earlier Flannel Boards section in this chapter.)

Sign Language

Over the past few years, teaching sign language to very young children has become more and more popular. Using sign language with very young children has also raised many questions. There are those who believe teaching hearing children to sign will delay their vocalization. Some believe only American Sign Language (ASL) should be taught, omitting any other kind of gestures. (The term "sign language" in this text refers to ASL.) Others feel sign language is too difficult and will confuse the children. Sign language does allow young children to communicate with adults before they have the ability to vocalize. It can ease the tension between adults and young children by enabling the children to convey what they want, need, or feel. Children will begin to imitate signs when they are able to sit independently with good stability, usually at six months of age or older, because their hands are then free to make the signs. Until then, the adults' use of sign language helps the children become familiar with it.

Research does not indicate that children who sign have difficulty communicating later in life. In fact, they seem to have a larger vocabulary and are better at expressing themselves. Drs. Linda Acredolo and Susan Goodwyn have presented studies that support this finding. To check out these studies and other research, visit the Baby Signs website (https://www.babysigns.com/index.cfm?id=64). The Early Head Start National Resource Center also offers information on many early-childhood topics, including the use of sign language, on its website (https://eclkc.ohs.acf.hhs.gov/hslc/tta-system/ehsnrc).

Using sign language as part of a program simply introduces it to adults who, if they so choose, may pursue additional information and instruction on their own. You can find classes for learning sign language at colleges (especially community colleges), hospitals, and online. Your local public library may also have resources in print, audio/text, and DVD format to help get you started.

To incorporate sign language into stories, do not try to interpret word for word; focus on nouns first and then verbs. This follows the natural pattern of how language is learned. Select the key word you want; prior to reading/reciting, say this word aloud as you sign it, and then incorporate the sign whenever the word occurs in the text. For example, you could use the sign for "apple" when reciting "Way Up High in the Apple Tree." *Brown Bear, Brown Bear, What Do You See?* by Bill Martin Jr. lends itself especially to animal signs. If this is a story you tend to use with each program, you can introduce new signs over time.

Children's musicians often add sign language with their songs, both traditional and original. Nancy Stewart, of Friends Street Music, often includes signing directions on her "Song of the Month" activity pages (http://nancymusic.com/SongMonth.htm) as well as links to such sites as American Sign Language Web and HandSpeak (http://nancymusic.com/contact.htm). On her website (http://drjean.org/), Dr. Jean Feldman offers signs to help children understand directions as well as links to YouTube clips of her presenting rhymes and songs.

Movement

Movement activities can be as varied as dancing or marching around the room, using your whole body to act out action rhymes, or even simple yoga positions. Children of this age are almost in constant motion and love to move. Incorporating movement into your program helps "get the wiggles" out.

Music is perfect to get the participants up and moving. Free dance is exactly that: everyone moves the way they want to or to general directions given by presenter, such as fast–slow or smooth–bouncy. Adults and children can move as partners or independently, depending on the children's standing ability or desire to move. The music can be anything the presenter would like to use, such as classical or country, jazz or rock, or even music designed for creative dance classes. Adults may be hesitant at first, so encourage them to relax and simply move to the music. Explain that there are no "proper" or designed steps for this activity; they just need to move along with the tempo of the music. Participants can waltz, hop, slide, rock back and forth, move all around, or stay in one spot—whatever they want is fine. Vary loud and soft music to change the intensity of the activity, going from large to small movements and from fast to slow movements. Stop the music and have the participants "freeze" in place until the music resumes. Children will joyfully anticipate the pause, which involves them even more. "The Silly Dance Contest" on *Jim Gill Sings the Sneezing Song and Other Contagious Tunes* is lots of fun. The field of dance also offers suitable music, such as "Rock 'n' Stop" on *Music for Creative Dance* by Eric Chappelle for moving and stopping and a wide variety of tempos. As presenter, you should model the movements, moving around along with the participants. While doing so, offer praise and encouragement to the group and to specific individuals, thereby lessening the self-consciousness adult participants may feel.

You can also use songs and rhymes to get the participants up and moving. "The Grand Old Duke of York" is good for marching around the room; "Shoo, Fly—Don't Bother Me" makes a fun circle dance; "Roll, Roll, Roll Your Hands" is adaptable to other body movements, such as stomp your feet, flap your arms, and so on. Instead of opening and shutting hands for "Patty Cake, Patty Cake," stretch your arms wide apart. Raffi's *More Singable Songs* includes a great version of "Shake Your Sillies Out" that participants are sure to enjoy. See the earlier Music section for Recommended Recordings and DVDs as well as the Music portion of the Resources section at the end of the chapter for additional print and online resources.

In recent years, yoga has become a popular activity, and some will include it as part of their programs for young children, although most books on yoga are designed for children three and older. There are no current studies as to its benefit for children, and although believed by some to be beneficial, others claim it can be harmful if presented incorrectly. Yoga must be performed correctly, safely, and in moderation, and previous experience is a must for those who are interested in providing yoga experiences as part of a program. Resources on yoga for young children are available; see the Movement portion of the Resources section.

Props

Balls and Blocks

Balls provide a variety of learning experiences. They reinforce recognition of the round circle shape, and identifying shapes is a necessary skill for letter recognition in the English language. Rolling a ball back and forth with an adult helps the child learn about following directions—"Roll the ball to me." Children learn about cause and effect when placing a ping-pong or plastic golf ball in one end of a cardboard packing tube and then seeing it roll out the other end when the tube is tipped. Such activities also help develop the child's vocabulary and eye-hand coordination.

There are many different kinds and sizes of balls. Inflatable beach balls come in various sizes and their bright colors always attract children's attention. Their light weight makes them safer than heavier playground balls, and they are also easier to store between programs because they deflate. The six-inch size is easy for a small child to handle. Make sure that smaller balls, such as ping-pong balls or plastic golf balls, do not present a choking or other hazard to the children in your group.

For more ideas on how to incorporate balls into you program, check out some of the Gymboree books (http://www.gymboree.com/) and sites such as Nurturing Pathways (http://www.nurturingpathways.com/), a program created by Christine Roberts that emphasizes growing the mind through movement. (See also the Movement portion of the Resources section at the end of the chapter.)

Children love to build things, and blocks help them with this endeavor. Commercially made blocks are available in wood, plastic, cloth, vinyl, cardboard, and other durable materials. You can make your own blocks of lighter weight from paper bags that have been stuffed with newspaper and taped shut. As children build with blocks, they learn about spatial relations, different shapes, and such things as cause and effect. They learn through experience what happens if you stack blocks on top of each other too high—they fall down! For a more overall view of the value of playing with blocks, see Karen Hewitt's article "Blocks as

a Tool for Learning: Historical and Contemporary Perspectives" (http://www
.naeyc.org/yc/pastissues/2001/january).

Bubbles

Bubbles fascinate both children and adults. Adding music enhances this simple,
yet fun activity. The presenter can blow bubbles into the air using a bubble wand
and solution while walking around the group. During this time, the adults can
interact with their children by talking to them about the bubbles, trying to catch
the bubbles, or dancing with their children through them. Various bubble-
blowing machines, battery-operated or plug-in, are now available for purchase
at party and department stores. Check the stability of the bubble solution container to ensure it is not prone to spilling. You can purchase bubble solution or
make it from scratch. You can use liquid dishwashing detergent (about 2 or 3
tablespoons) with 1 cup of water or tear-free baby shampoo. For more activity
suggestions and bubble recipes, check out children's craft magazines and search
online. Keep in mind that bubbles may leave surfaces slippery, so keep towels
around to wipe things off as necessary. If you want the participants to be able to
blow their own bubbles, either during the program or at home, you can provide
minibottles of bubbles; you can find these at party supply stores, often in the
bridal section, and at toy stores.

Playing music during this activity provides a backdrop for even more enjoyment. Add "bounce" to the fun by playing classical music, popular children's songs,
or even carousel music. *Bathtime Magic* by Joanie Bartels, an award-winning
children's artist, offers fun songs about baths, bubbles, and play (available on
iTunes; https://itunes.apple.com/us/album/bathtime-magic/id299028887).

Games

Very young children are likely to hesitate in joining group games, especially
with strangers. Let the adult-child couple be their own group and with time
larger groups will begin to develop. You can do "Ring around the Rosie" with
the child in the arms of the adult or the two facing each other. You can also use
props, such as hula hoops, scarves, or a parachute to obtain a circle shape. The
"Hokey Pokey" is another favorite that can lead to lots of giggles. John Feierabend's First Steps in Music curriculum offers simple circle games (http://www
.feierabendmusic.org/curriculum/). Turn action rhymes into games by marching
in a circle or around the room. Depending on the children's age, they can walk
facing forward holding an adult's hand, to the side, or simply follow the adult.
Songs such as "Here We Go 'round the Mulberry Bush" are easy to make into
circle games by circling during the chorus.

Parachutes, Scarves, and Streamers

You can purchase parachutes at toy stores, in early-childhood curriculum stores, and, of course, online. Choose a bright, colorful parachute and watch the children's faces light up with joy and excitement when you bring it out during the program. Parachutes range in diameter from small (6 feet) to large (45 feet). Select a size that fits your space without crowding. Keep in mind safety and the size of the group with which you intend to use it. Parachutes make circle games easier for young children because they can simply hold on to the parachute and not a stranger's hand. Sitting underneath the parachute is a sensory experience that involves the child's sight, hearing, physical sensations, and movement. The adults raise the parachute up and down over the children's heads and they see colors, feel the air movement, and experience the fun. Parachutes can also serve as the sitting area for the program. Remember, the very young child should have the choice to participate in the activity in the way he or she feels most comfortable, be it sitting under the parachute, holding on to the edges, sitting on top of it, or simply observing the activity from the sidelines.

Many early-childhood activity books include ideas for parachute activities, but CDs often are the best source for ideas and music. Resources for this type of activity typically target children three years of age and older because the activities may require the children to be able to hold on to the parachute or do things that are beyond the very young child's developmental ability. Keep these activities simple and fun. Sitting on the parachute could be exciting enough for the children. You can also create a game with lightweight balls, such as inflatable beach balls of different sizes or paper crumpled into balls. Roll or bounce these on the parachute while it is positioned very close to or on the floor, surrounded by the participants. Have the children keep the balls on top of the parachute while the adults move it around. As always, keep safety and participation utmost in mind when planning this kind of activity.

You can use some of the songs, rhymes, and games found in this book for parachute activities; here are some good ones to try:

- "Ring around the Rosie": Walk around in a circle while holding on to the parachute, following the actions of the words.
- "Pop! Goes the Weasel": Walk around in a circle while holding on to the parachute and jump up on the word "Pop" or just raise the parachute upward.
- "The Grand Old Duke of York": March in a circle while holding on to the parachute and then change directions with "left" and "right."
- "London Bridge": Gently raise and lower the parachute in time with the song.

- "Motor Boat": Shake the parachute in response to "slow," "fast," and "step on the gas."
- "Popcorn": Stand around the parachute, holding on to the edges, and then shake it up and down so that small inflatable beach balls or balls of crumpled paper placed on top will bounce up and down like popcorn.

Using scarves and streamers in a program introduces children to the world of color, air movement, and texture. Scarves come in chiffon, silk, satin, and many other materials. They can be see-through or solid, smooth or textured. Juggling scarves are the perfect size. Garage/yard sales often provide a place to find scarves, or you can cut the size you want from materials purchased at a craft/fabric store. Hem or serge the edges or use a product such as Fray Check to minimize fraying. Cut streamers from colorful fabric or use wide satin ribbon or blanket binding. Make sure that any ribbon you choose does not have wired edges or attached sparkles/glitter because these pose a health hazard to very young children. Paper streamers, often made from crepe paper, have colors that bleed when dampened by little mouths and edges that may cut tender skin. Always do this activity with adults present to monitor the children.

Here are a few ideas on how you can incorporate scarves and streamers into your program:

- Play peek-a-boo.
- Slide a scarf down the child's body to give a sense of rain while doing a rhyme or song. Two great rhymes to start with are "Rain, Rain, Go Away" and "Rain Is Falling Down."
- Play different kinds of music (classical, popular, folk, new age, etc.) and move the scarf to the tempo. Give directions to help the children follow the tempo (wave high, low, fast, slow, etc.). Try using popular children's songs, such as "Let's Go Fly a Kite" from Disney's *Mary Poppins* or "Alabama Mississippi" from *Jim Gill Sings the Sneezing Song and Other Contagious Tunes*.
- Have participants use the scarves as flags while marching around the room.
- Put scarves into a container with an opening on the lid so children can pull them out one at a time. Tissue boxes, oatmeal containers, and other small-sized containers will work. If doing an activity with adult-child pairs, you will need a container and scarf or scarves for each couple. You can also use a larger container and have the children come up to pull a scarf out to use during the program.

- Poke scarves or streamers in one end of a paper roll, leaving just a tip showing on the other end. Multiple scarves/streamers that are tied together end to end with loose knots give a slight resistance. The child will have a delightful time pulling it out of the roll.
- Use scarves/streamers as part of a story or song. Toss them in the air so they float down as rain when reading *Rain* by Robert Kalan; dance around with them to bring *Color Dance* by Ann Jonas to life; put a scarf or streamer in the circle for the "Hokey Pokey."
- Roll or scrunch up the scarves/streamers into a ball and toss the ball in the air.

Toys

There are many commercially made, age-appropriate toys on the market. In many cases, you will bring out these toys at the end of a program or when you want to speak specifically to the adults. Besides making sure they stay in good condition and safe for the children to play with, make sure they are cleaned between uses. Suggested toys include stacking toys, puzzles, cars and trucks, and so forth. See the Resources section at the end of the chapter for some companies that focus on this type of toy.

Play

Play is how children investigate and learn about the world around them and their place in it. The adult is their guide and partner in this venture. The following are activities that can be done in conjunction with a storytime or at home. By combining a play activity with storytime, the adult rediscovers how to play, why play is important, the benefits of play, and, for some adults, the permission to play.

Water Play

- Give children different temperatures or forms of water (warm, cold, ice) and use words to describe it. For example, "The ice is slippery and cold."
- Give them simple "toys" to use in the bathtub, such as a measuring cup or funnel.
- Have them give a baby doll a bath or perhaps help wash vegetables for eating.

- Fill a dishpan or sink with water and give the child different objects to see which ones float or sink.
- Use bubbles to hide an object in a tub of water or float boats on the surface.
- Use a sponge to soak up water and let the child discover what happens when it is squeezed.

Outings

- Visit a zoo, farm, grocery store, garden, nursery with lots of different flowers, playground, and so on. You could even read a story about such places before and after your visit.
- Go for a walk around the house, around the block, in the rain, to a park, and so forth. Talk about what you see, hear, feel, smell, and so on, along the way
- When driving, be a tour guide for your child. Describe where you are going, what you see along the way, and what you might do once you get there. You can make going to the Laundromat an adventure.
- Get down close to the grass and look at it. Talk about the creatures you might find.
- Plant a garden. It does not have to be big, perhaps just a small container. The child can even plant seeds in a cup, but be sure the seeds go in the cup and not in the child's mouth.
- Take a walk on bubble wrap. Talk about the sounds, the surface, and so forth.
- Collect leaves, rocks, and so on, while taking a walk. Talk about how they look, feel, and perhaps even sound.

Imaginary Play

Developmentally, most children of this age do not initiate imaginary play, so it is best if the adult acts as a role model, playing alongside the child to facilitate learning. Here are some ideas:

- Have a telephone conversation using a toy phone.
- Trains and trucks are fun to drive and manipulate. Create a ramp by using a cookie sheet, cardboard, or a large wrapping/mailing cardboard tube to roll objects through. Such objects may include plastic "whiffle" golf balls, trucks, or even stuffed toys. Adults can talk about size, speed, where the object is, and so on.
- Get a large box and help the child create a boat, house, cave, wagon, and so forth, with it.

- Large mirrors are fascinating to the very young child. Allow the child to use a large safety mirror (unbreakable) to discover his or her own self and body parts as well as to see facial reactions.
- Blow feathers, leaves, scarves, or bubbles. Talk about their textures and the types of wind (hard, soft, strong, etc.).
- Create a flannel board using cardboard (8-by-11 inches, or any size) covered with felt or flannel (or a clean pizza box with the lid covered). Cut out simple shapes drawn free hand or traced using cookie cutters, and the child can create his or her own stories and learn hand-eye coordination as well. You can also mount pictures from coloring books, magazines, and even photos on the felt or flannel. Store pieces in a ziplock bag or inside the pizza box.
- Draw a face on a wooden spoon or decorate a mitten to make a puppet. Use craft sticks, tongue depressors, straws, or stirring sticks to create stick puppets; simply place a sticker at one end or use a marker to draw a face on them. You can also mount pictures from magazines or photos on sturdy paper and glue to one end of the stick. Larger puppets, often commercially made, are great to use with the very young child. They encourage interaction between the child and puppet, who will often "talk" with the puppet without shyness.
- Play peek-a-boo. Using a chiffon scarf or other see-through material, "hide" by draping it over your head and then reappear. When placing over the child's head, use the see-through material, as this will reassure the child. Cover an object such as a stuffed toy, doll, or truck with the scarf and then make it reappear. Remember to talk about the object and what is happening.
- Play hide-and-seek. This childhood game works best when the very young child is the one who hides. Be sure to talk while looking for the child: "Now, where is Billy? I am going to look behind the chair." Many times, the child will pop out from the hiding place, bringing the game to a halt. You should react with appropriate surprise and joy.

Language

These activities are all related to language building and literacy:

- Greeting cards are wonderful things. Use ones that have no small, loose pieces or glitter on them. Take a collection of cards and place them in a dishpan or box. The child will enjoy taking them out, putting them in, opening and closing them, as well as looking at them. You can create stories about the pictures or just describe them, identifying objects, animals, flowers, and so forth.

- Junk mail is also fun. You can talk about the mail with the child and work together to sort it into boxes. Help create the letter-writing habit in the child by helping him or her to "write" a letter to someone and then mail it. Take the child with you and talk about what you are doing so he or she can learn the process of getting paper, writing, addressing, using the post office, mailbox, and so on.

- The round metal ends of frozen juice cans, which have no sharp edges, are great to help develop eye-hand control and coordination. Using fine-motor skills, the child can pick up a can cover and place it in a box or coffee can. If you make a slit or hole in the top of a box, the child can "mail" the juice cover. Children love the sound the lid makes when it is dropped in. Colorful stickers are fun to put on these juice lids, or you can use signal dots, which are available at most office supply stores. Later on, you can use the lids in a sorting or identification game.

- Create picture cards. Index cards work well for this project. Simply glue pictures or put stickers on the card and then lay it picture side down on clear contact paper. You can cover both sides of the card with clear contact paper, if desired. Cut the cards apart and use them as puzzles.

- Make your own books. Photo albums, especially the magnetic kind, allow for pictures to be moved and words written on the pages. Make a book about the child by taking and printing photos of his or her daily routine. A less sturdy option is to place thin cardboard in a ziplock bag to create a two-sided page, which can then be sewn together with others using strong thread or yarn, thus making a book.

- Play dress up. Children can be creative with scarves, hats, old slips, shoes, and so on, that you already have around the house. You do not need to put out a trunk load of clothes; the very young child does not need an unlimited number of things to select from, just a few.

- Create a play space. Small pop-up tents have become popular, but a bed sheet works just as well. Just make sure that it is draped securely over objects that will not fall over and cause injuries.

- Give the child a catalog to help him or her practice turning pages. Repetition is an essential part of learning. It is much better to practice this skill with an old catalog, probably ripping pages, than with a beautiful picture book.

- With your child, look at magazines, books, and other places where words and pictures may be found together. Talk about what you see and give the child time to absorb as much of what appears on the page as he or she wants. Reading time may be limited to only one page, but that is how it all begins.

- Let your child handle and discover different kinds of paper. Let him crunch it into a ball, tear it, and examine it. Use regular paper, wax paper, cardboard, newspaper, and so forth.
- Music can play a large part in children's language learning. There are many rhymes, songs, and so on, that reflect the daily activities of a very young child. Create rhythm instruments from pots, wooden spoons, plastic bowls, empty coffee cans, and the like.
- Exercise time is a wonderful opportunity to use language, especially songs that make the activity fun for both you and your child. Roll a ball back and forth between the child and yourself. Use different-sized balls or different colors to talk about concepts such as bouncing high or low, color, fast, slow, and so on.
- When baking, read the recipe to the child and name the ingredients and utensils as you get them out. Allow the child to decorate cookies, cupcakes (mini ones are best), or graham crackers with icing, fruit jam, or even peanut butter using a small plastic knife or ice cream stick.
- Puzzles are fun at this age as long as pieces are large and the number kept to a minimum. See the earlier Creative Activities section for directions on making puzzles.

Displays

Displays enable you to bring attention to materials, services, and ideas of which you want to make the participants aware. They can also help you add an educational component to your program. Having the display in the same area as the program makes it more likely that the adults will look at it. Displays can be as simple or elaborate as you desire, but it is important to remember that the adults will have very young children along, which may limit their ability to browse. Make sure to post a Check These Out sign on or near the table, as many adults may need a reminder to check out library material and not just walk off with it.

Planning Displays

Where will the display be located and how large will it be? Most displays are placed on tables, set back from the edge and out of the reach of curious little hands. Small tables, such as card tables, will work in place of oversized ones. The top of a bookcase or shelf will work if it is at least 29 inches high, the average table height. If there is room in the program area, locate the display by the entrance/exit and away from the program proper, where it will cause the least amount of distraction during the program. Avoid using tablecloths for safety reasons; children this age are practicing standing and walking, and they may grab at the cloth, bringing it and the display content down on top of themselves. If space does not allow for even a small display, create one outside the program area and tell the participants about it, encouraging them not only to go out and look at it but to explore the library/facility itself; an informal "tour" on the way might help them to become acquainted with the area as well. If this program is going to be done outside the library, check with the other location's facilitator about setting up a display.

How much time does the librarian/presenter have to gather display materials? Often a quick walk through the stacks will yield books that parents/caregivers/children will find useful. Displays should be a sampling of a subject, not everything on it. If the display is to focus on a specific topic, you may need to collect material over a longer period of time.

Ideas for Displays

- Parenting books: Include books on general parenting, grandparents parenting grandchildren, adoption, discipline, working parents, communicating with children, and the like.
- Books that support adults: Consider such topics as things to do with children, places to go in the local area, self-help, parks and recreation information, arts and crafts, how to start a play group, how to pick a day care center or preschool, and so forth.
- Materials on child development: Feature books and/or DVDs on early brain development, sign language instruction, and so on.
- Magazines: Include titles such as *Parenting* and *Family Fun* that are aimed directly at parents and families as well as those targeted to very young children, for example, *Babybug* and *Ladybug*. Early childhood education magazines, such as those in The Mailbox Magazines for Teachers and Educators series, are good also. Subscriptions to such magazines can be expensive, and having access to them through the library is a definite plus for adults with limited funds.
- Special collections at the library: Make the participants aware of collections they can access, for example, circulating puppets or toys or special kits, such as Books to Grow On and Books to Grow On for Toddlers (King County Library System, WA), that have been created specifically with very young children in mind.

- Books appropriate for very young children: Select materials that work well when read aloud. There is such a variety of board books now that this kind of display is not only easy to create but also colorful. Actually seeing, examining, and using books carefully chosen for this age group will help the adults recognize others.

- Variations on a theme: Display Mother Goose titles, which have always been popular material for reading to this age group. Today, there are many variations available with all styles of illustrations. Include other poetry books in addition to Mother Goose, such as *Catch Me and Kiss Me and Say It Again* by Cliye Watson (Collins + World, 1978) and *Read-Aloud Poems for the Very Young* by Jack Prelutsky (Knopf Books for Young Readers, 1986)—just two of the wonderful poetry books now in circulation. You could also focus on ABC books, for example, *26 Letters and 99 Cents* by Tana Hoban (Greenwillow, 1978), Wanda Gag's *The ABC Bunny* (Coward-McCann, 1933), and Bill Martin Jr.'s *Chicka Chicka, Boom Boom* (Simon and Schuster Books for Young Readers, 1989).

- Award-winning books: Feature old favorites that the adults may recognize from their own childhoods or books that reflect the theme of the program.

- Books that make a good "home library" for children and families: Include a variety of titles, such as classics like *Goodnight Moon* by Margaret Wise Brown (Harper Collins, 1947), *Where Is the Green Sheep?* by Mem Fox (Harcourt, 2004), *I Spy on the Farm* by Edward Gibbs (Templar Books, 2013), and *Brown Bear, Brown Bear, What Do You See?* by Bill Martin Jr. (Henry Holt, 1992); a book of Mother Goose rhymes; board books by Tan Hoban, Margaret Miller, or the Global Fund for Children; and other titles that you consider worthy of a place in someone's home library. For this type of display, I have gathered books from the collection my daughter had as a young child to show the adults. It reassures them to see board books, cloth or vinyl books, and books of "lesser literary quality" included and reminds them that worn and well-loved books have value too.

- Various types of nonprint material: Display quality recordings in different formats, such as cassettes, CDs, and DVDs. Keep near the display a tape/CD player so that the adults can preview a musical selection. Include DVDs that are fun viewing for both adults and children; remind adults that they should view the films with the children. If your library circulates artwork or other materials that adults may use at home, such as books on tape/CD, Playaways, or downloadable materials, do not forget to include resources to help adults select these materials, such as website addresses, magazines that review media, and books that offer ideas for using media to expand children's horizons.

Displays are not absolutely necessary, but they are a great way to inform and educate the adult participants. They also make browsing easier for the adults because appropriate materials have been preselected for them. Along with handouts, displays are tangible indicators to the participants that you believe they are worth the extra time and effort to make this the best language experience possible for them and their children.

Handouts

Handouts can be a blessing and a curse, not only for those who make them but also for those who receive them. There are so many topics important to serving very young children that it is easy to become overwhelmed. The time involved in creating handouts must be balanced with their value to those they are intended to serve. Handouts must be kept simple and easy to understand for them to be utilized effectively. Quite often, handouts serve simply as introductions to larger topics. Handouts can include guidelines for programs, child development points, reasons to read to children, suggested books for very young children, fingerplay lyrics, and program evaluations; see the handouts and templates in this book's appendix for some ideas. They can also be "souvenir" items, for instance, a drinking cup for toddlers, a bib, growth chart, placemat, bookmark, or other useful item, that feature the organization's name and program information. Since the items are intended for very young children, make sure they meet all safety regulations. Commercial companies and organizations offer these kinds of materials for purchase. See the E-resources for Handouts and Information section at the end of this chapter for some resources to get you started.

Many libraries and organizations have a variety of ready-made handouts that can be used to inform the participants of their services. The following are handouts that should be available at each program:

- The library's open hours and contact information: Adults need to know when and how they can access your facility. Include special phone numbers, such as the ready reference line, the number to use when renewing or requesting material, the Children's Department, and so on. Provide the library's website address. If available, also include a help line number.

- Library card applications: Not everyone who attends these programs has a library card. Because it might be difficult for participants to fill out the application while attending the program, due to carrying little ones or trying to keep an eye on them, make applications available for them to take home or fill out prior to entering the program area.
- Your business card, if you have one: Some people may be intimidated by libraries and may feel more welcome knowing the children's librarian's name the next time they come in or call.
- Newsletters or publications circulated by your library or facility: These help patrons become aware of what the library is doing beyond the early childhood area.

Knowing when the library or facility is available to them, available special services aimed directly at them, a contact person's name, and what the library/facility is doing for others in their community can encourage non–library users to begin utilizing the public library and its resources.

Guidelines or a welcome sheet can help participants understand what is going to happen during the program and what is expected of both the children and the adults (e.g., see the Program Guidelines handouts in the appendix). You can print program guidelines on a separate sheet of paper or include them as part of another handout. You can also use signs or posters in the program area, either in addition to or in place of handouts. You might also want to incorporate an explanation of guidelines into the welcome/introduction at the beginning of each program. Explaining guidelines does help to create a more relaxed atmosphere because the adults will fully understand the kind of behavior that is expected of them and their children (i.e., age-appropriate behavior). Sharing your knowledge of the developmental stages for very young children may also prove reassuring, as well as enlightening, for the adults.

Many adults have a hard time remembering everything that was said during a program or the exact words to a specific rhyme. Even though children this age do not mind if some of the words are not the "authentic" ones, providing a sheet of the most frequently used rhymes and their lyrics is a good idea (e.g., see the Fun Rhymes to Share handout in the appendix); participants can follow along during the program or use the sheet, again and again, with their children at home. You can create a small rhyming booklet for participants to take home by using the Rhyme Booklet templates in the appendix. Print the two documents on the front and back of one sheet of 8.5-by-11-inch paper, cut the printed sheet in half horizontally, stack the two sheets, fold them in half vertically, and then trim off any excess white space along the top, bottom, and side. You now have a roughly 5-by-4-inch booklet with eight pages, including the front and back covers. If you prefer theme programs, you can create a sheet with just the rhymes that reflect the theme (e.g., see the All Wet! and Things That Go handouts in the appendix). You can also include on these sheets suggested cassettes or CDs that feature rhymes, fingerplays, and songs. Another idea is to create a handout that includes the words to a fingerplay or song along with the outline of a finger puppet to use with it. For possible pattern templates, see the Flannel Boards and Puppets sections in the resources at the end of this chapter. A similar idea would be to give out a die-cut or cutout shape with an appropriate rhyme printed on it; for example, you could print the lyrics for "Two Little Apples" on a label and then stick it on an apple cutout—simple to make and just about guaranteed to get posted in the home. See Creative Rhyme Handout Ideas in the appendix for some ideas.

As previously stated, very young children learn in many ways. They use all their senses to explore their world and develop their skills. Arts and crafts handouts can help the adults who have limited time and funds to "be creative" with their children without spending a lot of money on elaborate toys or materials. Offer a few very simple and safe recipes, activities, or crafts, and then supply the participants with additional resources for more ideas (e.g., see the Art Activity Recipes, Craft Ideas, and Creative Play Ideas handouts in the appendix). If your time is really tight, look around to see what you have available in-house. Here are two ideas:

- Do you have extra book jackets? Take them to your program and offer them to participants. Give suggestions for using them, such as for posters to hang on the back of the child's door, by the changing table, or in the eating or quiet area, or for making placemats for the child's highchair.
- You can make picture cards from pictures cut from extra book jackets or magazines that are then glued onto index cards and covered with clear contact paper. Encourage a dialogue between the adult and child about what the picture depicts, perhaps offering the book it is from for checkout. This kind of activity involves both the adult and child in a shared experience and helps bring stories and books into the daily life of busy families.

Program outlines and a list of materials used can be a review sheet for adult participants (e.g., see the Handout Templates in the appendix). Bibliographies of recommended books for the 12-to-24-month age group can guide them in selecting books and should include resources they might find useful in reinforcing the language-learning experience with their children. You can also do a list of recommended titles for toddlers and/or of applicable electronic resources (e.g., the "Tell Me a Story" page from the King County Library System, WA, at http://wiki.kcls.org/tellmeastory/index.php/Main_Page).

Handouts that aid an understanding of child development are useful to many adults. Include a list of developmental stages the children must go through, benefits of reading to their children, and parenting tips. Help the adults identify developmental stages, stress the fact that each child develops at his or her own pace, and emphasize the important roles of adult interaction and language.

Evaluation handouts help you get feedback for your program, enabling you not only to assess your program but also to decide priorities for programming and services. The written support and comments of adults who want this kind of language experience are important. The evaluation needs to include some basic questions:

- How old is your child?
- What did you like best/least about the program?
- Have you used any of the ideas/materials at home?
- Was the time relatively convenient?
- Do you have any suggestions and/or comments?

See the Evaluation handouts in the appendix for two examples.

You do not need to make every handout from scratch, nor do they need to be elaborate. Investigate other sources for existing materials and/or handouts relevant to your program. In-house booklists and guides to your collection may already be available. Consider distributing multiple copies of newspapers or magazines aimed at parents or adults working with this age group. Include park district activity booklets, community college publications, and farm guides. These handouts help adults become aware of library and community services that they can share with their children. Other public and private agencies offer brochures that encourage adults to read to their very young children or provide information related to parenting. These ready-made handouts can save time but may also be costly, though some may be available for free as downloads from the Internet. The American Library Association (http://www.ala.org/), the National Association for the Education of Young Children (http://www.naeyc.org/), Zero to Three (http://www.zerotothree.org/), Talaris Institute (http://www.talaris.org/), and other groups offer handouts for download and/or purchase. Look to your state or local health department as a possible resource. With the increasing recognition of the importance of early literacy, many libraries have developed programs and have posted the supporting materials on their websites. Look at library websites that share handouts, booklists, and ideas, such as the King County Library System in Washington and the Hennepin County Library in Minnesota. Electronic discussion list members are often eager and willing to share their knowledge and materials with others in the field. See the Resources section at the end of this chapter for websites to get you started.

The sample handouts in this book's appendix are also available at alaeditions .org/webextras. You can use these as is, adapt for your own needs, or simply use them as idea starting points for your own work. Remember to include on them your library/facility identification information and any logo/trade brand. Extra space allows you to add decorative details, such as borders, clip art, stickers, stamps, and other decorations. Be aware of copyright laws and restrictions when using patterns and artwork other than your own. Various desktop software such as Microsoft Publisher, Microsoft Word, ClipArt, Print Shop, and so on, provide decorative artwork, which can be a real a time saver. If cut-and-paste is your preferred method of creating handouts, look for books with reproducible borders and artwork in bookstores and school supply stores.

Tips to Keep in Mind When Creating Handouts

Simplicity

Handouts that are too wordy or use too small a font will more than likely not be read. Consolidate rather than make lengthy lists. My program guidelines consist of three basic "rules":

- I don't expect the children to sit still, but I do expect their caregivers to keep them safe. Feel free to step out and "regroup" if necessary and then come back in or try another day.
- Sharing is not easy for this age group, so please put things away. There will be time after the program for relaxing and conversation. Set phones to mute or vibrate, please!
- Big people are expected to take part; the more the adults participate and have fun, the more the children will want to as well.

Identification

Know what your organization requires on a handout, such as name, address, phone number, logo/trade brand, or disclaimers. Including the presenter's name, contact information, program name, and date is also helpful.

Citation

It may seem like a small thing to include where the information, idea, or pattern came from, but it may prove invaluable. If the master is lost or destroyed and needs to be replicated, finding it again will be much easier. Give credit to the resources you use for your ideas, and take into account copyright laws when using someone else's material.

Attention Grabbers

Use color, size, and pictures to draw attention to handouts. Colors can reflect a season, a series, or a theme. The usual size for handouts is 8.5-by-11 inches, but half sheets might work better if you want to make a booklet. Heavier-weight paper will be more durable. If the program has a logo, use it repeatedly with handout materials. Consider using a folder or large envelope with the series logo for storing your handouts.

Disclaimers

Some organizations require disclaimers to be put on all materials that are distributed. An example of a disclaimer is a statement regarding the need to be contacted if arrangements for those with special needs must be made, such as providing an interpreter for the hearing impaired.

Reasons for Being

Handing out materials just so the child will have something to take home is not the best reason for creating handouts. Handouts that reinforce or enhance the program by providing book titles, rhymes, an educational/informative statement or fact, ways to continue the experience at home or that help in evaluation are worth the effort it takes to create them. Overall, handouts should have a purpose and value for those to whom they are given. Creating them takes your time and resources, so keep master copies that can be updated and reused.

Resources

Music

Print Resources

Bower, Bruce. "Birth of the Beat." *Science News*, August 14, 2010. http://www
.sciencenews.org/view/feature/id/61561/title/Birth_of_the_beat.

Cobb, Jane. *What'll I Do with the Baby-O? Nursery Rhymes, Songs, and Stories for Babies.* Vancouver, BC: Black Sheep Press, 2007.

Feierabend, John M. *The Book of Simple Songs and Circles.* Chicago: GIA First Steps, 2000.

Humpal, Marcia Earl, and Jan Wolf. "Music in the Inclusive Environment." *Young Children* 58, no. 2 (March 2003): 103–107.

Kleiner, Lynn. *Toddlers Make Music! Ones and Twos! for Parents and Their Toddlers.* Book and CD. Redondo Beach, CA: Alfred Publishing, 2000.

Levine-Gelb Communications, Claire Lerner, and Lynette A. Ciervo. *Getting in Tune: The Powerful Influence of Music on Young Children's Development.* Washington, DC: Zero to Three, 2002.

Shore, Rebecca. *Baby Teacher: Nurturing Neural Networks from Birth to Age Five.* Lanham, MD: Scarecrow Education, 2002.

Shore, Rebecca, and Janis Strasser. "Music for Their Minds." *Young Children* 61, no. 2 (March 2006): 62–67.

Silberg, Jackie. *The I Can't Sing Book: For Grownups Who Can't Carry a Tune in a Paper Bag . . . but Want to Do Music with Young Children.* Beltsville, MD: Gryphon House. 1998.

E-resources

Adventure Music. http://www.aventurinemusic.com/. This website for Eric Chappelle, creator of the Music for Creative Dance series, offers ideas for storytime creative movement activities.

KidzSing Garden of Song. http://gardenofsong.com/. Don't know the melody? This site features audio of tunes for English-language nursery rhymes and songs and links to other children's music websites.

King County Library System. "Tell Me a Story." http://wiki.kcls.org/tellmeastory/index.php/Main_Page. KCLS children's librarians have filmed hundreds of videos demonstrating rhymes and songs. The words to even more rhymes are made available for families to try at home.

Nancy Stewart. http://nancymusic.com/. This website of an award-winning professional musician and songwriter includes activity pages for making homemade instruments, games to play with music, information about how to share music with babies, and links to sites related to music and children. The "Song of the Month" page offers a new original song each month, along with the melody, lyrics, and activities, for free download.

National Institute of Environmental Health Sciences. "Kids's Pages." http://www.niehs.nih.gov/kids/musicchild.htm. This website, from a division of the National Institutes of Health, offers lyrics and MIDI (Musical Instrument Digital Interface) tunes for many popular children's songs.

Sally Jaeger. http://sallyjaeger.com/. This popular Canadian storyteller provides materials that are available in DVD and CD formats. The website offers lyrics to songs on CD as free downloads. *Here Comes Mr. Bear* and *From Wibbleton to Wobbleton* include songs, rhymes, bounces, tickles, hello songs, walking and galloping songs, and lullabies. *From Wibbleton to Wobbleton* on DVD is a live recording of an actual Music with Young Children program and is a good way to learn new ways of using traditional material.

Sing with Our Kids. http://singwithourkids.com/. This website offers free resources for early learning through community singing. Resources include song library, video library, community toolbox, grandparents' corner, tips and tricks from experts, and early learning and music information.

Texas State Library and Archives Commission. "El Día de Los Niños: El Día de Los Libros." https://www.tsl.state.tx.us/ld/projects/ninos/index.html. This site features traditional songs, rhymes, fingerplays, and games in Spanish and English, including lyrics and directions and some audio.

Zero to Three. http://www.zerotothree.org/. The mission of this website, from a national, nonprofit, multidisciplinary organization, is to inform, educate, and support adults who influence the lives of infants and toddlers. It offers well-documented and carefully written brochures to hand out; many can be downloaded and others purchased.

Distributors of Children's Media

Kimbo Educational: The Children's Music Company. http://kimboed.com/. Mail: PO Box 477M, Long Branch, NJ 07740-0477. Phone: 800-631-2187.

Music for Little People. http://www.mflpdistribution.com/. Mail: PO Box 757, Greenland, NH 03840. Phone: 800-409-2457.

Music In Motion. http://musicmotion.com/. Mail: PO Box 869231, Plano, TX 75086-9231. Phone: 972-943-8744; toll-free: 800-807-3520.

Flannel Boards

Print Resources

Briggs, Diane. *Toddler Storytimes II*. Lanham, MD: Scarecrow Press, 2008.

Carlson, Ann, and Mary Carlson. *Flannelboard Stories for Infants and Toddlers*. Chicago: American Library Association, 2005.

———. *Flannelboard Stories for Infants and Toddlers, Bilingual Edition*. Chicago: American Library Association, 2005.

Sierra, Judy. *The Flannel Board Storytelling Book*. 2nd ed. New York: H. W. Wilson, 1997.

Stewart, Nancy. *Little Songs for Little Me*. Activity Kit with CD or Cassette. Mercer Island, WA: Friends Street Music, 1992.

Distributors of Flannel-Board Supplies

AccuCut: Die Cutting Products for Craft, Education, and Custom Use. http://www.accucut.com/. Phone: 800-288-1670.

Beyond Play: Products for Early Childhood and Special Needs. http://www.beyondplay.com/. Phone: 877-428-1244.

Book Props (visual props based on children's stories). http://www.bookprops.com/ www.bookprops.com/Welcome.html. Mail: 1120 McVey Avenue, Lake Oswego, OR 97034. Phone: 503-636-0330.

ChildWood (wooden magnetic characters). http://www.childwood.com/. Mail: 8873 Woodbank Drive, Bainbridge Island, WA 98110. Phone: 800-362-9825.

Ellison (die-cut machines and dies). http://www.ellison.com/. Mail: Ellison Educational Equipment, Inc., 25862 Commercentre Drive, Lake Forest, CA 92630-8804. Phone: 800-253-2238 (toll-free in the United States).

The Felt Source. http://www.thefeltsource.com/index.html. Mail: 31256 Corte Talvera, Temecula, CA 92592-5469. Phone: 951-695-7440; toll-free (United States only): 877-463-1053.

Lakeshore Learning (educational materials for home and classroom). http://www.lakeshorelearning.com/. Mail: Lakeshore Learning Materials, 2695 East Dominguez Street, Carson, CA 90895.Phone: 800-421-5354.

Preschool Express by Jean Warren (preschool activities and ideas that include "Pattern Station," which is useful for making flannel-board pieces). http://www.preschoolexpress.com/.

Puppets

Print Resources

Briggs, Diane. *101 Fingerplays, Stories and Songs to Use with Finger Puppets*. Chicago: American Library Association, 1999.

Nichols, Judy. *Storytimes for Two-Year-Olds*. 3rd ed. Chicago: American Library Association, 2007.

Rottman, Fran. *Easy-to-Make Puppets and How to Use Them*. Ventura, CA: Gospel Light, 1995.

Distributors of Puppet Supplies

Crafts from Bolivia. (3 Bags Full Finger Puppet Pouches: theme sets of finger puppets with a storage bag that also serves as the story board). http://www.craftsfrombolivia.com/. Mail: 504-581 Avenue Road, Toronto, ON M4V 2K4, Canada. Phone: 416-481-40664.

Demco. http://www.demco.com/. Phone (toll-free): 800-962-4463.

Environments (children's furniture, educational equipment, toys, and curriculum materials). http://eichild.com/.

Folkmanis (puppets of all sorts), http://folkmanis.com/. Mail: 1219 Park Avenue, Emeryville, CA 94608. Phone: 800-654-8922.

Lakeshore Learning (educational materials for home and classroom). http://www.lakeshorelearning.com/. Mail: Lakeshore Learning Materials, 2695 East Dominguez Street, Carson, CA 90895. Phone: 800-421-5354.

School Specialty Marketplace (discount school supplies and teaching supplies). https://store.schoolspecialty.com/OA_HTML/ibeCCtpSctDspRte.jsp?minisite=10206. Mail: School Specialty, PO Box 1579, Appleton, WI 54912-1579. Phone: 1-888-388-3224.

Language

Print Resources

Bingham, Sara. *The Baby Signing Book: Includes 350 ASL Signs for Babies and Toddlers.* Toronto, ON: Robert Rose, 2007.

Miller, Anne Meeker. *Baby Sing and Sign: Communicate Early with Your Baby: Learning Signs the Fun Way through Music and Play.* New York: Marlowe, 2007.

———. *Toddler Sing and Sign: Improve your Child's Vocabulary and Verbal Skills the Fun Way through Music and Play.* New York: Da Capo Press, 2007.

Thompson, Rachel H., Nicole M. Cotnoir-Bichelman, Paige M. McKerchar, Trista L. Tate, and Kelly A. Dancho. "Enhancing Early Communication through Infant Sign Training." *Journal of Applied Behavior Analysis* 40, no. 1 (Spring 2007): 15–23.

Using ProQuest (http://www.proquest.com/), a database that indexes articles from over 4,000 magazines, journals, and newspapers, a search of the terms "infant" and "sign" will retrieve a list of articles from the *Alaska Daily News* to the *Bangor Daily News*, the *Washington Post* to *Psychology Today*, and even the *Tribune Business News*.

E-resources

Michigan State University Communication Technology Laboratory. American Sign Language Browser. http://commtechlab.msu.edu/sites/aslweb/browser.htm. This website is an online ASL browser of video of thousands of ASL signs being demonstrated. This site, although useful, links to a more up-to-date site called Signing Savvy (http://www.signingsavvy.com/).

HandSpeak. http://www.handspeak.com/. Created by Jolanta Lapiak, this is a content site on sign language, consisting of an ASL online dictionary, grammar tutorials, finger spelling, baby talk in ASL, literary arts (storytelling and poetry), and other features.

Movement

Print Resources

Garabedian, Helen. *Itsy Bitsy Yoga for Toddlers and Preschoolers.* Cambridge, MA: De Capo Press, 2008.

Miller, Karen. *Simple Steps: Developmental Activities for Infants, Toddlers, and Two-Year-Olds.* Beltsville, MD: Gryphon Press, 2005.

Stokes, Beverly. *Amazing Babies: Essential Movement for Your Baby in the First Year.* Toronto, ON: Move Alive Media, 2002.

Whitford, Rebecca, and Martina Selway. *Little Yoga: A Toddler's First Book of Yoga.* New York: Henry Holt, 2005.

E-resources

Nurturing Pathways Inc. http://www.nurturingpathways.com/. This creative dance program is based on scientific research that movement has an impact on a child's development.

Preschool Express by Jean Warren. http://preschoolexpress.com/. This free online activity resource is for parents, teachers, and grandparents of toddlers (ages 1–3) and preschoolers (ages 3–5).

Props: Parachutes/Scarves/Streamers

Print and Audio Resources

Downing, Johnette. *The Second Line: Scarf Activity Songs.* New Orleans: Johnette Downing, 2003.

Gill, Jim. *Jim Gill Sings the Sneezing Song and Other Contagious Tunes.* CD (suggested song: "Alabama Mississippi"). Oak Park, IL: Jim Gill Music, 1993.

Stewart, Georgiana Liccione. *Musical Scarves and Activities.* CD. Long Branch, NJ: Kimbo, 2002.

Creative Activities and Play

Print Resources

Ernst, Linda L. *Baby Rhyming Time.* New York: Neal-Schuman, 2008.

Hewitt, Karen. "Blocks as a Tool for Learning: Historical and Contemporary Perspectives." *Journal of the National Association for the Education of Young Children* 56, no. 1 (January 2001): 6–13. http://www.naeyc.org/yc/pastissues/ 2001/january.

Masi, Wendy S (ed.). *Gymboree Baby and Toddler Play: The Best 170 Fun-Filled Activities from Top-Selling Favorites Baby Play and Toddler Play.* San Francisco: Weldon Owen, 2011.

———. *Toddler Play: 100 Fun-Filled Activities to Maximize Your Toddler's Potential.* San Francisco: Creative Publishing, 2001.

McClure, Robin. *The Playskool Guide to Baby Play.* Naperville, IL: Sourcebooks, 2007.

Miller, Karen. *Simple Steps: Developmental Activities for Infants, Toddlers and Two-Year-Olds.* Beltsville, MD: Gryphon House, 1999.

Raines, Shirley, Karen Miller, and Leah Curry-Rood. *Story S-T-R-E-T-C-H-E-R-S for Infants, Toddlers, and Twos: Experiences, Activities, and Games for Popular Children's Books.* Beltsville, MD: Gryphon House, 2002.

Sasse, Margaret. *Active Baby, Healthy Brain: 135 Fun Exercises and Activities to Maximize Your Child's Brain Development from Birth through Age 5½.* New York: The Experiment, 2010.

Schiller, Pam. *The Complete Resource Book for Toddlers and Twos: Over 2000 Activities for Enriching Language and Developing Skills and Concepts.* Beltsville, MD: Gryphon House, 2002.

Silberg, Jackie. *Games to Play with Babies.* 3rd ed. Beltsville, MD: Gryphon House, 2001.

———. *Games to Play with Toddlers.* Revised ed. Beltsville, MD: Gryphon House, 2002.

———. *More Games to Play with Toddlers.* Beltsville, MD: Gryphon House, 2004.

E-resources

Beyond Play. http://beyondplay.com/. This website specializes in products for early
childhood and special-needs children.

Bright Ring Publishing. http://brightring.com/. This site offers award-winning art
activity books as well as free art activities and links to favorite websites.

Enchanted Learning. http://enchantedlearning.com/Home.html. This is a good
source for accessing curriculum material online.

Family Reading Partnership. http://www.familyreading.org. A nonprofit community
organization that promotes early literacy.

Kids Crafts Weekly. http://kidscraftweekly.com/. Here you will find free kids' craft ideas
and printable projects; they may need modifications for younger children.

Lakeshore Learning Materials. http://www.lakeshorelearning.com/. Lakeshore offers
products for infants through sixth grade.

Preschool Express by Jean Warren. http://preschoolexpress.com/. This is a free
online educational activity resource for parents, teachers, and grandparents
of toddlers (ages 1–3) and preschoolers (ages 3–5).

Handouts and Information for Displays

E-resources

Association for Library Service to Children. "Born to Read." http://www.ala.org/alsc/
issuesadv/borntoread. This site provides tips for reading, book sharing, websites,
information on emergent literacy, and booklists that can be shared with parents.

Association for Library Service to Children and Public Library Association. "Every
Child Ready to Read® @ your library®." http://www.everychildreadytoread
.org/. This site provides workshop information, handouts, and research on
the topic of early literacy.

Brooklyn Public Library. "Brooklyn Reads to Babies." http://www.bklynpubliclibrary
.org/first-5-years/read/baby. This campaign, aimed at parents and caregivers
of babies and toddlers, underscores the importance of reading aloud to
children during the first years of life.

———. "First 5 Years." http://www.bklynpubliclibrary.org/first-5-years/. This
page offers suggested books, rhymes, songs, and play activities for babies,
toddlers, and preschoolers.

———. "Read, Play, Grow!" http://www.bklynpubliclibrary.org/first-5-years/play/
baby. This program promotes play activities that help develop early literacy.

Hennepin County Library. "Birth to Six." http://www.hclib.org/BirthTo6. This site
offers suggestions and information on books, songs, rhymes, and other ways
of developing early literacy in conjunction with talking, singing, reading,
writing, and playing together.

King County Library System. "Parents and Care Givers." http://www.kcls.org/
 parents/. This page provides links to websites that would be of interest to
 parents, including child-care resources, families with special-needs children,
 government sites, and library system services and resources for families.
———. "Tell Me a Story." http://www.kcls.org/tellmeastory/. This site is a "storytime
 companion" for parents and caregivers. It provides the lyrics and videos of
 many rhymes and songs used in storytimes and allows families to see what
 was presented at storytime at their branch if they were unable to attend.
Multnomah County Library. "Early Literacy: Birth to Six." https://www.multcolib
 .org/birthtosix/. This library's website offers parent education, their "Every
 Child Initiative," and discussion of how reading, talking, singing, writing,
 and playing with children every day can help them get ready to read.
National Association for the Education of Young Children. http://www.naeyc
 .org/. This is the website of the world's largest organization advocating on
 behalf of young children and those who work with them. To find early
 learning information, enter the phrase "early years are learning years" in the
 search box at the top of the screen.
National Literacy Trust (Great Britain). "Talk to Your Baby." http://www
 .talktoyourbaby.org.uk/home. This campaign encourages parents and
 child-care providers to talk more to children from birth to three.
Reach Out and Read. http://www.reachoutandread.org/. This national nonprofit
 promotes early literacy by making books a routine part of pediatric care,
 including placing books in pediatric waiting rooms. It trains doctors and
 nurses to advise parents about the importance of reading aloud. The site
 features PDF handouts for downloading on many early childhood topics.
Reading Rockets. "Reading Topics A to Z." http://www.readingrockets.org/atoz/.
 This national multimedia project, funded by a grant from the U.S.
 Department of Education, provides information and resources to parents,
 teachers, child-care providers, administrators, and others who touch the life
 of a child about various topics regarding children and reading. They provide
 PDF handouts on many early childhood topics for downloading.
Talaris Institute. http://www.talaris.org/. The purpose of this nonprofit organization is
 to offer parents accurate information and research on topics of parenting in
 an understandable, concise way so it can be applied practically in their lives.
Zero to Three: National Center for Infants, Toddlers, and Families. http://www
 .zerotothree.org/. This national, nonprofit organization "informs, trains and
 supports professionals, policymakers and parents in their efforts to improve
 the lives of infants and toddlers."

Handouts and Templates

Appendix

The following sample handouts and templates, arranged alphabetically, are also available at alaeditions.org/webextras.

1	All Wet!	12	Handout Template—Stories and Stuff
2	Art Activity Recipes	13	Interesting Facts and Tips
3	Craft Ideas	14	Program Descriptions for Publicity Flyers
4	Creative Play Ideas	15	Program Guidelines Bookmarks
5	Creative Rhyme Handout Ideas	16	Program Guidelines Poster
6	Door Sign	17	Reading Aloud to Little Ones
7	Evaluation—Long	18	Rhyme Booklet, Page 1
8	Evaluation—Short	19	Rhyme Booklet, Page 2
9	Flannel-Board Fun	20	Sick Sign
10	Fun Rhymes to Share!	21	Things That Go
11	Handout Template—Generic		

Sample handouts can be found at **alaeditions.org/webextras**.

TIP

Use handouts as is, or copy and paste the text into your own. These handouts are intended to be examples. Feel free to modify them to suit your program needs.

Use these sample handouts as a starting point when creating your own. Many of these sample handouts include space for inserting your library/facility identification information and logo/trade brand. When creating your own handouts, use decorative elements, such as borders, clip art, stickers, stamps, and so forth. Keep in mind copyright laws when using patterns, artwork, and text other than your own because restrictions on their use, whether in house or for distribution, may apply. Some desktop software, such as Microsoft Publisher, Microsoft Word, ClipArt, and Print Shop, will include decorative artwork, which can be a real a time saver, but, again, be sure to read the user license agreements to determine any use restrictions.

Also included at alaeditions.org/webextras (but not in this book) is a complete file of the English lyrics for the rhymes appearing in chapter 4 of the book so that you can easily create your own handouts or substitute different rhymes on existing handouts.

All Wet!

Row, Row, Row Your Boat

Row, row, row
your boat,
Gently down
the stream.
Merrily, merrily,
merrily, merrily,
Life is
but a dream.

1, 2, 3, 4, 5, I Caught a Fish Alive

1, 2, 3, 4, 5,
I caught a fish alive!
6, 7, 8, 9, 10,
I let him go again!

Rub-a-Dub-Dub

Rub-a-dub-dub,
three men in a tub,
And who do you
think they be?
The butcher,
the baker,
the candlestick maker.
And all went
out to sea!

More Ideas!

- Put out a small pan of water and let your child wash some dishes or perhaps a baby doll. Children this age love to imitate the big people around them.

- Take a walk around a pond, lake, or stream in your area. Talk about what you see and hear.

- Sand is lots of fun for little ones, and it is best kept outside. You can use a simple dishpan to hold it or dump it in a box. Be sure to supply containers and digging tools.

- Bubbles can add a smile to any day. Put on some music and dance with your child amid this bubbly fun. This is best done outside or in a room that won't get damaged by the moisture.

Books to Share with Your Child!

Here are some fun picture books for sharing:

- *Have You Seen My Duckling?* by Nancy Tafuri
- *In the Small, Small Pond* by Denise Fleming
- *Splash!* by Flora McDonnell

 HANDOUT 1: All Wet! by Linda L. Ernst, *The Essential Lapsit Guide*, 2015 © American Library Association.

Art Activity Recipes

Children in this age group can be very creative. However, because many children still put things in their mouths, it is better not to use recipes that demand a great deal of salt, include tempera as a coloring agent, or have alum as an ingredient. Here are some simple and fast art recipes for you to try.

Playdough (This is firm and holds its shape.)

- 4 cups flour
- 1 cup salt
- 4 tablespoons of cooking oil or shortening
- 1 ½ cups water (If needed, add more a little at a time.)
- food coloring (about 1 fluid ounce for dark color)–optional

If adding color, put the food coloring in the water for ease in mixing. Mix dry ingredients together and add liquid until pliable, somewhat like a pie crust. Stored in a plastic bag, this will keep for about a month, depending on use. If it gets too sticky, just add more flour.

Playdough

- 1 cup flour
- ½ cup salt
- 2 teaspoons cream of tartar
- 1 cup boiling water
- 2 teaspoons cooking oil
- food coloring–optional

Mix dry ingredients together in a pot and add the water, cooking oil, and, if desired, the food coloring. Cook, stirring constantly, over medium heat for 3 to 4 minutes until it forms a ball. Store in a plastic bag or sealed container. This keeps well in the refrigerator.

Oatmeal Dough

- 1 cup flour
- 2 cups oatmeal
- 1 cup water

Mix ingredients and cook over medium heat, stirring constantly, for 3 minutes. Pour out mixture and knead well. When cool, store in a plastic bag with a tight seal.

Glue or Cornstarch Paste

- 3 tablespoons cornstarch
- 1 cup cold water

Mix the cornstarch into the water and boil the mixture until it thickens. Use when cool. This does separate over time, so reheat and cool before using again. This is one of the simplest pastes to make, but it does not keep well, so make small amounts at a time. For colored paste, add food coloring.

Finger Paint

- ½ cup cornstarch
- ¾ cup cold water
- 2 cups boiling water
- food coloring

Bring the cornstarch and cold water to a boil in a pot and then add the combined boiling water and food coloring. Cook until it boils clear. Cool mixture and then use. Children love to use finger paint and really get involved with it. If you prefer, use food as finger paint for your very young child. Applesauce, yogurt, canned pumpkin, sour cream, and cranberry sauce are only a few ideas to start with, then use your imagination.

Craft Ideas

It's fun to make things for you and your child to play with and enjoy together. Try out some of the following ideas.

Stick Puppets

Use a craft stick, ice cream stick, tongue depressor, or even a wooden spoon. For children not yet steady on their feet, use a straw or tightly rolled piece of paper. Cut a circle out of colored paper, tape it on one end of the stick, and decorate it. Use stickers or draw a face.

Picture Cards

Use unlined index cards. Glue pictures from magazines, decorative stickers, or even photographs you have taken to the card. Using clear contact paper, place the decorated side of the index card face down on the sticky surface. Cover both sides for durability. Sort into a dishpan or box, which can also be used for storage.

Can Lids

Clean juice lids from frozen juice cans are great for "mailing" into a coffee can with a hole cut in the top. You can decorate the lids with stickers or use them as is. The lids make a great sound when dropped in the can!

Squish Bags

For the "paint," you can use pudding. In a bowl, combine contents of one box of instant pudding mix with about 1⁄2 to 3⁄4 the amount of water usually required. Chocolate pudding makes great "dirt," or you can add food coloring to vanilla pudding. Mix well. Put about 1⁄4 cup mixture into a ziplock bag, press out as much air as possible, and seal well. Reinforce the bag by folding tape over edges.

Cream Bags

Use whipped cream or shaving cream (if your child has stopped chewing on everything). Fill a ziplock plastic bag about half full. Add a few drops of food coloring. Seal well and then squeeze to mix. Freezer bags work the best because they are the strongest. Taping the opening end shut helps keep them that way when children play with them.

Books

You can make books that follow your child through his or her day, illustrating things that go, a trip to the farm, favorite things, and the like. Glue pictures on lightweight tag board or construction paper. Insert into plastic page protectors or cover both sides with clear contact paper. Punch holes on one side if not using page protectors. Join the pages together in a three-ring binder, use ring fasteners, or tie with yarn. This gives your child his or her own very personal book. If using plastic bags, cut cardboard to fit, draw or glue pictures on the board, insert into the bag, and then sew bags together on one side with yarn to make a book.

Creative Play Ideas

Water-Related Play

- Give children different temperatures or forms of water (warm, cold, ice) and use words to describe it. For example, "The ice is slippery and cold."
- Give them simple "toys" to use in the bathtub, such as a measuring cup or funnel.
- Have them give a baby doll a bath or perhaps help wash vegetables for eating.
- Fill a dishpan or sink with water and give the child different objects to see which ones float or sink.
- Use bubbles to hide an object in the water or float boats on the surface.
- Use a sponge to soak up water and let the child discover what happens when it is squeezed.

Outings

- Visit a zoo, farm, grocery store, garden, nursery with lots of different flowers, playground, and so on. You could even read a story about such places before and after you go.
- Go for a walk around the house, around the block, in the rain, to a park, and so forth. Talk about what you see, hear, feel, smell, and so on.
- When driving, be a tour guide for your child. Describe where you are going, what you see along the way, and what you might do once you get there. You can even make going to the Laundromat an adventure.
- Get down close to the grass and look at it. Talk about the creatures you might find.
- Plant a garden. It does not have to be big, perhaps just a small container. The child can even plant seeds in a cup, but be sure the seeds go in the cup, not in the child's mouth.
- Take a walk on bubble wrap. Talk about the sounds, the surface, and so on.
- Collect leaves, rocks, and the like on your walk. Talk about what they look like, feel like, and perhaps even sound like.
- Take a bus ride.

Creative Play Ideas

Imagination Play

Children this age should not be expected to know how to "play," so be a role model playing alongside the child to facilitate learning.

- Have a telephone conversation using a toy phone.
- Trains and trucks are fun to drive and manipulate. Create a ramp by using a cookie sheet or cardboard or a large wrapping/mailing cardboard tube to drop objects through, such as plastic "whiffle" golf balls, trucks, or even stuffed toys. Talk about size, speed, where is it, and so forth.
- Get a large-sized box and help the child create a boat, house, cave, wagon, and so on, with it.
- Large mirrors fascinate the very young child. Allow the child to use a large safety mirror (unbreakable) to discover his or her own self and body parts as well as to see facial reactions.
- Blow feathers, leaves, scarves, or bubbles. Talk about textures and types of wind (hard, soft, strong, etc.).
- Create a flannel board by covering cardboard (8-by-11 inches or any size) with felt or flannel. You can also use the inside cover of a clean pizza box. Cut out simple shapes either free hand or using cookie cutters for outlines, and the child can create his or her own stories and learn hand-eye coordination as well. You can also mount pictures from coloring books and magazines and even photos on the felt or flannel. Store pieces in a ziplock bag or inside the pizza box.
- Make puppets using a wooden spoon as the base and decorate it with a face. You can do the same with mittens. Use craft sticks, tongue depressors, straws, or stirring sticks to create stick puppets. Simply place a sticker at one end or use a marker to draw a face on the stick. You can also mount pictures from magazines or photos on sturdy paper and then glue on one end of the stick. Larger puppets, often commercially made, are great to use with the very young child because they encourage interaction between the child and puppet, who often "talk" together without shyness.

- Play peek-a-boo. Using chiffon scarves or other see-through material, drape it over your own head and then reappear. When placing it over the child's head, the see-through material is best because it reassures the child. Cover an object such as a stuffed toy, doll, or truck with the scarf and then make it reappear. Remember to talk about the object and what is happening.
- Play hide-and-seek. This childhood game is best when the very young child is the one who hides. You should talk while looking for the child: "Now, where is Billy? I am going to look behind the chair." Many times, the child will pop out from the hiding place, bringing the game to a halt, but you should react with appropriate surprise and joy.

HANDOUT 4: Creative Play Ideas by Linda L. Ernst, *The Essential Lapsit Guide*, 2015 © American Library Association.

Creative Play Ideas

Language Play

- Greeting cards make wonderful activity materials. Use ones that have no small, loose pieces or glitter on them. Take a collection of cards and place them in a dishpan or box. The child will enjoy taking them out, putting them in, opening and closing them, as well as looking at them. You can create stories about the pictures or just describe what is on them. Identify objects, animals, flowers, and so forth, depicted on the cards.

- Junk mail is fun to use in activities with your child. You can talk with the child about the mail, put the mail into boxes, and sort the mail. Help create the letter-writing habit in your child by helping him or her to "write" a letter to someone and then mail it. Take the child with you throughout the process and talk about what you are doing so he or she can learn the process of getting paper, writing, addressing, and mailing the letter (post office, mailbox, etc.).

- Use plastic can covers to help the child develop eye-hand control and coordination. Using fine-motor skills, the child can pick up a can cover and place in a box or coffee can. If you make a slit or hole in the top of the container, the child can "mail" the juice cover. Children love the sound the lid makes when it is dropped in. Colorful stickers are fun to put on these juice lids, or you can use signal dots, which are available at most office supply stores. Later on, use the lids in a sorting or identification game.

- Make picture cards from index cards. Simply glue pictures on or use stickers to cover the cards and then lay them picture side down on clear contact paper. You can cover both sides of the card with clear contact paper, if so desired. Cut the cards apart and use them in the same manner as the greeting cards or juice lids.

- Make your own books. Photo albums, especially the magnetic kind, allow for pictures to be moved around and words written on the pages. Make a book about the child using photos of his or her daily routine. By placing thin cardboard in a ziplock bag, you can create two-sided pages that can then be sewn together using strong thread or yarn, making a book. This is not as sturdy as the photo album, but it will work.

- Play dress up. This does not mean you have to go out and buy these clothes. Children can be creative with scarves, hats, old slips, shoes, and the like. Don't put out a trunk load of clothes either. Very young children do not need an unlimited number of things to select from, just a few.

- Create a play space. Small pop-up tents have become popular to use, but a sheet works just as well. Just make sure that it is draped securely over objects that will not fall over on the child and cause injuries.

- Give the child his or her own catalog to help the child practice turning pages. Repetition is an essential part of learning. It is much better to practice with an old catalog, probably ripping pages, than with a beautiful picture book.

- Look at magazines, books, and other places where words and pictures may be found with your child. Talk about what you see and give the child time to absorb as much on the page as he or she wants. Reading time may be limited to only one page, but that is how it all begins.

- Let your child handle and discover different kinds of paper. Let the child crunch it into a ball, tear it, and examine it. Use regular paper, wax paper, cardboard, newspaper, and so on.

- Music can play a large part in the language learning of children. Many rhymes and songs reflect the daily activities of a very young child. Create rhythm instruments from pots, wooden spoons, plastic bowls, empty coffee cans, and the like.

- Exercise time is a wonderful time to use language, especially songs that make the activity fun for both you and your child. Roll a ball back and forth between you and the child. Use two different-sized balls (making the size difference distinct) or different colors and talk about concepts such as bouncing and color, high, low, fast and slow, and so forth.

- When baking, read the recipe to the child and name the ingredients and utensils as you get them out. Allow the child to decorate cookies, cupcakes (mini ones are best), or graham crackers with icing, fruit jam, or peanut butter using a small plastic knife or ice cream stick.

Creative Rhyme Handout Ideas

This sheet provides a shortcut for those who like to create handouts or give participants a souvenir at each storytime. The time involved is minimal, especially if you have the equipment or volunteers to assist you. Such handouts help to remind storytime participants to continue storytime at home because these will often find their way to the family "note board," like the front of the refrigerator, which encourages them to practice the rhyme at home. You can copy and paste the following rhymes onto an address label and then "stick" them onto a cutout shape, such as an Ellison die or a 2-by-8-inch rectangular piece of paper that can be used as a bookmark. I have not included the titles due to limited space. The cutout shape should reflect the rhyme (e.g., apple rhyme on an apple shape), and the bookmark shape can include the library logo or information on one end while the other end features a decoration, such as a stamp or sticker, that reflects the subject of the rhyme. I have found that Avery Label 5971–2.63-by-1 or 2.65-by-1 inches works well. After copying the rhyme to the label template, you can also change the type of font and center the words on the label for a more "finished" look. For a more dramatic impact, use a **bold** font. You can also use this handout to create a simple booklet: use a metal ring (like individual loose-leaf rings found at office supply stores) to join together the shapes or index cards with the rhymes. Pass out one of these at each program, and your participants will end up with a nice collection of materials for use at home.

An elephant goes like this and that.
He's terribly big and he's terribly fat.
He has no fingers!
He has no toes!
But goodness, gracious—what a nose!

"Gack-goon," went the little green frog one day.
"Gack-goon," went the little green frog.
"Gack-goon," went the little green frog one day,
And his eyes went "Gack-gack-goon."

Way up high in the apple tree,
Two little apples did I see.
So I shook that tree as hard as I could,
And d-o-w-n came the apples.
Umm! They were good!

Twinkle, twinkle, little star.
How I wonder what you are.
Up above the world so high, like a diamond in the sky.
Twinkle, twinkle little star.
How I wonder what you are.

This is the way we rake the leaves,
Rake the leaves, rake the leaves.
This is the way we rake the leaves,
So early in the morning.

Row, row, row your boat
Gently down the stream.
Merrily, merrily, merrily, merrily,
Life is but a dream.

The turkey is a funny bird.
His head goes wobble, wobble.
He only says a single word.
That's "Gobble! Gobble! Gobble!"

Warm hands, warm.
Do you know how?
If you want to warm your hands,
Blow on them now!

HANDOUT 5: Creative Rhyme Handout Ideas by Linda L. Ernst, *The Essential Lapsit Guide*, 2015 © American Library Association.

Door Sign

[Insert Title of Program]

**A special storytime
for children ages**
[insert age range]
**with caregivers.
Please keep door closed.**

THANK YOU!

[Insert Presenter's Name]

Evaluation–Long

Take a moment to let us know what you think.
Please fill out the evaluation below.
[Program name and date]

How old is your child? _____

How many programs did you and your child attend? _____

What did you like best about the program(s)? _____

_____

_____

What did you like least about the program(s)? _____

_____

_____

Did the program(s) meet your expectations? _____

_____

Have you used any of the ideas presented at home? _____

_____

Were the materials suitable for the age range? _____

_____

Was the time relatively convenient? _____

_____

If offered again, would you attend? _____

_____

Please include any suggestions and/or comments you may have: _____

_____

_____

_____

HANDOUT 7: Evaluation–Long by Linda L. Ernst, *The Essential Lapsit Guide,* 2015 © American Library Association.

Evaluation–Short

[Name of Program and Date]

How old is your child? _____

How did you hear about this program? _____
_____

Program was (circle one): _____ Great!   Okay   Could have been better   Not worth my time

Liked best: _____
_____

Liked least: _____
_____

Suggestions/comments: _____
_____

`CUT` ·

[Name of Program and Date]

How old is your child? _____

How did you hear about this program? _____
_____

Program was (circle one): _____ Great!   Okay   Could have been better   Not worth my time

Liked best: _____
_____

Liked least: _____
_____

Suggestions/comments: _____
_____

Flannel-Board Fun

Flannel boards or felt boards are interactive, and children love to play with them. Children can practice their fine motor skills by putting the pieces on the board and taking them off. Keep the pieces simple at this young age so your child will feel successful. Use rhymes, tell stories, or sing songs and illustrate them with simple pictures or shapes.

Materials

• Use felt, flannel, or fleece.

Backing

• Cut materials to size to fit either a piece of cardboard that can be inserted into a large ziplock bag, the top cover of an individual pizza box (inside or out), or the inside lid of a shoe box. Glue down securely and, if necessary, tape around the edges.

Pieces

• You can use simple cut-out shapes (circles, squares, triangles, etc.) or figures related to the story/rhyme/song. They should be large enough for your child to hold and still be able to place on the board. Use fun, bright colors.

Storage

• Keep pieces together by storing them inside the box or bag.

To get started, try *Brown Bear, Brown Bear, What Do You See?* by Bill Martin Jr. or the nursery rhyme "Two Little Blackbirds."

For more ideas, check out *The Flannel Board Storytelling Book* by Judy Sierra (H. W. Wilson, 1997) and *Little Songs for Little Me* by Nancy Stewart (Friends Street Music, 1992).

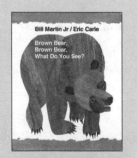

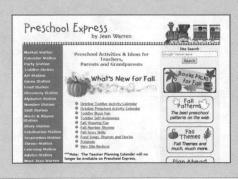

The Preschool Express website at www.preschoolexpress.com is another great place to look.

HANDOUT 9: Flannel-Board Fun by Linda L. Ernst, *The Essential Lapsit Guide*, 2015 © American Library Association.

Fun Rhymes to Share!

Include on the other side of this rhyme sheet information you would like your attendees to know about, for example, upcoming programs, activities in the area, new book titles, more rhymes, etc.

Way Up High in the Apple Tree

Way up high in the apple tree,
(*Hold arms above head,
fingers spread.*)
Two little apples did I see.
(*Make two fists.*)
So I shook that tree as
hard as I could,
(*Shake and wiggle body.*)
And d-o-w-n came the apples.
(*Lower arms.*)
Umm! They were good!
(*Rub tummy.*)

Mother and Father and Uncle John

Mother and Father and
Uncle John went
to town one by one.
Mother fell off.
And Father fell off.
But Uncle John went on and on
and on and on and on!
(*Bounce child on lap,
tipping child to side on "off,"
and lots of bounces on last line.*)

Criss-Cross Applesauce

Criss-cross applesauce,
(*Draw an X on child's back
with finger.*)
Spiders running up your back.
(*Walk fingers up child's back.*)
Cool breeze,
(*Blow gently on child's neck
and back of head.*)
Tight squeeze,
(*Give child a big hug.*)
Now you've got the shivers!
(*Tickle child gently all over.*)

I'm a Little Teapot

I'm a little teapot, short and stout.
Here is my handle;
(*Put one hand on hip.*)
Here is my spout.
(*Put other hand up in the air.*)
When I get all steamed up,
Hear me shout.
Tip me over and pour me out.
(*Bend over at waist to the side
and then stand upright again.*)
I'm a special teapot, it is true.
Here, let me show you
what I can do.
I can change my handle
and my spout.
(*Switch positions of arms.*)
Tip me over and pour me out.
(*Bend to the side at waistline.*)

Jack in the Box

Jack in the box, you sit so still.
(*Kneel on floor with head covered
by arms or hands.*)
Won't you come out? Yes, I will!
(*Pop up on last phrase.*)

Acka Backa

Acka backa soda cracker, Acka backa boo!
(*Rock, swing, or bounce child.*)
Acka backa soda cracker, I love you!
(*Pick up and give child a hug.*)
Acka backa soda cracker, Acka backa boo!
(*Rock, swing, or bounce child.*)
Acka backa soda cracker, Up goes you!
(*Lift child up into the air.*)

The Eency, Weency Spider

The eency, weency spider went up the waterspout.
Down came the rain and washed the spider out!
Out came the sun and dried up all the rain.
And the eency, weency spider went up the spout again!

Hickory, Dickory, Dock

Hickory, dickory, dock,
(*Clasp hands together and swing gently back and forth.*)
The mouse ran up the clock.
(*Run fingers up so hands end up above head.*)
The clock struck one,
(*Clap hands once.*)
The mouse ran down,
(*Bring arms back down in front.*)
Hickory, dickory, dock.
(*Clasp hands and swing gently back and forth.*)
(*You can also run fingers up child's arm and touch nose on "one."*)

Handout Template–Generic

[Title of Program]

Books We Read: _____

_____

_____

_____

Rhymes: _____

_____

_____

_____

Tip: _____

_____

_____

_____

_____

Contact Name _____

Library Information _____

INSERT PICTURE OR LOGO HERE.

_____

HANDOUT 11: Handout Template–Generic by Linda L. Ernst, *The Essential Lapsit Guide*, 2015 © American Library Association.

Handout Template–Stories and Stuff

[Title of Program]

Books we read today: _____

_____

_____

Bouncing rhyme: _____

_____

_____

Tickle rhyme: _____

_____

_____

Bouncing rhyme: _____

_____

_____

 TIP Using rhymes and songs is a great way to help your child learn the names of different body parts! "Head and Shoulders, Knees and Toes" is a fun song to use!

_____

(Presenter's name and contact information)

Interesting Facts and Tips

These suggestions are for your use when creating a mini poster/card for display or as filler on a take-home sheet. Copy them directly or rewrite them using your own words. Find more facts and tips to share with your community in the multiple sources listed in the text and from the newest early literacy information being published today.

General

- Children who are exposed to books early in life have better language skills than those who wait until later.

- Children who are read to three times per week or more do much better in later development than children who are read to less than three times per week.

- Your child does not need worksheets or flash cards to learn to read, but the more time you spend reading and playing sound games with your child will help him or her to learn reading skills.

- Let your child see you reading and writing or find interesting articles in the newspaper to share with him or her.

- Children develop much of their capacity for learning in the first three years of life, when their brains grow to 90 percent of their eventual adult weight.

- Promoting literacy does not mean creating a school-like setting in your home but, rather, taking advantage of the opportunities in your everyday life.

- The development of early literacy skills through early experiences with books and stories is critically linked to a child's success in learning to read.

- Development of literacy is a continuous process that begins at birth and depends heavily on environmental influences.

- Reading to children also impacts their emotional and social development, as they share stories with those they care for. Because brain development and early literacy follow the "use it or lose it" principle, exposure to reading should occur early and often.

- Have books in many different places in your home to show your child that reading is important.

- Keep books down low where your child can see and reach them. Encourage your child to read or pretend to read.

- Introduce yourself and your child to your librarian. Librarians can help you to select the best books that are both fun and suitable for your child's age level. They can also show you the other programs and services the library has to offer.

- In addition to a wealth of books, your library has tapes and CDs of books, musical CDs and tapes, movies, computers that you can use, and many more resources. You also might find books in languages other than English or programs to help adults improve their reading. If you would like reading help for yourself or your family, check with the librarian about literacy programs in your community.

- Reading to a child for thirty minutes per day from infancy helps prepare a child to learn. A five-year-old who has not been read to daily will enter kindergarten with far fewer hours of "literacy nutrition" than a child who has been read to daily from infancy. No teacher, no matter how talented, can make up for those lost hours.

- You are the key to your child's success in learning to read. When you read, talk, or play with your child, you're stimulating the growth of your child's brain and building the connections that will become the building blocks for reading. Brain development research shows that reading aloud to your child every day increases your child's brain's capacity for language and literacy skills and is the most important thing you can do to prepare him or her for learning to read.

Interesting Facts and Tips

Reading

- Reading books to children is a great way to build their vocabulary. Typically, books include a more diverse vocabulary than what we use in everyday conversation.

- Ask your child about the book you are reading together, instead of just having the child listen to you reading the story. This will help your child develop reading comprehension.

- How we read to children is as important as how frequently we read to them. Children learn most from books when they are actively involved. Ask your child lots of questions, pause to let him or her answer each question or finish talking, and then expand on his or her answer.

- Read for just a short time, many times a day. Make books part of your child's everyday life by having them available for his or her use.

- Read to your baby every day. You do not need to read the words; you can just point to the pictures and tell your baby what you see.

- Continue reading with enthusiasm even if your child walks away; he or she will still benefit from hearing the rich language.

- Share a book with your child every day. Make book sharing a positive experience. Share books when you and your child are in a good mood.

- When you are reading a book with your child, do not worry about whether you get to finish the book. If your child loses interest, just continue another time. By following your child's lead, you can make book sharing a positive experience.

- Read a variety of books with your child, both fiction and nonfiction.

- Reading aloud to children is the single most important activity for developing their literacy skills, according to a 1985 study by the National Commission on Reading.

- Before you start reading a book with your child, introduce the book. Read the title and the author's and illustrator's names. Look at the cover. Talk about what the book might be about. Suggest things to look and listen for. This will help your child develop essential early literacy skills.

- Make reading a part of every day. You can read at bedtime, after lunch, on the bus, or just take a story break.

- Have fun! Children who love books learn to read. Books can be part of special time with your child.

- Talk about the pictures. You do not have to read the book to tell a story.

- When you share books that include a repetitive or predictable phrase, pause and wait so your child can say the word that ends this phrase. This will help your child develop narrative skills.

- Read from a variety of children's books, including fairy tales, song books, poems, and information books.

Singing

- Singing songs and rhymes with your child is a great way to help him or her develop phonological awareness. Libraries have CDs and books with rhymes that you can check out.

- Begin talking and singing to your baby from birth. Your baby loves hearing your voice.

- Do fingerplays and songs like "The Eency Weency Spider" and "Where Is Thumbkin?" with your child. Libraries have books and CDs of fingerplays that you can check out. Sharing them with your child helps him or her develop phonological awareness.

- Simply singing with a child helps to connect neural pathways and increases the child's ability to retain information; in other words, it builds memory.

- Children and adults have favorite songs. Repeating these same songs gives children security and memories that can be called on to comfort for a lifetime.

- Songs naturally divide words into syllables and sounds, so they are internalized. The built-in repetition and rhyme increase understanding and retention.

Interesting Facts and Tips

Talking

- Pointing out print around you will help your child develop the print awareness, an essential early literacy skill. You can point out the signs in the library, at the grocery store, and while driving.

- Point out familiar pictures and name them; that's how your child's vocabulary grows.

- If you are more fluent in a language other than English, research shows that it is best for you to speak to your child in the language you know best.

- When you share books with the sounds of animals and other things, you help children develop their phonological awareness, an essential early literacy skill.

- Let your child ask questions about the story. Use the story as an opportunity to engage in conversation and to talk about familiar activities and objects.

- When you engage your child in conversation, you are helping him or her develop essential early literacy skills.

Writing

- Have your child be an author and illustrator. Encourage your child to make up his or her own story, dictate it to you, and draw the pictures to go with it.

- Follow up on the story. Invite your child to talk about, draw, paint, or pretend to be one of the characters in the story.

- The first letter of a child's first name is very important to him or her and is often the first letter the child will recognize. Make sure the writing surface is big because young children are still working on their fine-motor skills, and they use full arm movements when writing.

Playing

- You can help your child get ready to read by cooking with him or her. The library has cookbooks for children. You can show your child how to read a recipe and read the labels on the ingredients together.

- Follow up on the story. Invite your child to talk about, draw, paint, or pretend to be one of the characters in the story.

- To help your child develop letter knowledge, let him or her make letter shapes out WWof playdough or dim the lights and let him or her trace letter shapes on the wall with a flashlight.

Quotes to Remember

The single most significant factor influencing a child's early educational success is an introduction to books and being read to at home prior to beginning school.

–Richard C. Anderson and others, *Becoming a Nation of Readers: The Report of the Commission on Reading* (Center for the Study on Reading, 1985)

Although many experiences are said to contribute to early literacy, no other single activity is regarded as important as the shared book experience between caregivers and children.

–Susan B. Neuman, "Books Make a Difference: A Study of Access to Literacy" (*Reading Research Quarterly* 34, no. 3 [July–September 1999]: 286–311)

The relationship between the skills with which children enter a school and their later academic performance is strikingly stable. For instance, research has shown that there is nearly a 90% probability that a child will remain a poor reader at the end of the fourth grade if the child is a poor reader at the end of the first grade. Further, knowledge of alphabet letters at entry into kindergarten is a strong predictor of reading ability in 10th grade.

–Ernest L. Boyer, *Ready to Learn: A Mandate for the Nation* (Jossey-Bass, 1991)

Children who are read to three or more times a week are nearly twice as likely as other children to show three or more skills associated with emerging literacy.

–Christine W. Nord and others, "Home Literacy Activities and Signs of Children's Emerging Literacy" (*Statistics in Brief*, November 1999)

 HANDOUT 13: Interesting Facts and Tips by Linda L. Ernst, *The Essential Lapsit Guide*, 2015 © American Library Association.

Program Descriptions
for Publicity Flyers

Tickles, songs, and a short story
introduce very young children and their caregivers to the rhythm of words.
Bring a blanket to sit on and join us!

Join us for a story or two, rhymes, tickles, bounces, and bubbles.
This program is for children under 24 months with their caregivers.
Babies welcome!

Enjoy interactive storytelling and experience new ways of sharing picture books.
Children will develop essential early literacy skills as they and their caregivers
play through creative moment, music, and action rhymes.

Super stories and songs just for toddlers.
Lots of wiggling and giggling guaranteed!

Welcome little ones!
Enjoy stories, signs, puppets, movement, and music
designed specifically for new walkers.

Come join us as we explore the world of words
with stories, songs, rhymes, and more
in this special storytime with the very young child in mind!
Children ages 24 months and younger with their caregivers are invited.

Program Guidelines Bookmarks

Storytime Tips

Welcome to storytime—an early literacy experience you and your child share that is lots of fun!

- I don't expect the children to sit still, but I do expect you to keep them safe.
- If you and your child need a moment to "regroup," feel free to step out of the room and come back when you're ready. Some days are like that.
- We have time after class to talk and snack, so please wait till then so we can focus on the fun stuff.
- The big people take part—the more involved you are with your child and our program, the more fun it will be for everyone!

Have fun!

[Library Name]

[Website]

[Librarian's Name]

[Contact Info]

LOGO/ CLIPART

Storytime Tips

Welcome to storytime—an early literacy experience you and your child share that is lots of fun!

- I don't expect the children to sit still, but I do expect you to keep them safe.
- If you and your child need a moment to "regroup," feel free to step out of the room and come back when you're ready. Some days are like that.
- We have time after class to talk and snack, so please wait till then so we can focus on the fun stuff.
- The big people take part—the more involved you are with your child and our program, the more fun it will be for everyone!

Have fun!

[Library Name]

[Website]

[Librarian's Name]

[Contact Info]

LOGO/ CLIPART

Storytime Tips

Welcome to storytime—an early literacy experience you and your child share that is lots of fun!

- I don't expect the children to sit still, but I do expect you to keep them safe.
- If you and your child need a moment to "regroup," feel free to step out of the room and come back when you're ready. Some days are like that.
- We have time after class to talk and snack, so please wait till then so we can focus on the fun stuff.
- The big people take part—the more involved you are with your child and our program, the more fun it will be for everyone!

Have fun!

[Library Name]

[Website]

[Librarian's Name]

[Contact Info]

LOGO/ CLIPART

Program Guidelines Poster

Welcome Everybody!
How do you do?
This is a special library time just for you!

A few guidelines to keep in mind during our program:

Get Involved!
Parent participation is key to the success of this program! Your cooperation is important. Join in the activities and show your child that it is fun!

Please put toys and foods away and silence cell phones.
These may distract the children from the program. Something such as breast-feeding we understand, but please be discreet.

Save your comments for after the program.
You will probably have lots to share with the other adults. Your sharing time comes afterward. We like to do the program first, when the children are fresh.

Be considerate of others.
If your child is crying loudly or otherwise distracting the group, or in another way losing control, please feel free to step out and "regroup." Talk to me if you are unsure or concerned about your child's behavior.

Relax!
It is not expected that your child will sit still and participate in all the activities. Our goal is to have fun with rhymes, songs, books, and other language-building play.

_____   _____
[Librarian's Name]

_____   _____
[Library Name]

_____   _____
[E-mail address]   [Library/Library System's Information
                                          (name, address, etc.)]

Reading Aloud to Little Ones

Things to remember:

- It starts with YOU!
- Let your child see you reading at home.
- Have reading materials around the house.
- Make the time to share a story, rhyme, etc., with your child.
- Talk to your child about what is going on around him or her.
- Have fun with language and read with expression.
- Make the moment a comfortable one for you and your child.
- Let your child see how special books are by the way you handle them.

When selecting books, remember:

- Pick stories you like to hear because you'll end up reading them again and again.
- Encourage your child to point to the pictures and talk about them together.
- Select stories that have rhythm.
- Choose books with artwork that is bright, clear, and with white space for resting eyes.

Remember that your little one:

- May like to select the story for himself or herself.
- May only listen to a little at first, but will get better.
- Needs the adult to share the book with him or her; otherwise, it's just a toy.

Stories to Share:

Big Fat Hen .... by Keith Baker

Brown Bear, Brown Bear, What Do You See? .... by Bill Martin Jr.

Down on the Farm .... by Merrily Kutner

The Little Mouse, the Red Ripe Strawberry, and the Big Hungry Bear .... by Don and Audrey Wood

Little Robin Redbreast .... by Shari Halpern

"More More More," Said the Baby .... by Vera B. Williams

On Mother's Lap .... by Ann Herbert Scott

Sam Who Never Forgets .... by Eve Rice

Tickle, Tickle .... by Helen Oxenbury

Where's Spot? .... by Eric Hill

 HANDOUT 17: Reading Aloud to Little Ones by Linda L. Ernst, *The Essential Lapsit Guide*, 2015 © American Library Association.

Rhyme Booklet, Page 1

Storytime Rhymes

Print on one side of 8.5-by-11-inch paper; print Rhyme Booklet Back on the other side of the same sheet. Cut the sheet horizontally along the dotted line, stack the two sheets, fold vertically, and then trim off excess margin space as needed.

I went to the library today and had a great time!

[Library Name]   [Date]

Name:

Age:

My Favorites:

Song:

Rhyme:

Tickle:

Book:

Storytime Rhymes

Hickory, Dickory, Dock

Hickory, dickory, dock,

The mouse ran up
the clock.

The clock struck one,

The mouse ran down,

Hickory, dickory, dock.

Little Bo Peep

Little Bo Peep

Has lost her sheep

And doesn't know where
to find them.

Leave them alone

And they'll come home,

Wagging their tails behind them.

Rhyme Booklet, Page 2

This Little Piggy

This little piggy
went to market.

This little piggy
stayed home.

This little piggy
had roast beef

And this little piggy
had none.

And this little piggy ran
wee, wee, wee, wee, wee,
All the way home!

Humpty Dumpty

Humpty Dumpty sat on a wall.

Humpty Dumpty had a great fall.

All the king's horses
and all the king's men

Couldn't put Humpty
together again.

Hey, Diddle, Diddle

Hey, diddle, diddle,

The cat and the fiddle,

The cow jumped over the moon.

The little dog laughed
to see such sport,

And the dish ran away with
the spoon.

To Market, to Market

To market, to market,
to buy a fat pig,

Home again, home again,
jiggity jig.

To market, to market,
to buy a fat hog,

Home again, home again,
jiggity jog.

 HANDOUT 19: Rhyme Booklet, Page 2 by Linda L. Ernst, *The Essential Lapsit Guide*, 2015 © American Library Association.

Sick Sign

DON'T FEEL GOOD?

Help keep storytime a happy, healthy experience.

Please keep sick children home until they feel better.

[Library information]

Things That Go

Rhymes/Songs

- "Bumping Downtown in My Little Red Wagon"
- "Down by the Station"
- "I've Been Working on the Railroad"
- "Row, Row, Row Your Boat"
- "To Market, to Market"
- "Wheels on the Bus"

Things to Do!

- Use a large laundry basket as a car, boat, train, or other vehicle, and let your child "go somewhere."
- Give your child a box or laundry basket that he or she can push with a doll or toy in it and move it from one place to another.
- While driving, play tour guide for your child and describe what you see.
- Use a magnetic picture album to create a book about things that go from pictures in magazines.
- Take a bus or ferry ride.
- Whatever you do, remember to take along foods/drinks that can go too!

Books:

Freight Train .... by Donald Crews

Sheep in a Jeep .... by Nancy Shaw

Chugga-Chugga Choo-Choo .... by Kevin Lewis

Author/Title Index

A

The ABC Bunny (Gag), 76, 91, 108, 111, 151, 161, 209

"Ábranlas, Ciérrenlas" (Open, Shut Them), 117, 136, 164, 165, 166, 168, 169

"Acka Backa," 117, 157, 169, 237

Across the Stream (Ginsburg), 76, 91, 97, 99, 113, 151, 153, 156

Adler, Victoria, 67, 94, 96, 111

"Airplanes Fly in the Sky," 161

Alborough, Jez, 68, 92, 100, 112, 113

"All around the Mulberry Bush," 117, 158, 159, 160, 162

All Fall Down (Oxenbury), 168

All of Baby Nose to Toes (Adler), 67, 94, 96, 111

All You Need for a Snowman (Schertle), 86, 107, 110, 114

Allen, Jonathan, 68, 95, 96, 107, 154

Anderson, Peggy Perry, 68, 92, 101, 111, 113

Animals Speak (Prap), 85, 91, 111

"Arabella Miller," 158

Asch, Frank, 68, 95, 100, 101, 154, 156

Ask Mr. Bear (Flack), 74, 91, 95, 96, 102, 105, 151, 153, 155, 156, 189

B

"Baa, Baa, Black Sheep," 118, 152, 161

Baby Faces (Miller), 83, 94, 96, 99

Baby Loves (Lawrence), 81, 94, 99, 100, 156

Baby Says "Moo!" (Macken), 82, 91, 111, 168

"Baby's Nap," 119, 154

The Baby Record (McGrath and Smithrim), 115, 152

Baicker, Karen, 68, 99, 100

Baker, Keith, 68, 97, 99, 106, 108, 111, 156, 246

"Ball for Baby," 119, 162

Bang, Molly, 68, 95, 99, 106, 112, 154

Barnyard Banter (Fleming), 74, 91, 94, 101, 109, 111, 151

Barry, Francis, 68, 98, 100, 156

Bear Snores On (Wilson), 90, 91, 95, 102, 109, 114

"Bear Went over the Mountain," 154, 164

"Beehive," 119

Beetle Bop (Fleming), 74, 96, 111

Bell, Babs, 69, 92, 102, 112, 161, 189

"Bend and Stretch," 119

Berger, Barbara, 69, 95, 154

Big Fat Hen (Baker), 68, 97, 99, 106, 108, 111, 156, 246

The Big Storm: A Very Soggy Counting Book (Tafuri), 87, 91, 99, 106, 108, 113, 114, 166

"Bingo," 119, 152, 155

Birds (Henkes), 77, 96, 154

Bloom, Suzanne, 69, 94, 95, 96, 97, 103, 108, 112

Blue Goose (Tafuri), 87, 91, 98, 101

Blue Sea (Kalan), 80, 98, 102, 110, 113, 153, 166, 189

Blue Sky (Wood), 90, 98, 99, 106, 109, 114, 163

Book! Book! Book! (Bruss), 70, 92, 96, 101, 111

Bornstein, Ruth, 69, 93, 94, 96, 103, 110, 152, 154, 155

Boynton, Sandra, 69, 92, 95, 112, 151, 154

Braun, Sebastien, 69–70, 93, 95, 97, 104, 106, 108, 111, 113

The Bridge Is Up! (Bell), 69, 92, 102, 112, 161, 189

Brown Bear, Brown Bear, What Do You See? (Martin), 24, 58, 59, 66, 82, 92, 98, 102, 107, 108, 109, 110, 111, 151, 164, 165, 166, 167, 169, 189, 209, 236, 246

Brown , Margaret Wise, 65, 70, 92, 95, 100, 102, 108, 112, 151, 154, 156, 160, 209
Browne, Anthony, 70, 92, 96, 105, 160
Bruss, Deborah, 70, 92, 96, 101, 111
"Bump'n Downtown in My Little Red Wagon," 162, 166, 167, 250
The Bus for Us (Bloom), 69, 97, 112
The Busy Little Squirrel (Tafuri), 87, 92, 100, 109, 110, 114
Butler, John, 70, 94, 108
Butterworth, Nick, 70, 97, 113, 162, 167

C

Can You Make a Scary Face? (Thomas), 88, 92, 96, 102, 103
Can You Moo? (Wojtowycz), 90, 92, 111
Carle, Eric, 71, 92, 94, 96, 98, 100, 106, 107, 109, 111, 114, 151, 158, 163
Carlson, Nancy, 71, 92, 103, 107, 160
The Carrot Seed (Krauss), 80, 103, 158, 166, 189
Carter, David, 71, 93, 103, 105, 106, 109, 110, 111, 112, 152, 162, 165, 179, 182
Cat the Cat, Who Is That? (Willems), 89, 92, 97, 102
"Catch Me and Kiss Me and Say It Again," 153
Catch Me and Kiss Me and Say It Again (Watson), 24, 156, 160, 162, 167, 209
Caterpillar's Wish (Murphy), 84, 96, 97, 109, 111
Cauley, Lorinda Bryan, 71, 106, 107, 112, 162
"Charlie over the Water," 153
Chick (Vere), 89, 92, 97, 105
Chicka Chicka, Boom Boom (Martin), 209
The Chick and the Duckling (Suteyev), 87, 91, 92, 97, 99, 151, 156
Chicky Chicky Chook Chook (MacLennan), 82, 92, 97, 101, 109, 111, 114, 158, 165
"Choo-Choo Train," 120, 161
Chorao, Kay, 71, 107, 108
Chuck's Truck (Anderson), 68, 92, 101, 111, 113
Chugga-Chugga Choo-Choo (Lewis), 81, 112, 113, 161, 162, 250
Church, Caroline, 71, 93, 95, 105, 106
Cimarusti, Marie Torres, 72, 93, 101, 103, 104, 111, 152, 162, 168

"Cinco Calabacitas" (Five Little Pumpkins), 120, 123
"Clap Your Hands," 121, 165, 168
Clap Your Hands (Cauley), 71, 106, 107, 112, 162
Clip-Clop (Smee), 86, 92, 101, 102, 104, 108, 165
"Cobbler, Cobbler," 121, 159, 165, 168, 171
Come Along, Daisy! (Simmons), 86, 91, 99, 100, 105, 156
"Come'a Look'a See, Here's My Mama," 157
Cony, Frances, 72, 93, 94, 101, 105, 110, 151
Costello, David Hyde, 72, 92, 103
Cousins, Lucy, 72, 93, 97, 98, 100, 101, 102, 105, 106, 107, 109, 112, 113, 161
Cowell, Cressida, 72, 94, 95, 103
The Cow Loves Cookies (Wilson), 90, 99, 101, 102, 157
Craig, Lindsey, 72–73, 92, 94, 95, 100, 101, 106, 108, 112, 151, 154
Crews, Donald, 73, 98, 102, 113, 161, 165, 189, 250
"Criss-Cross Applesauce," 121, 157, 159, 165, 166, 167, 170, 237
Cronin, Doreen, 73, 93, 106, 111
"Cup of Tea," 157

D

"Dance to your Daddy," 121, 161
Dancing Feet! (Craig), 72, 92, 100, 106, 108
Demarest, Chris L., 73, 92, 94, 100, 101, 105, 111, 151, 156
"Did You Ever See a Pumpkin?," 170
"Do You Know the Muffin Man," 157, 159
Dodd, Emma, 73, 96, 112
Dog Wants to Play (McDonnell), 83, 92, 99, 101, 102, 103, 112, 155, 162
Dogs (Gravett), 77, 92, 98, 99, 107
"Dos Pajaritos" (Two Little Birds), 121, 154
"Down at the Station," 122, 161, 250
Down on the Farm (Kutner), 80, 92, 101, 107, 111, 167, 246
"Dr. Foster," 163
"Drums," 122, 162
Duck and Goose Find a Pumpkin (Hills), 78, 92, 99, 100, 108, 109, 154, 163
Duck in the Truck (Alborough), 68, 92, 100, 112, 113
Duckie's Splash (Barry), 68, 98, 100, 156

E

"The Eency Weency Spider," 122, 237
Ehlert, Lois, 73, 100, 110, 112, 114
"An Elephant Goes Like This and That," 152, 165
Elgar, Rebecca, 73, 92, 94, 100, 103, 105, 108, 109, 152, 162, 165
Eliot, Lise, 7
Emberley, Ed, 73, 98, 104, 170, 189
"The Engine," 122, 161

F

Farmyard Beat (Craig), 73, 94, 95, 101, 106, 112, 151, 154
Faulkner, Keith, 65, 74, 94, 102, 103, 105, 157
"Fee-Fi-Fo-Fum," 122
Fernandes, Eugenie, 74, 93, 97, 100, 101, 102, 110, 111, 112
Ferri, Francesca, 74, 93, 101, 103, 104
The First Snowfall (Rockwell and Rockwell), 85, 98, 110, 114
"Fishies," 123, 153
"Five Little Boats," 161
Five Little Chicks (Tafuri), 87, 92, 97, 101
Five Little Ducks (Raffi), 85, 99, 100, 106, 110, 156, 179, 182
"Five Little Ducks Went Out One Day," 156
"Five Little Pigs," 160
"Five Little Pumpkins" (Cinco Calabacitas), 120, 123
"Five Plump Peas," 123, 157, 158, 167
The Five Little Pumpkins (Van Rynbach), 89, 104, 109, 112, 163, 189
Flack, Marjorie, 74, 91, 95, 96, 102, 105, 151, 154, 155, 156, 189
Fleming, Denise, 74–75, 91, 92, 93, 94, 95, 96, 97, 98, 100, 101, 102, 104, 105, 107, 109, 111, 112, 113, 151, 153, 157, 158, 159, 163, 189, 226
Fox, Mem, 75, 94, 95, 96, 98, 99, 101, 106, 110, 112, 154, 161, 166, 209
Freight Train (Crews), 73, 98, 102, 113, 161, 165, 189, 250
From Head to Toe (Carle), 71, 92, 100, 106, 107, 151
"From Wibbleton to Wobbleton," 124

G

"Gack-Goon," 124, 153, 158
Gag, Wanda, 76, 91, 108, 111, 151, 160, 209

Galdone, Paul, 76, 93, 97, 103, 114
Garcia, Emma, 76, 98, 111, 113
George, Lindsay Barrett, 76, 93, 99, 103, 108, 113, 162, 165
"Georgie Porgie," 157
Gibbs, Edward, 209
Ginsburg, Mirra, 76, 91, 92, 94, 97, 99, 101, 113, 151, 153, 156
Giving (Hughes), 79, 103, 110
Go Away, Big Green Monster! (Emberley), 73, 98, 104, 170, 189
"Going on a Bear Hunt," 154
The Golden Egg Book (Brown), 70, 92, 100, 102, 108, 151, 156, 161
A Good Day (Henkes), 78, 92, 96, 99, 102, 154, 155
Good Morning, Chick (Ginsburg), 76, 92, 94, 97, 101
Good Night, Good Night (Boynton), 69, 92, 95, 112, 154
Goodnight Moon (Brown), 65, 70, 95, 108, 112, 154, 161, 209
"The Grand Old Duke of York," 124, 161, 198, 201
Grandfather Twilight (Berger), 69, 95, 154
Gravett, Emily, 77, 92, 98, 99, 107
Gray, Nigel, 77, 101, 104, 108, 112, 162
"Gray Squirrel," 124, 152, 158
"The Great Big Spider," 125, 153, 158, 163, 166, 167, 168, 170

H

Hacohen, Dean, 77, 94, 95, 104, 154
Hale, Sarah Josepha, 77, 108, 110, 112, 161, 167
Hall, Michael, 77, 93, 98, 99, 102, 106, 110, 114
Halpern, Shari, 77, 96, 97, 108, 112, 154, 246
"Happy Birthday to You," 155
A Hat for Minerva Louise (Stoeke), 87, 92, 97, 98, 101, 109, 114
Have You Seen My Duckling? (Tafuri), 87, 91, 100, 105, 113, 153, 156, 226
"Head and Shoulders, Knees and Toes," 24, 125, 155, 159, 166, 167, 168, 170
Hello, Day! (Lobel), 82, 92, 101, 111
Henkes, Kevin, 77–78, 92, 93, 95, 96, 97, 98, 99, 102, 104, 105, 106, 108, 109, 110, 114, 154, 155
"Here Are Baby's Fingers," 159

Here Are My Hands (Martin), 82, 96, 112
"Here Comes a Mouse," 24, 125, 156, 160, 162, 167
"Here Comes the Choo-Choo Train," 161
"Here Is a Beehive," 125, 158
"Here Is a Bunny," 126, 152, 161, 167
"Here Is a Choo-Choo Train," 126, 161
"Here Is a Nest for a Robin," 152, 154, 161
"Here is Baby," 126
"Here Is the Engine," 126, 161, 189
"Here We Go 'round the Mulberry Bush," 200
"Here We Go Up-Up-Up," 127, 162, 165
"Here's a Ball," 127, 162, 164
"Here's a Cup," 127, 155
"Hey, Diddle, Diddle," 127, 155, 248
"Hickety, Pickety, My Black Hen," 128, 154, 156
"Hickory, Dickory, Dock," 23, 128, 152, 156, 160, 162, 164, 165, 166, 167, 237, 247
Hill, Eric, 78, 99, 104, 105, 108, 109, 155, 166, 246
Hillenbrand, Will, 78, 93, 103, 109, 111
Hills, Tad, 78, 92, 99, 100, 108, 109, 154, 163
Hoban, Tana, 209
"Hokey Pokey!," 168, 200
Home for a Bunny (Brown), 70, 92, 102, 108, 161
Honk! (Demarest), 73, 92, 94, 100, 101, 105, 111, 151, 156
Hooray for Fish! (Cousins), 72, 102, 106, 112
Hopgood, Tim, 79, 96, 98, 107
Horáček, Petr, 79, 93, 94, 104, 105, 159
"Hot Cross Buns," 157
How Kind! (Murphy), 84, 92, 101, 104
"How Much is That Doggie in the Window?," 128, 156
Hubbell, Patricia, 79, 95, 103, 104, 106, 108, 111, 157, 159, 162
Hughes, Shirley, 79, 103, 110
"Humpty Dumpty," 23, 128, 157, 159, 162, 165, 166, 168, 248
Hutchins, Pat, 79, 101, 103, 113, 158, 162, 167

I

I Can Do It Too! (Baicker), 68, 99, 100
I Can Help (Costello), 72, 92, 103
"I Hear Thunder," 129, 163, 166
I Kissed the Baby! (Murphy), 84, 94, 99
I Like Books (Browne), 70, 92, 96, 105, 160

I Like It When . . . (Murphy), 84, 96, 105
I Like Me! (Carlson), 71, 92, 103, 107, 160
I Love Animals (McDonnell), 83, 92, 94, 101, 151
I Love Bugs! (Dodd), 73, 112
I Spy on the Farm (Gibbs), 209
I Went Walking (Williams), 89, 91, 92, 94, 107, 108, 109, 112, 158, 189
If You're Happy and You Know It, Clap Your Hands! A Pop-Up Book (Carter), 71, 105, 106, 109, 110, 112, 165, 179, 182
"If You're Happy and You Know It," 129, 155, 166, 169, 171
If You're Hoppy (Sayre), 86, 92, 106, 110, 112
"If You're Wearing Red Today," 129, 159
"I'll Drive a Dump Truck," 129, 162
"I'm a Little Teapot," 130, 153, 155, 157, 168, 237
I'm Not Sleepy (Allen), 68, 95, 96, 107, 154
In the Small, Small Pond (Fleming), 74, 92, 107, 109, 112, 113, 151, 153, 158, 163, 226
In the Tall, Tall Grass (Fleming), 75, 91, 92, 96, 107, 112, 151, 158
Is That an Elephant Over There? (Elgar), 73, 92, 94, 100, 103, 105, 108, 109, 162, 165
Isadora, Rachel, 79, 95, 99, 101, 103, 106
It's My Birthday! (Oxenbury), 84, 92, 96, 99, 102, 103, 155
"It's Raining, It's Pouring," 130, 163
"I've Been Working on the Railroad," 250

J

"Jack and Jill," 130, 153
"Jack Be Nimble," 130, 154, 162
"Jack in the Box," 131, 162, 164, 165, 167, 237
"Jeremiah, Blow the Fire," 131
"Johnny Hammers One Hammer," 131, 162
Jonas, Ann, 79, 93, 99, 106, 114
Jump, Frog, Jump! (Kalan), 80, 92, 103, 107, 108, 109, 113, 153
Just Like Daddy (Asch), 68, 95, 100, 101, 153, 156
Just Like Jasper! (Butterworth), 70, 97, 113, 162, 167

K

Kalan, Robert, 80, 92, 98, 102, 103, 107, 108, 109, 110, 113, 114, 153, 163, 166, 189
Katz, Karen, 80, 95, 98, 103, 104

A Kiss Like This (Murphy), 84, 93, 102, 105, 156

A Kitten's Tale (Rohann), 85, 93, 97, 108, 109, 110, 114

Kitten's Autumn (Fernandes), 74, 93, 97, 100, 101, 102, 110, 111

Kitten's First Full Moon (Henkes), 78, 97, 105, 106

Kitten's Spring (Fernandes), 74, 93, 97, 101, 110, 111, 112

Kitty Cat, Kitty Cat, Are You Waking Up? (Martin), 82, 93, 97, 99, 112, 155

Knock at the Door and Other Baby Action Rhymes (Chorao), 71, 107, 108

Knock! Knock! (Tidholm), 88, 98, 111

Kraus, Robert, 80, 91, 95, 101, 103, 105, 157, 159

Krauss, Ruth, 80, 158, 166, 189

Kuskin, Karla, 80, 98, 102, 108, 109, 114, 189

Kutner, Merrily, 80, 92, 101, 107, 112, 167, 246

L

Langstaff, John, 81, 91, 93, 99, 106, 110, 112, 151, 152, 179, 182, 189

Lawrence, Michael, 81, 94, 99, 100, 156

Lear, Edward, 81, 93, 96, 97, 107, 108, 112, 152, 154

"Leg Over Leg," 131, 152, 156, 165, 166

"Let Everyone Clap Hands Like Me," 162

Let's Go Visiting (Williams), 89, 93, 94, 99, 106, 109, 112, 189

Lewis, Kevin, 81, 112, 113, 161, 162, 250

Lewison, Wendy Cheyette, 81, 109, 112, 114, 163

Light, Steve, 81, 111, 113, 161

"Little Bo Peep," 247

"Little Boy Blue," 131, 152, 161

Little Cloud (Carle), 71, 98, 109, 114, 163

Little Gorilla (Bornstein), 69, 93, 94, 96, 103, 110, 155

"Little Miss Muffet," 132

The Little Mouse, the Red Ripe Strawberry, and the Big Hungry Bear (Wood and Wood), 90, 95, 102, 104, 154, 157, 159, 164, 166, 246

The Little Red Hen (Galdone), 76, 93, 97, 103, 114

Little Robin Redbreast: A Mother Goose Rhyme (Halpern), 77, 96, 97, 108, 112, 154, 246

Little Songs for Little Me (Stewart), 182

Little Tug (Savage), 85, 113, 161

"Little Turtle," 132, 152, 153, 158

"Little White Duck," 154

Little White Duck (Whippo), 89, 93, 106, 110, 179

Little White Rabbit (Henkes), 78, 93, 98, 104, 108

Litwin, Eric, 82, 93, 97, 98, 104, 106, 107, 110, 155, 159

Lobel, Anita, 82, 92, 101, 111

"London Bridge Is Falling Down," 132, 201

"Lots of Cars," 24, 133, 162

Lunch (Fleming), 75, 98, 102, 104, 105, 157, 159, 189

M

Macken, JoAnn Early, 82, 91, 111, 168

MacLennan, Cathy, 82, 92, 96, 97, 101, 109, 111, 114, 158, 165

Maggie's Ball (George), 76, 93, 99, 103, 108, 113, 162, 165

Maisy Dresses Up (Cousins), 72, 93, 98, 100, 105, 107, 109, 159

Maisy Drives the Bus (Cousins), 72, 93, 96, 105, 113, 161

Maisy's Morning on the Farm (Cousins), 72, 93, 101, 104

Mama Cat Has Three Kittens (Fleming), 75, 94, 97, 100, 105

Mama's Little Bears (Tafuri), 88, 91, 93, 95, 100, 105, 108, 153

"Mama's Taking Us to the Zoo Tomorrow," 153

Martin, Bill, Jr., 24, 58, 59, 66, 82–83, 92, 93, 96, 97, 98, 99, 102, 107, 108, 109, 110, 111, 112, 151, 155, 158, 164, 165, 166, 167, 169, 189, 191, 209, 236, 246

"Mary Had a Little Lamb," 133, 152, 161

Mary Had a Little Lamb (Hale), 77, 108, 110, 112, 161, 167

"Mary, Mary, Quite Contrary," 133, 158

McDonnell, Christine, 83, 92, 99, 101, 102, 103, 112, 155, 162

McDonnell, Flora, 83, 92, 94, 100, 101, 108, 114, 151, 152, 153, 226

McGrath, Bob, 115, 152

Meeow and the Big Box (Braun), 69, 93, 97, 104, 106, 113

Meeow and the Pots and Pans (Braun), 70, 108, 111

Menchin, Scott, 73, 93, 106, 111

Miller, Margaret, 83, 94, 95, 96, 99, 107, 209

Miller, Virginia, 83, 93, 94, 95, 99, 100, 106, 109

Millions of Snowflakes (Siddals), 86, 102, 110, 112, 114, 189

"Mix a Pancake," 155

Mommies Say Shh! (Polacco), 85, 93, 105

"More More More," Said the Baby (Williams), 90, 94, 100, 157, 246

More Singable Songs (Raffi), 170, 198

"The More We Get Together," 133, 164, 165, 166, 167, 168, 171

"Mother and Father and Uncle John," 134, 157, 165, 169, 237

"Motor Boat," 134, 202

Mouse's First Fall (Thompson), 88, 93, 100, 103, 105, 108, 109, 159

Mouse's First Snow (Thompson), 88, 93, 105, 109, 110, 114

Mouse's First Spring (Thompson), 88, 93, 105, 109, 111

Mr. Cookie Baker (Wellington), 89, 102, 106

"Mr. Turkey and Mr. Duck," 134, 152, 154, 156, 164, 166

"The Muffin Man," 155

Murphy, Mary, 84, 92, 93, 94, 96, 97, 99, 101, 102, 104, 105, 109, 111, 156

Murray, Alison, 84, 99, 112, 155

My Heart Is Like a Zoo (Hall), 77, 93, 98, 99, 102, 106, 110, 114

My Many Colored Days (Seuss), 86, 98, 102, 112, 189

"My Pony Macaroni," 134, 166

"My Wiggles," 135

N

A New House for Mouse (Horáček), 79, 93, 94, 104, 105, 159

O

Oh, A-Hunting We Will Go (Langstaff), 81, 91, 93, 110, 112, 151, 179, 189

Oh! (Henkes), 78, 93, 108, 109, 110, 114

Old Bear (Henkes), 78, 93, 95, 109

"Old MacDonald Had a Farm," 135, 152, 165, 167, 189

Old MacDonald Had a Farm (Cony), 72, 93, 94, 101, 105, 110, 151

On Mother's Lap (Scott), 86, 94, 100, 105, 157, 168, 246

On Our Way Home (Braun), 70, 93, 95

"One, Two," 135

"One, Two, Buckle My Shoe," 136, 154, 156

"1, 2, 3, 4, 5, I Caught a Fish Alive," 23, 136, 153, 166, 167, 168, 170, 226

One More Hug for Madison (Church), 71, 93, 95, 105, 106

One Two That's My Shoe! (Murray), 84, 99, 112, 155

"Open, Shut Them" (Ábranlas, Ciérrenlas), 117, 136, 164, 165, 166, 168, 169

Over in the Meadow (Langstaff), 81, 93, 99, 106, 110, 112, 151, 182, 189

The Owl and the Pussycat (Lear), 81, 93, 96, 97, 107, 108, 112, 151, 154

Owl Babies (Waddell), 89, 96, 102, 105, 107

Oxenbury, Helen, 84, 92, 95, 96, 99, 102, 103, 155, 157, 168, 246

P

"Pancake," 137, 157

Patricelli, Leslie, 84, 98, 102, 107

"Patty Cake, Patty Cake," 137, 155, 157, 159, 164, 165, 169, 198

"Pease Porridge Hot," 137, 155, 158

Peek-a-Boo (Ferri), 74, 93, 101, 103, 104

Peek-a-Moo! (Cimarusti), 72, 93, 101, 103, 104, 111, 151, 162, 168

Peekaboo Morning (Isadora), 79, 95, 99, 103, 106

Perfect Square (Hall), 77, 98, 102, 110

Pete the Cat: I Love My White Shoes (Litwin), 82, 93, 97, 98, 104, 106, 107, 110, 155, 159

Peterson, Mary, 85, 91, 98, 101, 107, 160

Piggies in the Pumpkin Patch (Peterson and Rofé), 85, 91, 98, 101, 107, 160

Piggies (Wood and Wood), 90, 95, 96, 103, 107, 154, 160, 162, 165

"Plant a Little Seed," 137, 152, 158, 167

Plant a Little Seed (Stewart), 24, 183

Polacco, Patricia, 85, 93, 105, 111

"Pop! Goes the Weasel," 23, 137, 201

"Popcorn," 138, 201

Pots and Pans (Hubbell), 79, 95, 103, 104, 106, 108, 111, 157, 159, 162

Prap, Lila, 85, 91, 111

Prelutsky, Jack, 209

Pumpkin Trouble (Thomas), 88, 93, 100, 101, 104, 105, 107

"Pussy Cat, Pussy Cat," 138, 153, 156, 160

R

Raffi, 85, 99, 100, 106, 110, 156, 170, 179, 182, 198

"Rain Is Falling Down," 138, 153, 163, 165, 166, 171, 202

Rain (Kalan), 80, 98, 108, 109, 114, 163

"Rain on the Green Grass," 138, 163

"Rain, Rain, Go Away," 138, 153, 163, 202

Raindrop, Plop! (Lewison), 81, 109, 112, 114, 163

"Reach for the Ceiling," 139

Read-Aloud Poems for the Very Young (Prelutsky), 209

Red Light, Green Light (Suen), 87, 96, 112, 113

Rice, Eve, 85, 93, 100, 102, 114, 152, 157, 165, 246

"Ride a Cock Horse," 139

"Ride, Baby, Ride," 139

"Riding on My Pony," 140

"Ring Around the Rosie," 140, 162, 165, 201

Rockwell, Anne, 85, 98, 110, 114

Rockwell, Harlow, 85, 98, 110, 114

Rofé, Jennifer, 85, 91, 98, 101, 107

Rohann, Eric, 85, 93, 97, 108, 109, 110, 114

"Roll, Roll, Roll Your Hands," 198

"Roly-Poly," 23, 140, 166, 168

"Rooster Crows (Or 1, 2, 3, Baby's on my Knee)," 140, 152, 154

Rosen, Michael, 85, 91, 94, 95, 103, 107, 154, 164

"Round and 'Round the Garden," 141, 154, 158, 164, 166, 167, 170

"Row, Row, Row Your Boat," 141, 153, 162, 164, 167, 168, 170, 226, 250

"Rub-a-Dub-Dub," 141, 153, 226

S

Sam Who Never Forgets (Rice), 85, 93, 100, 102, 114, 152, 157, 165, 246

Savage, Stephen, 85, 113, 161

Sayre, April Pulley, 86, 92, 106, 110, 112

Says Who? (Carter), 71, 93, 103, 105, 109, 111, 151, 162

Scharschmidt, Sherry, 77, 94, 95, 104

Schertle, Alice, 86, 107, 110, 114

Scott, Ann Herbert, 86, 94, 100, 105, 157, 168, 246

"See My Pony, My Jet Black Pony," 162

Seuss, Dr., 86, 98, 102, 112, 189

"Shake Your Sillies Out," 170, 198

Shaw, Nancy, 86, 110, 112, 113, 161, 250

Sheep in a Jeep (Shaw), 86, 110, 112, 113, 161, 250

"Shoe the Old Horse," 141, 152, 159

"Shoo, Fly-Don't Bother Me," 198

Siddals, Mary McKenna, 86, 102, 110, 112, 114, 189

Simmons, Jane, 86, 91, 99, 100, 105, 156

"Sing a Song of Sixpence," 141, 155, 158

"Skinnamarink," 169

Sleepy, Oh So Sleepy (Fleming), 75, 93, 95

"Slowly, Slowly, Very Slowly Creeps the Garden Snail," 158, 160

Smee, Nicola, 86, 92, 101, 102, 104, 108, 165

Smithrim, Katharine, 115, 152

"Snow Is Falling Down," 142, 163

Snowballs (Ehlert), 73, 100, 110, 112, 114

"Sometimes I Am Tall," 142, 155, 164

Splash! (Jonas), 79, 93, 99, 106, 114

Splash! (McDonnell), 83, 94, 100, 108, 114, 153, 226

Spring Is Here (Hillenbrand), 78, 93, 103, 109, 111

"Star Light, Star Bright," 142, 154

Stewart, Nancy, 24, 182, 183

Stoeke, Janet, 87, 92, 97, 98, 101, 109, 114

Stretch (Cronin and Menchin), 73, 93, 106, 111

Suen, Anastasia, 87, 97, 112, 113

"Suppose," 142, 155, 167

Suteyev, V., 87, 91, 92, 97, 99, 151, 156

T

Taback, Simms, 91, 94, 101, 104, 111

Tafuri, Nancy, 87–88, 91, 92, 93, 94, 95, 97, 98, 99, 100, 101, 105, 106, 108, 109, 110, 111, 113, 114, 152, 153, 154, 156, 166, 226

"Tall as a Tree," 143, 155, 158, 166, 167, 171

Tap, Tap, Bang, Bang (Garcia), 76, 98, 111, 113

"Teddy Bear, Teddy Bear," 143, 154, 162, 164

Ten Little Caterpillars (Martin), 83, 96, 97, 99, 107, 112, 158

Ten Little Fingers and Ten Little Toes (Fox), 75, 95, 96, 99, 106

"Ten Little Firemen," 143

Ten, Nine, Eight (Bang), 68, 95, 99, 106, 112, 154

Ten Red Apples: A Bartholomew Bear Counting Book (Miller), 83, 93, 94, 95, 99, 100, 106, 109

"There Was a Little Man," 143, 157, 158, 166

"There Was a Little Turtle," 158, 162

"There Were Five in the Bed," 154

"These Are Baby's Fingers," 24, 144, 155, 157, 164

"These Are Grandma's Glasses," 144, 157, 159

"This Is My Father, This Is My Mother," 157

"This Is My Garden," 144, 158

This Is the Farmer (Tafuri), 88, 94, 101, 105, 151, 159

"This Is the Way the Ladies Ride," 145, 152, 162, 163, 167, 170

"This Is the Way We Wash Our Face," 153

"This Little Pig Had a Scrub-a-Dub-Dub," 152, 160

"This Little Piggy," 145, 152, 153, 160, 248

Thomas, Jan, 88, 92, 93, 96, 100, 101, 102, 103, 104, 105, 107

Thompson, Lauren, 88, 93, 100, 103, 105, 108, 109, 110, 111, 114, 159

"Three Green and Speckled Frogs," 145, 153, 158

"Three Little Ducks Went Out One Day," 152, 155

"Three Little Monkeys," 145, 153, 154, 160, 163, 165

"Thumbs in the Thumb Place," 159, 163

"Tick-Tock," 146

Tickle, Tickle (Oxenbury), 84, 94, 103, 157, 246

Tidholm, Anna-Clara, 88, 98, 111

Time for Bed (Fox), 75, 95, 101, 112, 154

Time to Play! (Gray), 77, 101, 104, 108, 112, 162

Tip, Tip, Dig, Dig (Garcia), 76, 98, 111, 113

Titch (Hutchins), 79, 101, 103, 113, 158, 162, 167

"To Market, to Market," 146, 152, 158, 160, 167, 248, 250

"Tommy Thumbs Up," 146, 157, 159, 166, 167

"Tortillas Tortillas," 158

Trains Go (Light), 81, 111, 113, 161

Treasure (Bloom), 69, 94, 95, 96, 103, 108

"Trot, Trot to Boston," 147, 162

Truck Stuck (Wolf), 90, 112, 113

Tuck Me In! (Hacohen and Scharschmidt), 77, 93, 95, 104, 154

26 Letters and 99 Cents (Hoban), 209

"Twinkle, Twinkle, Little Star," 147, 154

"Two Little Birds" (Dos Pajaritos), 121, 153, 154

"Two Little Blackbirds," 23, 147, 152, 153, 155, 163, 164, 165, 166, 236

U

Uh-oh! (Isadora), 79, 95, 99, 101, 106

Under My Hood I Have a Hat (Kuskin), 80, 98, 102, 108, 109, 114, 159, 189

V

Van Rynbach, Iris, 89, 104, 109, 112, 163, 189

Vere, Ed, 89, 92, 97, 105

The Very Quiet Cricket (Carle), 71, 93, 96, 111, 158

W

Waddell, Martin, 89, 96, 102, 105, 107

"Warm Hands Warm," 148, 159, 163

"Wash the Dishes," 148, 158

Watson, Clyde, 24, 156, 160, 162, 167, 209

"Way Up High in the Apple Tree," 148, 152, 155, 158, 164, 166, 168, 170, 237

"We Are Marching to the Drum," 169

"Welcome, Welcome, Everyone," 168, 169

Wellington, Monica, 89, 102, 106

We're Going on a Bear Hunt (Rosen), 85, 91, 94, 95, 103, 107, 153, 164

What Shall We Do with the Boo-Hoo Baby? (Cowell), 72, 94, 95, 103

What's on My Head? (Miller), 83, 95, 96, 107, 159

"Wheels on the Bus" (or Car, Truck, etc.), 149, 162, 163, 164, 165, 166, 167, 169, 250

"When Ducks Get Up in the Morning," 149, 152, 156, 183

Where Is Baby's Bellybutton? (Katz), 80, 95, 98, 103, 104

"Where Is Grandma? Where Is Grandma?," 157

Where Is the Green Sheep? (Fox), 75, 94, 98, 101, 110, 161, 166, 209

"Where is Thumbkin?," 149

Where's Spot? (Hill), 78, 99, 104, 105, 108, 109, 155, 166, 246

Whippo, Walt, 89, 93, 100, 106, 110, 179

Who Said Moo? (Ziefert and Taback), 91, 94, 101, 104, 111

"Whoops, Johnny!," 150

Whose Chick Are You? (Tafuri), 88, 94, 95, 101, 111

Whose Mouse Are You? (Kraus), 80, 91, 95, 101, 105, 157, 159

Whose Nose and Toes? (Butler), 70, 94, 108

The Wide-Mouthed Frog: A Pop-Up Book (Faulkner), 65, 74, 94, 102, 103, 105, 157

"Wiggle Your Fingers," 150, 160, 161, 163, 167, 168

Willems, Mo, 89, 92, 97, 102

Williams, Sue, 89, 91, 92, 93, 94, 99, 106, 107, 108, 109, 112, 158, 189

Williams, Vera B., 90, 94, 100, 157, 246

Wilson, Karma, 90, 91, 95, 99, 101, 102, 109, 114, 157

Wojtowycz, David, 90, 92, 111

Wolf, Sallie, 90, 112, 113

Wood, Audrey, 90, 95, 96, 98, 99, 102, 103, 104, 106, 107, 109, 114, 154, 157, 159, 160, 162, 163, 164, 165, 166, 246

Wood, Don, 90, 95, 96, 102, 103, 104, 107, 154, 157, 159, 160, 162, 164, 165, 166, 246

Wow! Said the Owl (Hopgood), 79, 96, 98, 107

Y

Yummy, YUCKY (Patricelli), 84, 98, 102, 107

Z

Ziefert, Harriet, 91, 94, 104, 111

"Zoom Down the Freeway," 150, 162

Theme Index

A

adventure

    Across the Stream (Ginsburg), 76, 91, 97, 99, 113, 151, 153, 156

    The Chick and the Duckling (Suteyev), 87, 91, 92, 97, 99, 151, 156

    Come Along, Daisy! (Simmons), 86, 91, 99, 100, 105, 156

    Have You Seen My Duckling? (Tafuri), 87, 91, 100, 105, 113, 153, 156, 226

    I Went Walking (Williams), 89, 91, 92, 94, 107, 108, 109, 112, 158, 189

    In the Tall, Tall Grass (Fleming), 75, 91, 92, 96, 107, 112, 151, 158

    Mama's Little Bears (Tafuri), 88, 91, 93, 95, 100, 105, 108, 153

    Oh, A-Hunting We Will Go (Langstaff), 81, 91, 93, 110, 112, 151, 179, 189

    Piggies in the Pumpkin Patch (Peterson and Rofé), 85, 91, 98, 101, 107, 160

    We're Going on a Bear Hunt (Rosen), 85, 91, 94, 95, 103, 107, 153, 164

    Whose Mouse Are You? (Kraus), 80, 91, 95, 101, 105, 157, 159

animals. *See also* animals, farm; animals, jungle; specific animals

    The ABC Bunny (Gag), 76, 91, 108, 111, 151, 161, 209

    Across the Stream (Ginsburg), 76, 91, 97, 99, 113, 151, 153, 156

    Animals Speak (Prap), 85, 91, 111

    Ask Mr. Bear (Flack), 74, 91, 95, 96, 102, 105, 151, 153, 155, 156, 189

    "Baa, Baa, Black Sheep," 118, 152, 161

    Baby Says "Moo!" (Macken), 82, 91, 111, 168

    Barnyard Banter (Fleming), 74, 91, 94, 101, 109, 111, 151

    Bear Snores On (Wilson), 90, 91, 95, 102, 109, 114

    The Big Storm: A Very Soggy Counting Book (Tafuri), 87, 91, 99, 106, 108, 113, 114, 166

    "Bingo," 119, 152, 155

    Blue Goose (Tafuri), 87, 91, 98, 101

    Book! Book! Book! (Bruss), 70, 92, 96, 101, 111

    The Bridge Is Up! (Bell), 69, 92, 102, 112, 161, 189

    Brown Bear, Brown Bear, What Do You See? (Martin), 24, 58, 59, 66, 82, 92, 98, 102, 107, 108, 109, 110, 111, 151, 164, 165, 166, 167, 169, 189, 209, 236, 246

    The Busy Little Squirrel (Tafuri), 87, 92, 100, 109, 110, 114

    Can You Make a Scary Face? (Thomas), 88, 92, 96, 102, 103

    Can You Moo? (Wojtowycz), 90, 92, 111

    Cat the Cat, Who Is That? (Willems), 89, 92, 97, 102

    The Chick and the Duckling (Suteyev), 87, 91, 92, 97, 99, 151, 156

    Chick (Vere), 89, 92, 97, 105

    Chicky Chicky Chook Chook (MacLennan), 82, 92, 97, 101, 109, 111, 114, 158, 165

    Chuck's Truck (Anderson), 68, 92, 101, 111, 113

    Clip-Clop (Smee), 86, 92, 101, 102, 104, 108, 165

    Dancing Feet! (Craig), 72, 92, 100, 106, 108

    Dog Wants to Play (McDonnell), 83, 92, 99, 101, 102, 103, 112, 155, 162

Dogs (Gravett), 77, 92, 98, 99, 107

Down on the Farm (Kutner), 80, 92, 101, 107, 111, 167, 246

Duck and Goose Find a Pumpkin (Hills), 78, 92, 99, 100, 108, 109, 154, 163

Duck in the Truck (Alborough), 68, 92, 100, 112, 113

Farmyard Beat (Craig), 73, 94, 95, 101, 106, 112, 151, 154

Five Little Chicks (Tafuri), 87, 92, 97, 101

From Head to Toe (Carle), 71, 92, 100, 106, 107, 151

The Golden Egg Book (Brown), 70, 92, 100, 102, 108, 151, 156, 161

A Good Day (Henkes), 78, 92, 96, 99, 102, 154, 155

Good Morning, Chick (Ginsburg), 76, 92, 94, 97, 101

Good Night, Good Night (Boynton), 69, 92, 95, 112, 154

"Gray Squirrel," 124, 152, 158

A Hat for Minerva Louise (Stoeke), 87, 92, 97, 98, 101, 109, 114

Hello, Day! (Lobel), 82, 92, 101, 111

"Here Is a Bunny," 126, 152, 161, 167

Home for a Bunny (Brown), 70, 92, 102, 108, 161

Honk! (Demarest), 73, 92, 94, 100, 101, 105, 111, 151, 156

How Kind! (Murphy), 84, 92, 101, 104

I Can Help (Costello), 72, 92, 103

I Like Books (Browne), 70, 92, 96, 105, 160

I Like Me! (Carlson), 71, 92, 103, 107, 160

I Love Animals (McDonnell), 83, 92, 94, 101, 151

I Went Walking (Williams), 89, 91, 92, 94, 107, 108, 109, 112, 158, 189

If You're Hoppy (Sayre), 86, 92, 106, 110, 112

In the Small, Small Pond (Fleming), 74, 92, 107, 109, 112, 113, 151, 153, 158, 163, 226

In the Tall, Tall Grass (Fleming), 75, 91, 92, 96, 107, 112, 151, 158

Is That an Elephant Over There? (Elgar), 73, 92, 94, 100, 103, 105, 108, 109, 162, 165

It's My Birthday! (Oxenbury), 84, 92, 96, 99, 102, 103, 155

Jump, Frog, Jump! (Kalan), 80, 92, 103, 107, 108, 109, 113, 153

A Kiss Like This (Murphy), 84, 93, 102, 105, 156

Kitten's Autumn (Fernandes), 74, 93, 97, 100, 101, 102, 110, 111

Kitten's Spring (Fernandes), 74, 93, 97, 101, 110, 111, 112

A Kitten's Tale (Rohann), 85, 93, 97, 108, 109, 110, 114

Kitty Cat, Kitty Cat, Are You Waking Up? (Martin), 82, 93, 97, 99, 112, 155

Let's Go Visiting (Williams), 89, 93, 94, 99, 106, 109, 112, 189

"Little Boy Blue," 131, 152, 161

Little Gorilla (Bornstein), 69, 93, 94, 96, 103, 110, 155

The Little Red Hen (Galdone), 76, 93, 97, 103, 114

"Little Turtle," 132, 152, 153, 158

Little White Duck (Whippo), 89, 93, 106, 110, 179

Little White Rabbit (Henkes), 78, 93, 98, 104, 108

Maggie's Ball (George), 76, 93, 99, 103, 108, 113, 162, 165

Maisy Dresses Up (Cousins), 72, 93, 98, 100, 105, 107, 109, 159

Maisy Drives the Bus (Cousins), 72, 93, 96, 105, 113, 161

Maisy's Morning on the Farm (Cousins), 72, 93, 101, 104

Mama's Little Bears (Tafuri), 88, 91, 93, 95, 100, 105, 108, 153

"Mary Had a Little Lamb," 133, 152, 161

Meeow and the Big Box (Braun), 69, 93, 97, 104, 106, 113

Mommies Say Shh! (Polacco), 85, 93, 105

Mouse's First Fall (Thompson), 88, 93, 100, 103, 105, 108, 109, 159

Mouse's First Snow (Thompson), 88, 93, 105, 109, 110, 114

Mouse's First Spring (Thompson), 88, 93, 105, 109, 111

"Mr. Turkey and Mr. Duck," 134, 152, 154, 156, 164, 166

My Heart Is Like a Zoo (Hall), 77, 93, 98, 99, 102, 106, 110, 114

A New House for Mouse (Horáček), 79, 93, 94, 104, 105, 159

Oh, A-Hunting We Will Go (Langstaff), 81, 91, 93, 110, 112, 151, 179, 189

Oh! (Henkes), 78, 93, 108, 109, 110, 114

Old Bear (Henkes), 78, 93, 95, 109

"Old MacDonald Had a Farm," 135, 152, 165, 167, 189

Old MacDonald Had a Farm (Cony), 72, 93, 94, 101, 105, 110, 151

One More Hug for Madison (Church), 71, 93, 95, 105, 106

On Our Way Home (Braun), 70, 93, 95

Over in the Meadow (Langstaff), 81, 93, 99, 106, 110, 112, 151, 182, 189

The Owl and the Pussycat (Lear), 81, 93, 96, 97, 107, 108, 112, 151, 154

Peek-a-Boo (Ferri), 74, 93, 101, 103, 104

Peek-a-Moo! (Cimarusti), 72, 93, 101, 103, 104, 111, 151, 162, 168

Pete the Cat: I Love My White Shoes (Litwin), 82, 93, 97, 98, 104, 106, 107, 110, 155, 159

"Plant a Little Seed," 137, 152, 158, 167

Pumpkin Trouble (Thomas), 88, 93, 100, 101, 104, 105, 107

"Rooster Crows," 140, 152, 154

Sam Who Never Forgets (Rice), 85, 93, 100, 102, 114, 152, 157, 165, 246

Says Who? (Carter), 71, 93, 103, 105, 109, 111, 151, 162

"Shoe the Old Horse," 141, 152, 159

Sleepy, Oh So Sleepy (Fleming), 75, 93, 95

Splash! (Jonas), 79, 93, 99, 106, 114

Spring Is Here (Hillenbrand), 78, 93, 103, 109, 111

Stretch (Cronin and Menchin), 73, 93, 106, 111

Ten Red Apples: A Bartholomew Bear Counting Book (Miller), 83, 93, 94, 95, 99, 100, 106, 109

This Is the Farmer (Tafuri), 88, 94, 101, 105, 151, 159

"This Is the Way the Ladies Ride," 145, 152, 162, 163, 167, 170

"This Little Pig Had a Scrub-a-Dub-Dub," 152, 160

"This Little Piggy," 145, 152, 153, 160, 248

"Three Little Ducks Went Out One Day," 152, 155

"To Market, to Market," 146, 152, 158, 160, 167, 248, 250

Treasure (Bloom), 69, 94, 95, 96, 103, 108

Tuck Me In! (Hacohen and Scharschmidt), 77, 93, 95, 104, 154

"Two Little Blackbirds," 23, 147, 152, 153, 155, 163, 164, 165, 166, 236

The Very Quiet Cricket (Carle), 71, 93, 96, 111, 158

"Way Up High in the Apple Tree," 148, 152, 155, 158, 164, 166, 168, 170, 237

We're Going on a Bear Hunt (Rosen), 85, 91, 94, 95, 103, 107, 153, 164

What Shall We Do with the Boo-Hoo Baby? (Cowell), 72, 94, 95, 103

"When Ducks Get Up in the Morning," 149, 152, 156, 183

Where Is the Green Sheep? (Fox), 75, 94, 98, 101, 110, 161, 166, 209

Who Said Moo? (Ziefert and Taback), 91, 94, 101, 104, 111

Whose Chick Are You? (Tafuri), 88, 94, 95, 101, 111

Whose Nose and Toes? (Butler), 70, 94, 108

The Wide-Mouthed Frog: A Pop-Up Book (Faulkner), 65, 74, 94, 102, 103, 105, 157

animals, farm. *See also* specific farm animals

The ABC Bunny (Gag), 76, 91, 108, 111, 151, 161, 209

Across the Stream (Ginsburg), 76, 91, 97, 99, 113, 151, 153, 156

Ask Mr. Bear (Flack), 74, 91, 95, 96, 102, 105, 151, 153, 155, 156, 189

"Baa, Baa, Black Sheep," 118, 152, 161

Barnyard Banter (Fleming), 74, 91, 94, 101, 109, 111, 151

"Bingo," 119, 152, 155

Brown Bear, Brown Bear, What Do You See? (Martin), 24, 58, 59, 66, 82, 92, 98, 102, 107, 108, 109, 110, 111, 151, 164, 165, 166, 167, 169, 189, 209, 236, 246

The Chick and the Duckling (Suteyev), 87, 91, 92, 97, 99, 151, 156

Farmyard Beat (Craig), 73, 94, 95, 101, 106, 112, 151, 154

The Golden Egg Book (Brown), 70, 92, 100, 102, 108, 151, 156, 161

Good Morning, Chick (Ginsburg), 76, 92, 94, 97, 101

"Gray Squirrel," 124, 152, 158

From Head to Toe (Carle), 71, 92, 100, 106, 107, 151

"Here Is a Bunny," 126, 152, 161, 167

Honk! (Demarest), 73, 92, 94, 100, 101, 105, 111, 151, 156

I Love Animals (McDonnell), 83, 92, 94, 101, 151

I Went Walking (Williams), 89, 91, 92, 94, 107, 108, 109, 112, 158, 189

In the Small, Small Pond (Fleming), 74, 92, 107, 109, 112, 113, 151, 153, 158, 163, 226

In the Tall, Tall Grass (Fleming), 75, 91, 92, 96, 107, 112, 151, 158

Let's Go Visiting (Williams), 89, 93, 94, 99, 106, 109, 112, 189

"Little Boy Blue," 131, 152, 161

"Little Turtle," 132, 152, 153, 158

"Mary Had a Little Lamb," 133, 152, 161

"Mr. Turkey and Mr. Duck," 134, 152, 154, 156, 164, 166

Oh, A-Hunting We Will Go (Langstaff), 81, 91, 93, 110, 112, 151, 179, 189

"Old MacDonald Had a Farm," 135, 152, 165, 167, 189

Old MacDonald Had a Farm (Cony), 72, 93, 94, 101, 105, 110, 151

Over in the Meadow (Langstaff), 81, 93, 99, 106, 110, 112, 151, 182, 189

The Owl and the Pussycat (Lear), 81, 93, 96, 97, 107, 108, 112, 151, 154

Peek-a-Moo! (Cimarusti), 72, 93, 101, 103, 104, 111, 151, 162, 168

"Plant a Little Seed," 137, 152, 158, 167

"Rooster Crows," 140, 152, 154

Says Who? (Carter), 71, 93, 103, 105, 109, 111, 151, 162

"Shoe the Old Horse," 141, 152, 159

This Is the Farmer (Tafuri), 88, 94, 101, 105, 151, 159

"This Is the Way the Ladies Ride," 145, 152, 162, 163, 167, 170

"This Little Pig Had a Scrub-a-Dub-Dub," 152, 160

"This Little Piggy," 145, 152, 153, 160, 248

"Three Little Ducks Went Out One Day," 152, 155

"To Market, to Market," 146, 152, 158, 160, 167, 248, 250

"Two Little Blackbirds," 23, 147, 152, 153, 155, 163, 164, 165, 166, 236

"Way Up High in the Apple Tree," 148, 152, 155, 158, 164, 166, 168, 170, 237

"When Ducks Get Up in the Morning," 149, 152, 156, 183

animals, jungle. *See also specific jungle animals*

"An Elephant Goes Like This and That," 152, 165

"Here Is a Bunny," 126, 152, 161, 167

"Here Is a Nest for a Robin," 152, 154, 161

"Hickory, Dickory, Dock," 23, 128, 152, 156, 160, 162, 164, 165, 166, 167, 237, 247

Is That an Elephant Over There? (Elgar), 73, 92, 94, 100, 103, 105, 108, 109, 162, 165

"Leg Over Leg," 131, 152, 156, 165, 166

Little Gorilla (Bornstein), 69, 93, 94, 96, 103, 110, 155

"Mama's Taking Us to the Zoo Tomorrow," 153

"Pussy Cat, Pussy Cat," 138, 153, 156, 160

Sam Who Never Forgets (Rice), 85, 93, 100, 102, 114, 152, 157, 165, 246

Splash! (McDonnell), 83, 94, 100, 108, 114, 153, 226

"This Little Piggy," 145, 152, 153, 160, 248

"Three Little Monkeys," 145, 153, 154, 160, 163, 165

"Two Little Blackbirds," 23, 147, 152, 153, 155, 163, 164, 165, 166, 236

apples

A New House for Mouse (Horáček), 79, 93, 94, 104, 105, 159

Ten Red Apples: A Bartholomew Bear Counting Book (Miller), 83, 93, 94, 95, 99, 100, 106, 109

autumn. *See* fall

B

babies. *See* families/babies/mothers/fathers bathtime/water

Across the Stream (Ginsburg), 76, 91, 97, 99, 113, 151, 153, 156

The Big Storm: A Very Soggy Counting Book (Tafuri), 87, 91, 99, 106, 108, 113, 114, 166

Blue Sea (Kalan), 80, 98, 102, 110, 113, 153, 166, 189

"Catch Me and Kiss Me and Say It Again," 153

"Charlie over the Water," 153

"Fishies," 153

"Gack-Goon," 124, 153, 158

"The Great Big Spider," 125, 153, 158, 163, 166, 167, 168, 170

Have You Seen My Duckling? (Tafuri), 87, 91, 100, 105, 113, 153, 156, 226

"I'm a Little Teapot," 130, 153, 155, 157, 168, 237

In the Small, Small Pond (Fleming), 74, 92, 107, 109, 112, 113, 151, 153, 158, 163, 226

"Jack and Jill," 130, 153

Jump, Frog, Jump! (Kalan), 80, 92, 103, 107, 108, 109, 113, 153

"Little Turtle," 132, 152, 153, 158

"1, 2, 3, 4, 5, I Caught a Fish Alive," 23, 136, 153, 166, 167, 168, 170, 226

"Rain Is Falling Down," 138, 153, 163, 165, 166, 171, 202

"Rain, Rain, Go Away," 138, 153, 163, 202

"Row, Row, Row Your Boat," 141, 153, 162, 164, 167, 168, 170, 226, 250

"Rub-a-Dub-Dub," 141, 153, 226

Splash! (Jonas), 79, 93, 99, 106, 114

Splash! (McDonnell), 83, 94, 100, 108, 114, 153, 226

"This Is the Way We Wash Our Face," 153

"Three Green and Speckled Frogs," 145, 153, 158

bears

Ask Mr. Bear (Flack), 74, 91, 95, 96, 102, 105, 151, 153, 155, 156, 189

Bear Snores On (Wilson), 90, 91, 95, 102, 109, 114

"Bear Went over the Mountain," 154, 164

"Going on a Bear Hunt," 154

Just Like Daddy (Asch), 68, 95, 100, 101, 153, 156

The Little Mouse, the Red Ripe Strawberry, and the Big Hungry Bear (Wood and Wood), 90, 95, 102, 104, 154, 157, 159, 164, 166, 246

Mama's Little Bears (Tafuri), 88, 91, 93, 95, 100, 105, 108, 153

Old Bear (Henkes), 78, 93, 95, 109

On Our Way Home (Braun), 70, 93, 95

"Round and 'Round the Garden," 141, 154, 158, 164, 166, 167, 170

"Teddy Bear, Teddy Bear," 143, 154, 162, 164

Ten Red Apples: A Bartholomew Bear Counting Book (Miller), 83, 93, 94, 95, 99, 100, 106, 109

Treasure (Bloom), 69, 94, 95, 96, 103, 108

We're Going on a Bear Hunt (Rosen), 85, 91, 94, 95, 103, 107, 153, 164

bedtime

"Baby's Nap," 119, 154

Farmyard Beat (Craig), 73, 94, 95, 101, 106, 112, 151, 154

Good Night, Good Night (Boynton), 69, 92, 95, 112, 154

Goodnight Moon (Brown), 65, 70, 95, 108, 112, 154, 161, 209

Grandfather Twilight (Berger), 69, 95, 154

I'm Not Sleepy (Allen), 68, 95, 96, 107, 154

"Jack Be Nimble," 130, 154, 162

One More Hug for Madison (Church), 71, 93, 95, 105, 106

On Our Way Home (Braun), 70, 93, 95

Piggies (Wood and Wood), 90, 95, 96, 103, 107, 154, 160, 162, 165

Sleepy, Oh So Sleepy (Fleming), 75, 93, 95

"Star Light, Star Bright," 142, 154

"Teddy Bear, Teddy Bear," 143, 154, 162, 164

Ten, Nine, Eight (Bang), 68, 95, 99, 106, 112, 154

"There Were Five in the Bed," 154

"Three Little Monkeys," 145, 153, 154, 160, 163, 165

Time for Bed (Fox), 75, 95, 101, 112, 154

Tuck Me In! (Hacohen and Scharschmidt), 77, 93, 95, 104, 154

"Twinkle, Twinkle, Little Star," 147, 154

birds

Birds (Henkes), 77, 96, 154

"Dos Pajaritos (Two Little Birds)," 121, 154

Duck and Goose Find a Pumpkin (Hills), 78, 92, 99, 100, 108, 109, 154, 163

A Good Day (Henkes), 78, 92, 96, 99, 102, 154, 155

"Here Is a Nest for a Robin," 152, 154, 161

"Hickety, Pickety, My Black Hen," 128, 154, 156

I Like It When . . . (Murphy), 84, 96, 105

I'm Not Sleepy (Allen), 68, 95, 96, 107, 154

Little Robin Redbreast: A Mother Goose Rhyme (Halpern), 77, 96, 97, 108, 112, 154, 246

"Little White Duck," 154

"Mr. Turkey and Mr. Duck," 134, 152, 154, 156, 164, 166

"One, Two, Buckle My Shoe," 136, 154, 156

The Owl and the Pussycat (Lear), 81, 93, 96, 97, 107, 108, 112, 151, 154

Owl Babies (Waddell), 89, 96, 102, 105, 107

"Rooster Crows," 140, 152, 154

"Sing a Song of Sixpence," 141, 155, 158

"Tall as a Tree," 143, 155, 158, 166, 167, 171

"Three Little Ducks Went Out One Day," 152, 155

Treasure (Bloom), 69, 94, 95, 96, 103, 108

"Two Little Blackbirds," 23, 147, 152, 153, 155, 163, 164, 165, 166, 236

"Way Up High in the Apple Tree," 148, 152, 155, 158, 164, 166, 168, 170, 237

Wow! Said the Owl (Hopgood), 79, 96, 98, 107

birthdays/growing up

Ask Mr. Bear (Flack), 74, 91, 95, 96, 102, 105, 151, 153, 155, 156, 189

"Happy Birthday to You," 155

"Head and Shoulders, Knees and Toes," 24, 125, 155, 159, 166, 167, 168, 170

"Here's a Cup," 127, 155

"If You're Happy and You Know It," 129, 155, 166, 169, 171

"I'm a Little Teapot," 130, 153, 155, 157, 168, 237

It's My Birthday! (Oxenbury), 84, 92, 96, 99, 102, 103, 155

Little Gorilla (Bornstein), 69, 93, 94, 96, 103, 110, 155

"Mix a Pancake," 155

"The Muffin Man," 155

"Patty Cake, Patty Cake," 137, 155, 157, 159, 164, 165, 169, 198

"Pease Porridge Hot," 137, 155, 158

"Sometimes I Am Tall," 142, 155, 164

"Suppose," 142, 155, 167

"Tall as a Tree," 143, 155, 158, 166, 167, 171

"These Are Baby's Fingers," 24, 144, 155, 157, 164

Titch (Hutchins), 79, 101, 103, 113, 158, 162, 167

boats. *See* things that go/boats/trains

body

    All of Baby Nose to Toes (Adler), 67, 94, 96, 111

    Baby Faces (Miller), 83, 94, 96, 99

    Here Are My Hands (Martin), 82, 96, 112

    Piggies (Wood and Wood), 90, 95, 96, 103, 107, 154, 160, 162, 165

    Ten Little Fingers and Ten Little Toes (Fox), 75, 95, 96, 99, 106

    What's on My Head? (Miller), 83, 95, 96, 107, 159

books

    Book! Book! Book! (Bruss), 70, 92, 96, 101, 111

    I Like Books (Browne), 70, 92, 96, 105, 160

bugs. *See* gardens/bugs/outside

bus

    The Bus for Us (Bloom), 69, 97, 112

    Maisy Drives the Bus (Cousins), 72, 93, 96, 105, 113, 161

C

cars

    Red Light, Green Light (Suen), 87, 96, 112, 113

caterpillars

    Caterpillar's Wish (Murphy), 84, 96, 97, 109, 111

    Ten Little Caterpillars (Martin), 83, 96, 97, 99, 107, 112, 158

cats. *See* dogs/cats

chickens/ducks

    Across the Stream (Ginsburg), 76, 91, 97, 99, 113, 151, 153, 156

    Big Fat Hen (Baker), 68, 97, 99, 106, 108, 111, 156, 246

    The Chick and the Duckling (Suteyev), 87, 91, 92, 97, 99, 151, 156

    Chick (Vere), 89, 92, 97, 105

    Chicky Chicky Chook Chook (MacLennan), 82, 92, 97, 101, 109, 111, 114, 158, 165

    Come Along, Daisy! (Simmons), 86, 91, 99, 100, 105, 156

    Duck and Goose Find a Pumpkin (Hills), 78, 92, 99, 100, 108, 109, 154, 163

    Duck in the Truck (Alborough), 68, 92, 100, 112, 113

    Duckie's Splash (Barry), 68, 98, 100, 156

    Five Little Chicks (Tafuri), 87, 92, 97, 101

    Five Little Ducks (Raffi), 85, 99, 100, 106, 110, 156, 179, 182

    "Five Little Ducks Went Out One Day," 156

    The Golden Egg Book (Brown), 70, 92, 100, 102, 108, 151, 156, 161

    Good Morning, Chick (Ginsburg), 76, 92, 94, 97, 101

    A Hat for Minerva Louise (Stoeke), 87, 92, 97, 98, 101, 109, 114

    Have You Seen My Ducklling? (Tafuri), 87, 91, 100, 105, 113, 153, 156, 226

    "Hickety, Pickety, My Black Hen," 128, 154, 156

    The Little Red Hen (Galdone), 76, 93, 97, 103, 114

    "Mr. Turkey and Mr. Duck," 134, 152, 154, 156, 164, 166

    "One, Two, Buckle My Shoe," 136, 154, 156

    Pumpkin Trouble (Thomas), 88, 93, 100, 101, 104, 105, 107

    "When Ducks Get Up in the Morning," 149, 152, 156, 183

clothes. *See also* getting dressed/hats

    The First Snowfall (Rockwell and Rockwell), 85, 98, 110, 114

    A Hat for Minerva Louise (Stoeke), 87, 92, 97, 98, 101, 109, 114

    Maisy Dresses Up (Cousins), 72, 93, 98, 100, 105, 107, 109, 159

    Under My Hood I Have a Hat (Kuskin), 80, 98, 102, 108, 109, 114, 159, 189

clouds. *See* weather/clouds/rain/seasons

colors

    Blue Goose (Tafuri), 87, 91, 98, 101

    Brown Bear, Brown Bear, What Do You See? (Martin), 24, 58, 59, 66, 82, 92, 98, 102, 107, 108, 109, 110, 111, 151, 164, 165, 166, 167, 169, 189, 209, 236, 246

    Freight Train (Crews), 73, 98, 102, 113, 161, 165, 189, 250

    Go Away, Big Green Monster! (Emberley), 73, 98, 104, 170, 189

    Knock! Knock! (Tidholm), 88, 98, 111

    Lunch (Fleming), 75, 98, 102, 104, 105, 157, 159, 189

    My Heart Is Like a Zoo (Hall), 77, 93, 98, 99, 102, 106, 110, 114

    My Many Colored Days (Seuss), 86, 98, 102, 112, 189

    Pete the Cat: I Love My White Shoes (Litwin), 82, 93, 97, 98, 104, 106, 107, 110, 155, 159

    Rain (Kalan), 80, 98, 108, 109, 114, 163

    Where Is the Green Sheep? (Fox), 75, 94, 98, 101, 110, 161, 166, 209

concepts

    Blue Sea (Kalan), 80, 98, 102, 110, 113, 153, 166, 189

    Dogs (Gravett), 77, 92, 98, 99, 107

    Duckie's Splash (Barry), 68, 98, 100, 156

    Little White Rabbit (Henkes), 78, 93, 98, 104, 108

    Perfect Square (Hall), 77, 98, 102, 110

    Pete the Cat: I Love My White Shoes (Litwin), 82, 93, 97, 98, 104, 106, 107, 110, 155, 159

    Piggies in the Pumpkin Patch (Peterson and Rofé), 85, 91, 98, 101, 107, 160

    Where Is Baby's Bellybutton? (Katz), 80, 95, 98, 103, 104

    Where Is the Green Sheep? (Fox), 75, 94, 98, 101, 110, 161, 166, 209

    Yummy, YUCKY (Patricelli), 84, 98, 102, 107

construction

    Tap, Tap, Bang, Bang (Garcia), 76, 98, 111, 113

    Tip, Tip, Dig, Dig (Garcia), 76, 98, 111, 113

counting. *See also* numbers

    Big Fat Hen (Baker), 68, 97, 99, 106, 108, 111, 156, 246

    The Big Storm: A Very Soggy Counting Book (Tafuri), 87, 91, 99, 106, 108, 113, 114, 166

Five Little Ducks (Raffi), 85, 99, 100, 106, 110, 156, 179, 182

Let's Go Visiting (Williams), 89, 93, 94, 99, 106, 109, 112, 189

My Heart Is Like a Zoo (Hall), 77, 93, 98, 99, 102, 106, 110, 114

One Two That's My Shoe! (Murray), 84, 99, 112, 155

Over in the Meadow (Langstaff), 81, 93, 99, 106, 110, 112, 151, 182, 189

Splash! (Jonas), 79, 93, 99, 106, 114

Ten, Nine, Eight (Bang), 68, 95, 99, 106, 112, 154

Ten Little Caterpillars (Martin), 83, 96, 97, 99, 107, 112, 158

Ten Red Apples: A Bartholomew Bear Counting Book (Miller), 83, 93, 94, 95, 99, 100, 106, 109

cows

The Cow Loves Cookies (Wilson), 90, 99, 101, 102, 157

D

daily life

Baby Faces (Miller), 83, 94, 96, 99

Baby Loves (Lawrence), 81, 94, 99, 100, 156

Blue Sky (Wood), 90, 98, 99, 106, 109, 114, 163

I Can Do It Too! (Baicker), 68, 99, 100

I Kissed the Baby! (Murphy), 84, 94, 99

It's My Birthday! (Oxenbury), 84, 92, 96, 99, 102, 103, 155

Kitty Cat, Kitty Cat, Are You Waking Up? (Martin), 82, 93, 97, 99, 112, 155

Peekaboo Morning (Isadora), 79, 95, 99, 103, 106

Ten Little Fingers and Ten Little Toes (Fox), 75, 95, 96, 99, 106

Uh-oh! (Isadora), 79, 95, 99, 101, 106

dogs/cats

"Bingo," 119, 152, 155

Cat the Cat, Who Is That? (Willems), 89, 92, 97, 102

Chicky Chicky Chook Chook (MacLennan), 82, 92, 97, 101, 109, 111, 114, 158, 165

Dog Wants to Play (McDonnell), 83, 92, 99, 101, 102, 103, 112, 155, 162

Dogs (Gravett), 77, 92, 98, 99, 107

A Good Day (Henkes), 78, 92, 96, 99, 102, 154, 155

"Here Comes a Mouse," 24, 125, 156, 160, 162, 167

"Hey, Diddle, Diddle," 127, 155, 248

"Hickory, Dickory, Dock," 23, 128, 152, 156, 160, 162, 164, 165, 166, 167, 237, 247

"How Much Is That Doggie in the Window," 128, 156

Just Like Jasper! (Butterworth), 70, 97, 113, 162, 167

Kitten's Autumn (Fernandes), 74, 93, 97, 100, 101, 102, 110, 111

Kitten's First Full Moon (Henkes), 78, 97, 105, 106

Kitten's Spring (Fernandes), 74, 93, 97, 101, 110, 111, 112

A Kitten's Tale (Rohann), 85, 93, 97, 108, 109, 110, 114

Kitty Cat, Kitty Cat, Are You Waking Up? (Martin), 82, 93, 97, 99, 112, 155

"Leg Over Leg," 131, 152, 156, 165, 166

Little Robin Redbreast: A Mother Goose Rhyme (Halpern), 77, 96, 97, 108, 112, 154, 246

Maggie's Ball (George), 76, 93, 99, 103, 108, 113, 162, 165

Mama Cat Has Three Kittens (Fleming), 75, 94, 97, 100, 105

Meeow and the Big Box (Braun), 69, 93, 97, 104, 106, 113

One Two That's My Shoe! (Murray), 84, 99, 112, 155

The Owl and the Pussycat (Lear), 81, 93, 96, 97, 107, 108, 112, 151, 154

Pete the Cat: I Love My White Shoes (Litwin), 82, 93, 97, 98, 104, 106, 107, 110, 155, 159

"Pussy Cat, Pussy Cat," 138, 153, 156, 160

Where's Spot? (Hill), 78, 99, 104, 105, 108, 109, 155, 166, 246

ducks. *See* chickens/ducks

E

elephants

Dancing Feet! (Craig), 72, 92, 100, 106, 108

"An Elephant Goes Like This and That," 152, 165

"Here Is a Bunny," 126, 152, 161, 167

"Here Is a Nest for a Robin," 152, 154, 161

"Hickory, Dickory, Dock," 23, 128, 152, 156, 160, 162, 164, 165, 166, 167, 237, 247

Is That an Elephant Over There? (Elgar), 73, 92, 94, 100, 103, 105, 108, 109, 162, 165

"Leg Over Leg," 131, 152, 156, 165, 166

Little Gorilla (Bornstein), 69, 93, 94, 96, 103, 110, 155

"Mama's Taking Us to the Zoo Tomorrow," 153

"Pussy Cat, Pussy Cat," 138, 153, 156, 160

Sam Who Never Forgets (Rice), 85, 93, 100, 102, 114, 152, 157, 165, 246

Splash! (McDonnell), 83, 94, 100, 108, 114, 153, 226

"This Little Piggy," 145, 152, 153, 160, 248

"Three Little Monkeys," 145, 153, 154, 160, 163, 165

"Two Little Blackbirds," 121, 153, 154

exercise

From Head to Toe (Carle), 71, 92, 100, 106, 107, 151

exploring

Come Along, Daisy! (Simmons), 86, 91, 99, 100, 105, 156

Five Little Ducks (Raffi), 85, 99, 100, 106, 110, 156, 179, 182

Have You Seen My Duckling? (Tafuri), 87, 91, 100, 105, 113, 153, 156, 226

F

fall

The Busy Little Squirrel (Tafuri), 87, 92, 100, 109, 110, 114

Duck and Goose Find a Pumpkin (Hills), 78, 92, 99, 100, 108, 109, 154, 163

Kitten's Autumn (Fernandes), 74, 93, 97, 100, 101, 102, 110, 111

Maisy Dresses Up (Cousins), 72, 93, 98, 100, 105, 107, 109, 159

Mouse's First Fall (Thompson), 88, 93, 100, 103, 105, 108, 109, 159

Ten Red Apples: A Bartholomew Bear Counting Book (Miller), 83, 93, 94, 95, 99, 100, 106, 109 families/babies/mothers/fathers

All of Baby Nose to Toes (Adler), 67, 94, 96, 111

Ask Mr. Bear (Flack), 74, 91, 95, 96, 102, 105, 151, 153, 155, 156, 189

Baby Faces (Miller), 83, 94, 96, 99

Baby Loves (Lawrence), 81, 94, 99, 100, 156

Come Along, Daisy! (Simmons), 86, 91, 99, 100, 105, 156

"Come'a Look'a See, Here's My Mama," 157

Have You Seen My Duckling? (Tafuri), 87, 91, 100, 105, 113, 153, 156, 226

Honk! (Demarest), 73, 92, 94, 100, 101, 105, 111, 151, 156

I Can Do It Too! (Baicker), 68, 99, 100

I Kissed the Baby! (Murphy), 84, 94, 99

I Like It When . . . (Murphy), 84, 96, 105

Just Like Daddy (Asch), 68, 95, 100, 101, 153, 156

A Kiss Like This (Murphy), 84, 93, 102, 105, 156

Mama Cat Has Three Kittens (Fleming), 75, 94, 97, 100, 105

Mama's Little Bears (Tafuri), 88, 91, 93, 95, 100, 105, 108, 153

Mommies Say Shh! (Polacco), 85, 93, 105

"More More More," Said the Baby (Williams), 90, 94, 100, 157, 246

"Mother and Father and Uncle John," 134, 157, 165, 169, 237

On Mother's Lap (Scott), 86, 94, 100, 105, 157, 168, 246

Owl Babies (Waddell), 89, 96, 102, 105, 107

"Patty Cake, Patty Cake," 137, 155, 157, 159, 164, 165, 169, 198

Peekaboo Morning (Isadora), 79, 95, 99, 103, 106

Pots and Pans (Hubbell), 79, 95, 103, 104, 106, 108, 111, 157, 159, 162

Snowballs (Ehlert), 73, 100, 110, 112, 114

Ten Little Fingers and Ten Little Toes (Fox), 75, 95, 96, 99, 106

"There Was a Little Man," 143, 157, 158, 166

"These Are Baby's Fingers," 24, 144, 155, 157, 164

"These Are Grandma's Glasses," 144, 157, 159

"This Is My Father, This Is My Mother," 157

Tickle, Tickle (Oxenbury), 84, 94, 103, 157, 246

Time for Bed (Fox), 75, 95, 101, 112, 154

Time to Play! (Gray), 77, 101, 104, 108, 112, 162

Titch (Hutchins), 79, 101, 103, 113, 158, 162, 167

"Tommy Thumbs Up," 146, 157, 159, 166, 167

Uh-oh! (Isadora), 79, 95, 99, 101, 106

What Shall We Do with the Boo-Hoo Baby? (Cowell), 72, 94, 95, 103

What's on My Head? (Miller), 83, 95, 96, 107, 159

Where Is Baby's Bellybutton? (Katz), 80, 95, 98, 103, 104

"Where Is Grandma? Where Is Grandma?," 157

Whose Chick Are You? (Tafuri), 88, 94, 95, 101, 111

Whose Mouse Are You? (Kraus), 80, 91, 95, 101, 105, 157, 159

farm animals. *See* animals, farm

farms

The ABC Bunny (Gag), 76, 91, 108, 111, 151, 161, 209

Across the Stream (Ginsburg), 76, 91, 97, 99, 113, 151, 153, 156

Ask Mr. Bear (Flack), 74, 91, 95, 96, 102, 105, 151, 153, 155, 156, 189

"Baa, Baa, Black Sheep," 118, 152, 161

Barnyard Banter (Fleming), 74, 91, 94, 101, 109, 111, 151

"Bingo," 119, 152, 155

Blue Goose (Tafuri), 87, 91, 98, 101

Book! Book! Book! (Bruss), 70, 92, 96, 101, 111

Brown Bear, Brown Bear, What Do You See? (Martin), 24, 58, 59, 66, 82, 92, 98, 102, 107, 108, 109, 110, 111, 151, 164, 165, 166, 167, 169, 189, 209, 236, 246

The Chick and the Duckling (Suteyev), 87, 91, 92, 97, 99, 151, 156

Chicky Chicky Chook Chook (MacLennan), 82, 92, 97, 101, 109, 111, 114, 158, 165

Chuck's Truck (Anderson), 68, 92, 101, 111, 113

Clip-Clop (Smee), 86, 92, 101, 102, 104, 108, 165

The Cow Loves Cookies (Wilson), 90, 99, 101, 102, 157

Dog Wants to Play (McDonnell), 83, 92, 99, 101, 102, 103, 112, 155, 162

Down on the Farm (Kutner), 80, 92, 101, 107, 111, 167, 246

Farmyard Beat (Craig), 73, 94, 95, 101, 106, 112, 151, 154

Five Little Chicks (Tafuri), 87, 92, 97, 101

From Head to Toe (Carle), 71, 92, 100, 106, 107, 151

The Golden Egg Book (Brown), 70, 92, 100, 102, 108, 151, 156, 161

Good Morning, Chick (Ginsburg), 76, 92, 94, 97, 101

"Gray Squirrel," 124, 152, 158

A Hat for Minerva Louise (Stoeke), 87, 92, 97, 98, 101, 109, 114

Hello, Day! (Lobel), 82, 92, 101, 111

"Here Is a Bunny," 126, 152, 161, 167

Honk! (Demarest), 73, 92, 94, 100, 101, 105, 111, 151, 156

How Kind! (Murphy), 84, 92, 101, 104

I Love Animals (McDonnell), 83, 92, 94, 101, 151

In the Small, Small Pond (Fleming), 74, 92, 107, 109, 112, 113, 151, 153, 158, 163, 226

In the Tall, Tall Grass (Fleming), 75, 91, 92, 96, 107, 112, 151, 158

Kitten's Autumn (Fernandes), 74, 93, 97, 100, 101, 102, 110, 111

Kitten's Spring (Fernandes), 74, 93, 97, 101, 110, 111, 112

"Little Boy Blue," 131, 152, 161

"Little Turtle," 132, 152, 153, 158

Maisy's Morning on the Farm (Cousins), 72, 93, 101, 104

"Mary Had a Little Lamb," 133, 152, 161

"Mr. Turkey and Mr. Duck," 134, 152, 154, 156, 164, 166

Oh, A-Hunting We Will Go (Langstaff), 81, 91, 93, 110, 112, 151, 179, 189

"Old MacDonald Had a Farm," 135, 152, 165, 167, 189

Old MacDonald Had a Farm (Cony), 72, 93, 94, 101, 105, 110, 151

Over in the Meadow (Langstaff), 81, 93, 99, 106, 110, 112, 151, 182, 189

The Owl and the Pussycat (Lear), 81, 93, 96, 97, 107, 108, 112, 151, 154

Peek-a-Boo (Ferri), 74, 93, 101, 103, 104

Peek-a-Moo! (Cimarusti), 72, 93, 101, 103, 104, 111, 151, 162, 168

Piggies in the Pumpkin Patch (Peterson and Rofé), 85, 91, 98, 101, 107, 160

"Plant a Little Seed," 137, 152, 158, 167

Pumpkin Trouble (Thomas), 88, 93, 100, 101, 104, 105, 107

"Rooster Crows," 140, 152, 154

Says Who? (Carter), 71, 93, 103, 105, 109, 111, 151, 162

"Shoe the Old Horse," 141, 152, 159

This Is the Farmer (Tafuri), 88, 94, 101, 105, 151, 159

"This Is the Way the Ladies Ride," 145, 152, 162, 163, 167, 170

"This Little Pig Had a Scrub-a-Dub-Dub," 152, 160

"This Little Piggy," 145, 152, 153, 160, 248

"Three Little Ducks Went Out One Day," 152, 155

"To Market, to Market," 146, 152, 158, 160, 167, 248, 250

"Two Little Blackbirds," 23, 147, 152, 153, 155, 163, 164, 165, 166, 236

"Way Up High in the Apple Tree," 148, 152, 155, 158, 164, 166, 168, 170, 237

"When Ducks Get Up in the Morning," 149, 152, 156, 183

Where Is the Green Sheep? (Fox), 75, 94, 98, 101, 110, 161, 166, 209

Who Said Moo? (Ziefert and Taback), 91, 94, 101, 104, 111

Whose Chick Are You? (Tafuri), 88, 94, 95, 101, 111

fathers. *See* families/babies/mothers/fathers

feelings

Can You Make a Scary Face? (Thomas), 88, 92, 96, 102, 103

A Good Day (Henkes), 78, 92, 96, 99, 102, 154, 155

A Kiss Like This (Murphy), 84, 93, 102, 105, 156

My Heart Is Like a Zoo (Hall), 77, 93, 98, 99, 102, 106, 110, 114

My Many Colored Days (Seuss), 86, 98, 102, 112, 189

Owl Babies (Waddell), 89, 96, 102, 105, 107

Perfect Square (Hall), 77, 98, 102, 110

fish

Blue Sea (Kalan), 80, 98, 102, 110, 113, 153, 166, 189

Hooray for Fish! (Cousins), 72, 102, 106, 112

flannel board

Ask Mr. Bear (Flack), 74, 91, 95, 96, 102, 105, 151, 153, 155, 156, 189

The Bridge Is Up! (Bell), 69, 92, 102, 112, 161, 189

Brown Bear, Brown Bear, What Do You See? (Martin), 24, 58, 59, 66, 82, 92, 98, 102, 107, 108, 109, 110, 111, 151, 164, 165, 166, 167, 169, 189, 209, 236, 246

Freight Train (Crews), 73, 98, 102, 113, 161, 165, 189, 250

It's My Birthday! (Oxenbury), 84, 92, 96, 99, 102, 103, 155

Lunch (Fleming), 75, 98, 102, 104, 105, 157, 159, 189

Under My Hood I Have a Hat (Kuskin), 80, 98, 102, 108, 109, 114, 159, 189

food/messes

"Acka Backa," 117, 157, 169, 237

The Cow Loves Cookies (Wilson), 90, 99, 101, 102, 157

"Criss-Cross Applesauce," 121, 157, 159, 165, 166, 167, 170, 237

"Cup of Tea," 157

"Do You Know the Muffin Man," 157, 159

"Five Plump Peas," 123, 157, 158, 167

"Georgie Porgie," 157

"Hot Cross Buns," 157

"Humpty Dumpty," 23, 128, 157, 159, 162, 165, 166, 168, 248

"I'm a Little Teapot," 130, 153, 155, 157, 168, 237

It's My Birthday! (Oxenbury), 84, 92, 96, 99, 102, 103, 155

Kitten's Autumn (Fernandes), 74, 93, 97, 100, 101, 102, 110, 111

The Little Mouse, the Red Ripe Strawberry, and the Big Hungry Bear (Wood and Wood), 90, 95, 102, 104, 154, 157, 159, 164, 166, 246

Lunch (Fleming), 75, 98, 102, 104, 105, 157, 159, 189

Mr. Cookie Baker (Wellington), 89, 102, 106

"Pancake," 137, 157

"Patty Cake, Patty Cake," 137, 155, 157, 159, 164, 165, 169, 198

"Pease Porridge Hot," 137, 155, 158

Pete the Cat: I Love My White Shoes (Litwin), 82, 93, 97, 98, 104, 106, 107, 110, 155, 159

Pots and Pans (Hubbell), 79, 95, 103, 104, 106, 108, 111, 157, 159, 162

Sam Who Never Forgets (Rice), 85, 93, 100, 102, 114, 152, 157, 165, 246

"Sing a Song of Sixpence," 141, 155, 158

"There Was a Little Man," 143, 157, 158, 166

"To Market, to Market," 146, 152, 158, 160, 167, 248, 250

"Tortillas Tortillas," 158

"Wash the Dishes," 148, 158

"Way Up High in the Apple Tree," 148, 152, 155, 158, 164, 166, 168, 170, 237

The Wide-Mouthed Frog: A Pop-Up Book (Faulkner), 65, 74, 94, 102, 103, 105, 157

Yummy, YUCKY (Patricelli), 84, 98, 102, 107

friends

Bear Snores On (Wilson), 90, 91, 95, 102, 109, 114

Cat the Cat, Who Is That? (Willems), 89, 92, 97, 102

Clip-Clop (Smee), 86, 92, 101, 102, 104, 108, 165

Dog Wants to Play (McDonnell), 83, 92, 99, 101, 102, 103, 112, 155, 162

The Golden Egg Book (Brown), 70, 92, 100, 102, 108, 151, 156, 161

Home for a Bunny (Brown), 70, 92, 102, 108, 161

I Can Help (Costello), 72, 92, 103

I Like Me! (Carlson), 71, 92, 103, 107, 160

It's My Birthday! (Oxenbury), 84, 92, 96, 99, 102, 103, 155

Maggie's Ball (George), 76, 93, 99, 103, 108, 113, 162, 165

Mouse's First Fall (Thompson), 88, 93, 100, 103, 105, 108, 109, 159

Spring Is Here (Hillenbrand), 78, 93, 103, 109, 111

Treasure (Bloom), 69, 94, 95, 96, 103, 108

frogs

Can You Make a Scary Face? (Thomas), 88, 92, 96, 102, 103

Jump, Frog, Jump! (Kalan), 80, 92, 103, 107, 108, 109, 113, 153

The Wide-Mouthed Frog: A Pop-Up Book (Faulkner), 65, 74, 94, 102, 103, 105, 157

G

games. *See* toys/play/games

gardens/bugs/outside

"All around the Mulberry Bush," 117, 158, 159, 160, 162

"Arabella Miller," 158

Beetle Bop (Fleming), 74, 96, 111

Can You Make a Scary Face? (Thomas), 88, 92, 96, 102, 103

The Carrot Seed (Krauss), 80, 103, 158, 166, 189

Caterpillar's Wish (Murphy), 84, 96, 97, 109, 111

Chicky Chicky Chook Chook (MacLennan), 82, 92, 97, 101, 109, 111, 114, 158, 165

"Five Plump Peas," 123, 157, 158, 167

"Gack-Goon," 124, 153, 158

"Gray Squirrel," 124, 152, 158

"The Great Big Spider," 125, 153, 158, 163, 166, 167, 168, 170

"Here Is a Beehive," 125, 158

I Went Walking (Williams), 89, 91, 92, 94, 107, 108, 109, 112, 158, 189

In the Small, Small Pond (Fleming), 74, 92, 107, 109, 112, 113, 151, 153, 158, 163, 226

In the Tall, Tall Grass (Fleming), 75, 91, 92, 96, 107, 112, 151, 158

"Little Turtle," 132, 152, 153, 158

"Mary, Mary, Quite Contrary," 133, 158

"Plant a Little Seed," 137, 152, 158, 167

"Round and 'Round the Garden," 141, 154, 158, 164, 166, 167, 170

"Slowly, Slowly, Very Slowly Creeps the Garden Snail," 158, 160

"Tall as a Tree," 143, 155, 158, 166, 167, 171

Ten Little Caterpillars (Martin), 83, 96, 97, 99, 107, 112, 158

"There Was a Little Turtle," 158, 162

"This Is My Garden," 144, 158

"Three Green and Speckled Frogs," 145, 153, 158

Titch (Hutchins), 79, 101, 103, 113, 158, 162, 167

The Very Quiet Cricket (Carle), 71, 93, 96, 111, 158

"Way Up High in the Apple Tree," 148, 152, 155, 158, 164, 166, 168, 170, 237

getting dressed/hats

"All around the Mulberry Bush," 117, 158, 159, 160, 162

"Cobbler, Cobbler," 121, 159, 165, 168, 171

"Head and Shoulders, Knees and Toes," 24, 125, 155, 159, 166, 167, 168, 170

"Here Are Baby's Fingers," 159

"If You're Wearing Red Today," 129, 159

Maisy Dresses Up (Cousins), 72, 93, 98, 100, 105, 107, 109, 159

Under My Hood I Have a Hat (Kuskin), 80, 98, 102, 108, 109, 114, 159, 189

"Shoe the Old Horse," 141, 152, 159

"These Are Grandma's Glasses," 144, 157, 159

"Thumb in the Thumb Place," 159, 163

"Tommy Thumbs Up," 146, 157, 159, 166, 167

"Warm Hands Warm," 148, 159, 163

What's on My Head? (Miller), 83, 95, 96, 107, 159

giving

Giving (Hughes), 79, 103, 110

growing up. *See* birthdays/growing up

H

hats. *See* getting dressed/hats

helping

I Can Help (Costello), 72, 92, 103

The Little Red Hen (Galdone), 76, 93, 97, 103, 114

What Shall We Do with the Boo-Hoo Baby? (Cowell), 72, 94, 95, 103

holidays

The Five Little Pumpkins (Van Rynbach), 89, 104, 109, 112, 163, 189

Pumpkin Trouble (Thomas), 88, 93, 100, 101, 104, 105, 107

horses

Clip-Clop (Smee), 86, 92, 101, 102, 104, 108, 165

houses

A New House for Mouse (Horáček), 79, 93, 94, 104, 105, 159

I

imagination

Little White Rabbit (Henkes), 78, 93, 98, 104, 108

Meeow and the Big Box (Braun), 69, 93, 97, 104, 106, 113

interactive books

Go Away, Big Green Monster! (Emberley), 73, 98, 104, 170, 189

Peek-a-Moo! (Cimarusti), 72, 93, 101, 103, 104, 111, 151, 162, 168

J

jungle animals. *See* animals, jungle

K

kindness

How Kind! (Murphy), 84, 92, 101, 104

L

lift-the-flap books

Peek-a-Boo (Ferri), 74, 93, 101, 103, 104

Peek-a-Moo! (Cimarusti), 72, 93, 101, 103, 104, 111, 151, 162, 168

Time to Play! (Gray), 77, 101, 104, 108, 112, 162

Tuck Me In! (Hacohen and Scharschmidt), 77, 93, 95, 104, 154

Where Is Baby's Bellybutton? (Katz), 80, 95, 98, 103, 104

Where's Spot? (Hill), 78, 99, 104, 105, 108, 109, 155, 166, 246

Who Said Moo? (Ziefert and Taback), 91, 94, 101, 104, 111

M

manners

Lunch (Fleming), 75, 98, 102, 104, 105, 157, 159, 189

messes. *See* food/messes

mice

"Here Comes a Mouse," 24, 125, 156, 160, 162, 167

"Hickory, Dickory, Dock," 23, 128, 152, 156, 160, 162, 164, 165, 166, 167, 237, 247

The Little Mouse, the Red Ripe Strawberry, and the Big Hungry Bear (Wood and Wood), 90, 95, 102, 104, 154, 157, 159, 164, 166, 246

Lunch (Fleming), 75, 98, 102, 104, 105, 157, 159, 189

Maisy Dresses Up (Cousins), 72, 93, 98, 100, 105, 107, 109, 159

Maisy Drives the Bus (Cousins), 72, 93, 96, 105, 113, 161

Maisy's Morning on the Farm (Cousins), 72, 93, 101, 104

Mouse's First Fall (Thompson), 88, 93, 100, 103, 105, 108, 109, 159

Mouse's First Snow (Thompson), 88, 93, 105, 109, 110, 114

Mouse's First Spring (Thompson), 88, 93, 105, 109, 111

A New House for Mouse (Horáček), 79, 93, 94, 104, 105, 159

One More Hug for Madison (Church), 71, 93, 95, 105, 106

Pumpkin Trouble (Thomas), 88, 93, 100, 101, 104, 105, 107

"Pussy Cat, Pussy Cat," 138, 153, 156, 160

"Slowly, Slowly, Very Slowly Creeps the Garden Snail," 158, 160

This Is the Farmer (Tafuri), 88, 94, 101, 105, 151, 159

Whose Mouse Are You? (Kraus), 80, 91, 95, 101, 105, 157, 159

"Wiggle Your Fingers," 150, 160, 161, 163, 167, 168

monkeys
"All around the Mulberry Bush," 117, 158, 159, 160, 162

I Like Books (Browne), 70, 92, 96, 105, 160

"Three Little Monkeys," 145, 153, 154, 160, 163, 165

"Wiggle Your Fingers," 150, 160, 161, 163, 167, 168

moon
Kitten's First Full Moon (Henkes), 78, 97, 105, 106

mothers. *See* families/babies/mothers/fathers

movable books
Chick (Vere), 89, 92, 97, 105

Honk! (Demarest), 73, 92, 94, 100, 101, 105, 111, 151, 156

If You're Happy and You Know It, Clap Your Hands! A Pop-Up Book (Carter), 71, 105, 106, 109, 110, 112, 165, 179, 182

Is That an Elephant Over There? (Elgar), 73, 92, 94, 100, 103, 105, 108, 109, 162, 165

Old MacDonald Had a Farm (Cony), 72, 93, 94, 101, 105, 110, 151

Says Who? (Carter), 71, 93, 103, 105, 109, 111, 151, 162

Where's Spot? (Hill), 78, 99, 104, 105, 108, 109, 155, 166, 246

The Wide-Mouthed Frog: A Pop-Up Book (Faulkner), 65, 74, 94, 102, 103, 105, 157

movement
Clap Your Hands (Cauley), 71, 106, 107, 112, 162

Dancing Feet! (Craig), 72, 92, 100, 106, 108

Farmyard Beat (Craig), 73, 94, 95, 101, 106, 112, 151, 154

From Head to Toe (Carle), 71, 92, 100, 106, 107, 151

If You're Hoppy (Sayre), 86, 92, 106, 110, 112

Mr. Cookie Baker (Wellington), 89, 102, 106

Stretch (Cronin and Menchin), 73, 93, 106, 111

multicultural stories
Peekaboo Morning (Isadora), 79, 95, 99, 103, 106

Ten Little Fingers and Ten Little Toes (Fox), 75, 95, 96, 99, 106

Uh-oh! (Isadora), 79, 95, 99, 101, 106

music
If You're Happy and You Know It, Clap Your Hands! A Pop-Up Book (Carter), 71, 105, 106, 109, 110, 112, 165, 179, 182

If You're Hoppy (Sayre), 86, 92, 106, 110, 112

Little White Duck (Whippo), 89, 93, 106, 110, 179

Meeow and the Big Box (Braun), 69, 93, 97, 104, 106, 113

Pete the Cat: I Love My White Shoes (Litwin), 82, 93, 97, 98, 104, 106, 107, 110, 155, 159

Pots and Pans (Hubbell), 79, 95, 103, 104, 106, 108, 111, 157, 159, 162

N

night
Blue Sky (Wood), 90, 98, 99, 106, 109, 114, 163

Kitten's First Full Moon (Henkes), 78, 97, 105, 106

One More Hug for Madison (Church), 71, 93, 95, 105, 106

numbers. *See also* counting
Big Fat Hen (Baker), 68, 97, 99, 106, 108, 111, 156, 246

The Big Storm: A Very Soggy Counting Book (Tafuri), 87, 91, 99, 106, 108, 113, 114, 166

Five Little Ducks (Raffi), 85, 99, 100, 106, 110, 156, 179, 182

Let's Go Visiting (Williams), 89, 93, 94, 99, 106, 109, 112, 189

My Heart Is Like a Zoo (Hall), 77, 93, 98, 99, 102, 106, 110, 114

Over in the Meadow (Langstaff), 81, 93, 99, 106, 110, 112, 151, 182, 189

Splash! (Jonas), 79, 93, 99, 106, 114

Ten, Nine, Eight (Bang), 68, 95, 99, 106, 112, 154

Ten Red Apples: A Bartholomew Bear Counting Book (Miller), 83, 93, 94, 95, 99, 100, 106, 109

O

ocean
Hooray for Fish! (Cousins), 72, 102, 106, 112

opposites
Dogs (Gravett), 77, 92, 98, 99, 107

Yummy, YUCKY (Patricelli), 84, 98, 102, 107

outside. *See* gardens/bugs/outside

owls
I'm Not Sleepy (Allen), 68, 95, 96, 107, 154

The Owl and the Pussycat (Lear), 81, 93, 96, 97, 107, 108, 112, 151, 154
Owl Babies (Waddell), 89, 96, 102, 105, 107
Wow! Said the Owl (Hopgood), 79, 96, 98, 107

P

participation
Brown Bear, Brown Bear, What Do You See? (Martin), 24, 58, 59, 66, 82, 92, 98, 102, 107, 108, 109, 110, 111, 151, 164, 165, 166, 167, 169, 189, 209, 236, 246
Clap Your Hands (Cauley), 71, 106, 107, 112, 162
Down on the Farm (Kutner), 80, 92, 101, 107, 111, 167, 246
From Head to Toe (Carle), 71, 92, 100, 106, 107, 151
Jump, Frog, Jump! (Kalan), 80, 92, 103, 107, 108, 109, 113, 153
Knock at the Door and Other Baby Action Rhymes (Chorao), 71, 107, 108
Pete the Cat: I Love My White Shoes (Litwin), 82, 93, 97, 98, 104, 106, 107, 110, 155, 159
We're Going on a Bear Hunt (Rosen), 85, 91, 94, 95, 103, 107, 153, 164
parties
Maisy Dresses Up (Cousins), 72, 93, 98, 100, 105, 107, 109, 159
photographs
What's on My Head? (Miller), 83, 95, 96, 107, 159
pigs
"Five Little Pigs," 160
I Like Me! (Carlson), 71, 92, 103, 107, 160
Piggies in the Pumpkin Patch (Peterson and Rofé), 85, 91, 98, 101, 107, 160
Piggies (Wood and Wood), 90, 95, 96, 103, 107, 154, 160, 162, 165
Pumpkin Trouble (Thomas), 88, 93, 100, 101, 104, 105, 107
"This Little Pig Had a Scrub-a-Dub," 152, 160
"This Little Piggy," 145, 152, 153, 160, 248
"To Market, to Market," 146, 152, 158, 160, 167, 248, 250
play. *See* toys/play/games

poetry
Big Fat Hen (Baker), 68, 97, 99, 106, 108, 111, 156, 246
Knock at the Door and Other Baby Action Rhymes (Chorao), 71, 107, 108
Little Robin Redbreast: A Mother Goose Rhyme (Halpern), 77, 96, 97, 108, 112, 154, 246
Mary Had a Little Lamb (Hale), 77, 108, 110, 112, 161, 167
The Owl and the Pussycat (Lear), 81, 93, 96, 97, 107, 108, 112, 151, 154
pop-up books. *See* movable books

Q

question-and-answer stories
Brown Bear, Brown Bear, What Do You See? (Martin), 24, 58, 59, 66, 82, 92, 98, 102, 107, 108, 109, 110, 111, 151, 164, 165, 166, 167, 169, 189, 209, 236, 246
Dancing Feet! (Craig), 72, 92, 100, 106, 108
Duck and Goose Find a Pumpkin (Hills), 78, 92, 99, 100, 108, 109, 154, 163
I Went Walking (Williams), 89, 91, 92, 94, 107, 108, 109, 112, 158, 189
Is That an Elephant Over There? (Elgar), 73, 92, 94, 100, 103, 105, 108, 109, 162, 165
Mama's Little Bears (Tafuri), 88, 91, 93, 95, 100, 105, 108, 153
Where's Spot? (Hill), 78, 99, 104, 105, 108, 109, 155, 166, 246
Whose Nose and Toes? (Butler), 70, 94, 108

R

rabbits
The ABC Bunny (Gag), 76, 91, 108, 111, 151, 161, 209
The Golden Egg Book (Brown), 70, 92, 100, 102, 108, 151, 156, 161
Goodnight Moon (Brown), 65, 70, 95, 108, 112, 154, 161, 209
"Here Is a Bunny," 126, 152, 161, 167
"Here Is a Nest for a Robin," 152, 154, 161
Home for a Bunny (Brown), 70, 92, 102, 108, 161

Little White Rabbit (Henkes), 78, 93, 98, 104, 108
"Wiggle Your Fingers," 150, 160, 161, 163, 167, 168
rain. *See* weather/clouds/rain/seasons
response books
Barnyard Banter (Fleming), 74, 91, 94, 101, 109, 111, 151
Brown Bear, Brown Bear, What Do You See? (Martin), 24, 58, 59, 66, 82, 92, 98, 102, 107, 108, 109, 110, 111, 151, 164, 165, 166, 167, 169, 189, 209, 236, 246
I Went Walking (Williams), 89, 91, 92, 94, 107, 108, 109, 112, 158, 189
If You're Happy and You Know It, Clap Your Hands! A Pop-Up Book (Carter), 71, 105, 106, 109, 110, 112, 165, 179, 182
Is That an Elephant Over There? (Elgar), 73, 92, 94, 100, 103, 105, 108, 109, 162, 165
Jump, Frog, Jump! (Kalan), 80, 92, 103, 107, 108, 109, 113, 153
Let's Go Visiting (Williams), 89, 93, 94, 99, 106, 109, 112, 189
Says Who? (Carter), 71, 93, 103, 105, 109, 111, 151, 162
Where's Spot? (Hill), 78, 99, 104, 105, 108, 109, 155, 166, 246
rhyming stories. *See* stories in rhyme

S

seasons. *See* weather/clouds/rain/seasons; *specific seasons*
shapes
Little Cloud (Carle), 71, 98, 109, 114, 163
My Heart Is Like a Zoo (Hall), 77, 93, 98, 99, 102, 106, 110, 114
Perfect Square (Hall), 77, 98, 102, 110
sharing
Giving (Hughes), 79, 103, 110
sheep
"Baa, Baa, Black Sheep," 118, 152, 161
"Little Boy Blue," 131, 152, 161
"Mary Had a Little Lamb," 133, 152, 161
Mary Had a Little Lamb (Hale), 77, 108, 110, 112, 161, 167
Sheep in a Jeep (Shaw), 86, 110, 112, 113, 161, 250

Where Is the Green Sheep? (Fox), 75, 94, 98, 101, 110, 161, 166, 209

sign language

Brown Bear, Brown Bear, What Do You See? (Martin), 24, 58, 59, 66, 82, 92, 98, 102, 107, 108, 109, 110, 111, 151, 164, 165, 166, 167, 169, 189, 209, 236, 246

The Busy Little Squirrel (Tafuri), 87, 92, 100, 109, 110, 114

Kitten's Autumn (Fernandes), 74, 93, 97, 100, 101, 102, 110, 111

Kitten's Spring (Fernandes), 74, 93, 97, 101, 110, 111, 112

size

Blue Sea (Kalan), 80, 98, 102, 110, 113, 153, 166, 189

Little Gorilla (Bornstein), 69, 93, 94, 96, 103, 110, 155

snow

All You Need for a Snowman (Schertle), 86, 107, 110, 114

The First Snowfall (Rockwell and Rockwell), 85, 98, 110, 114

A Kitten's Tale (Rohann), 85, 93, 97, 108, 109, 110, 114

Millions of Snowflakes (Siddals), 86, 102, 110, 112, 114, 189

Mouse's First Snow (Thompson), 88, 93, 105, 109, 110, 114

Oh! (Henkes), 78, 93, 108, 109, 110, 114

Snowballs (Ehlert), 73, 100, 110, 112, 114

songs

Five Little Ducks (Raffi), 85, 99, 100, 106, 110, 156, 179, 182

If You're Happy and You Know It, Clap Your Hands! A Pop-Up Book (Carter), 71, 105, 106, 109, 110, 112, 165, 179, 182

If You're Hoppy (Sayre), 86, 92, 106, 110, 112

Little White Duck (Whippo), 89, 93, 106, 110, 179

Mary Had a Little Lamb (Hale), 77, 108, 110, 112, 161, 167

Oh, A-Hunting We Will Go (Langstaff), 81, 91, 93, 110, 112, 151, 179, 189

Old MacDonald Had a Farm (Cony), 72, 93, 94, 101, 105, 110, 151

Over in the Meadow (Langstaff), 81, 93, 99, 106, 110, 112, 151, 182, 189

Pete the Cat: I Love My White Shoes (Litwin), 82, 93, 97, 98, 104, 106, 107, 110, 155, 159

sounds

Animals Speak (Prap), 85, 91, 111

Baby Says "Moo!" (Macken), 82, 91, 111, 168

Barnyard Banter (Fleming), 74, 91, 94, 101, 109, 111, 151

Book! Book! Book! (Bruss), 70, 92, 96, 101, 111

Can You Moo? (Wojtowycz), 90, 92, 111

Hello, Day! (Lobel), 82, 92, 101, 111

Honk! (Demarest), 73, 92, 94, 100, 101, 105, 111, 151, 156

Kitten's Autumn (Fernandes), 74, 93, 97, 100, 101, 102, 110, 111

Kitten's Spring (Fernandes), 74, 93, 97, 101, 110, 111, 112

Knock! Knock! (Tidholm), 88, 98, 111

Meeow and the Pots and Pans (Braun), 70, 108, 111

Peek-a-Moo! (Cimarusti), 72, 93, 101, 103, 104, 111, 151, 162, 168

Pots and Pans (Hubbell), 79, 95, 103, 104, 106, 108, 111, 157, 159, 162

Says Who? (Carter), 71, 93, 103, 105, 109, 111, 151, 162

Stretch (Cronin and Menchin), 73, 93, 106, 111

Tap, Tap, Bang, Bang (Garcia), 76, 98, 111, 113

Tip, Tip, Dig, Dig (Garcia), 76, 98, 111, 113

Trains Go (Light), 81, 111, 113, 161

The Very Quiet Cricket (Carle), 71, 93, 96, 111, 158

Who Said Moo? (Ziefert and Taback), 91, 94, 101, 104, 111

Whose Chick Are You? (Tafuri), 88, 94, 95, 101, 111

spring

Caterpillar's Wish (Murphy), 84, 96, 97, 109, 111

Kitten's Spring (Fernandes), 74, 93, 97, 101, 110, 111, 112

Mouse's First Spring (Thompson), 88, 93, 105, 109, 111

Spring Is Here (Hillenbrand), 78, 93, 103, 109, 111

stories in rhyme

The ABC Bunny (Gag), 76, 91, 108, 111, 151, 161, 209

All of Baby Nose to Toes (Adler), 67, 94, 96, 111

Barnyard Banter (Fleming), 74, 91, 94, 101, 109, 111, 151

Beetle Bop (Fleming), 74, 96, 111

Big Fat Hen (Baker), 68, 97, 99, 106, 108, 111, 156, 246

Brown Bear, Brown Bear, What Do You See? (Martin), 24, 58, 59, 66, 82, 92, 98, 102, 107, 108, 109, 110, 111, 151, 164, 165, 166, 167, 169, 189, 209, 236, 246

Chicky Chicky Chook Chook (MacLennan), 82, 92, 97, 101, 109, 111, 114, 158, 165

Chuck's Truck (Anderson), 68, 92, 101, 111, 113

Chugga-Chugga Choo-Choo (Lewis), 81, 112, 113, 161, 162, 250

Clap Your Hands (Cauley), 71, 106, 107, 112, 162

Dog Wants to Play (McDonnell), 83, 92, 99, 101, 102, 103, 112, 155, 162

Down on the Farm (Kutner), 80, 92, 101, 107, 111, 167, 246

Duck in the Truck (Alborough), 68, 92, 100, 112, 113

Farmyard Beat (Craig), 73, 94, 95, 101, 106, 112, 151, 154

The Five Little Pumpkins (Van Rynbach), 89, 104, 109, 112, 163, 189

Good Night, Good Night (Boynton), 69, 92, 95, 112, 154

Goodnight Moon (Brown), 65, 70, 95, 108, 112, 154, 161, 209

Here Are My Hands (Martin), 82, 96, 112

Hooray for Fish! (Cousins), 72, 102, 106, 112

I Love Bugs! (Dodd), 73, 112

I Went Walking (Williams), 89, 91, 92, 94, 107, 108, 109, 112, 158, 189

If You're Happy and You Know It, Clap Your Hands! A Pop-Up Book (Carter), 71, 105, 106, 109, 110, 112, 165, 179, 182

If You're Hoppy (Sayre), 86, 92, 106, 110, 112

In the Small, Small Pond (Fleming), 74, 92, 107, 109, 112, 113, 151, 153, 158, 163, 226

In the Tall, Tall Grass (Fleming), 75, 91, 92, 96, 107, 112, 151, 158

Kitten's Spring (Fernandes), 74, 93, 97, 101, 110, 111, 112

Kitty Cat, Kitty Cat, Are You Waking Up? (Martin), 82, 93, 97, 99, 112, 155

Let's Go Visiting (Williams), 89, 93, 94, 99, 106, 109, 112, 189

Little Robin Redbreast: A Mother Goose Rhyme (Halpern), 77, 96, 97, 108, 112, 154, 246

Mary Had a Little Lamb (Hale), 77, 108, 110, 112, 161, 167

Millions of Snowflakes (Siddals), 86, 102, 110, 112, 114, 189

My Many Colored Days (Seuss), 86, 98, 102, 112, 189

Oh, A-Hunting We Will Go (Langstaff), 81, 91, 93, 110, 112, 151, 179, 189

One Two That's My Shoe! (Murray), 84, 99, 112, 155

Over in the Meadow (Langstaff), 81, 93, 99, 106, 110, 112, 151, 182, 189

The Owl and the Pussycat (Lear), 81, 93, 96, 97, 107, 108, 112, 151, 154

Raindrop, Plop! (Lewison), 81, 109, 112, 114, 163

Red Light, Green Light (Suen), 87, 96, 112, 113

Sheep in a Jeep (Shaw), 86, 110, 112, 113, 161, 250

Snowballs (Ehlert), 73, 100, 110, 112, 114

Ten, Nine, Eight (Bang), 68, 95, 99, 106, 112, 154

Ten Little Caterpillars (Martin), 83, 96, 97, 99, 107, 112, 158

Time for Bed (Fox), 75, 95, 101, 112, 154

Time to Play! (Gray), 77, 101, 104, 108, 112, 162

Truck Stuck (Wolf), 90, 112, 113

T

themes for programs (overview), 151

things that go/boats/trains

"Airplanes Fly in the Sky," 161

The Bridge Is Up! (Bell), 69, 92, 102, 112, 161, 189

The Bus for Us (Bloom), 69, 97, 112

"Choo-Choo Train," 120, 161

Chuck's Truck (Anderson), 68, 92, 101, 111, 113

Chugga-Chugga Choo-Choo (Lewis), 81, 112, 113, 161, 162, 250

"Dance to Your Daddy," 121, 161

"Down at the Station," 122, 161, 250

Duck in the Truck (Alborough), 68, 92, 100, 112, 113

"The Engine," 122, 161

"Five Little Boats," 161

Freight Train (Crews), 73, 98, 102, 113, 161, 165, 189, 250

"The Grand Old Duke of York," 124, 161, 198, 201

"Here Comes the Choo-Choo Train," 161

"Here Is a Choo-Choo Train," 126, 161

"Here Is the Engine," 126, 161, 189

"I'll Drive a Dump Truck," 129, 162

Little Tug (Savage), 85, 113, 161

"Lots of Cars," 24, 133, 162

Maisy Drives the Bus (Cousins), 72, 93, 96, 105, 113, 161

Meeow and the Big Box (Braun), 69, 93, 97, 104, 106, 113

Red Light, Green Light (Suen), 87, 96, 112, 113

"Row, Row, Row Your Boat," 141, 153, 162, 164, 167, 168, 170, 226, 250

Sheep in a Jeep (Shaw), 86, 110, 112, 113, 161, 250

"This Is the Way the Ladies Ride," 145, 152, 162, 163, 167, 170

Tip, Tip, Dig, Dig (Garcia), 76, 98, 111, 113

Trains Go (Light), 81, 111, 113, 161

"Trot, Trot to Boston," 147, 162

Truck Stuck (Wolf), 90, 112, 113

"The Wheels on the Bus" (or Car, Truck, etc.), 149, 162, 163, 164, 165, 166, 167, 169, 250

"Zoom down the Freeway," 150, 162

tools

Tap, Tap, Bang, Bang (Garcia), 76, 98, 111, 113

toys/play/games

"All around the Mulberry Bush," 117, 158, 159, 160, 162

All You Need for a Snowman (Schertle), 86, 107, 110, 114

"Ball for Baby," 119, 162

"Bump'n Downtown in My Little Red Wagon," 162, 166, 167, 250

Chugga-Chugga Choo-Choo (Lewis), 81, 112, 113, 161, 162, 250

Clap Your Hands (Cauley), 71, 106, 107, 112, 162

Clip-Clop (Smee), 86, 92, 101, 102, 104, 108, 165

Dog Wants to Play (McDonnell), 83, 92, 99, 101, 102, 103, 112, 155, 162

"Drums," 122, 162

"Here Comes a Mouse," 24, 125, 156, 160, 162, 167

"Here We Go Up-Up-Up," 127, 162, 165

"Here's a Ball," 127, 162, 164

"Hickory, Dickory, Dock," 23, 128, 152, 156, 160, 162, 164, 165, 166, 167, 237, 247

"Humpty Dumpty," 23, 128, 157, 159, 162, 165, 166, 168, 248

Is That an Elephant Over There? (Elgar), 73, 92, 94, 100, 103, 105, 108, 109, 162, 165

"Jack Be Nimble," 130, 154, 162

"Jack in the Box," 131, 162, 164, 165, 167, 237

"Johnny Hammers One Hammer," 131, 162

Jump, Frog, Jump! (Kalan), 80, 92, 103, 107, 108, 109, 113, 153

Just Like Jasper! (Butterworth), 70, 97, 113, 162, 167

A Kitten's Tale (Rohann), 85, 93, 97, 108, 109, 110, 114

"Let Everyone Clap Hands Like Me," 162

Maggie's Ball (George), 76, 93, 99, 103, 108, 113, 162, 165

Meeow and the Pots and Pans (Braun), 70, 108, 111

Mouse's First Fall (Thompson), 88, 93, 100, 103, 105, 108, 109, 159

Under My Hood I Have a Hat (Kuskin), 80, 98, 102, 108, 109, 114, 159, 189

Oh! (Henkes), 78, 93, 108, 109, 110, 114

Peek-a-Boo (Ferri), 74, 93, 101, 103, 104

Peek-a-Moo! (Cimarusti), 72, 93, 101, 103, 104, 111, 151, 162, 168

Peekaboo Morning (Isadora), 79, 95, 99, 103, 106

Piggies (Wood and Wood), 90, 95, 96, 103, 107, 154, 160, 162, 165

Pots and Pans (Hubbell), 79, 95, 103, 104, 106, 108, 111, 157, 159, 162

"Ring around the Rosie," 140, 162, 165, 201

Says Who? (Carter), 71, 93, 103, 105, 109, 111, 151, 162

"See My Pony, My Jet Black Pony," 162

Splash! (McDonnell), 83, 94, 100, 108, 114, 153, 226

"Teddy Bear, Teddy Bear," 143, 154, 162, 164

"There Was a Little Turtle," 158, 162

"This Is the Way the Ladies Ride," 145, 152, 162, 163, 167, 170

"Three Little Monkeys," 145, 153, 154, 160, 163, 165

Tickle, Tickle (Oxenbury), 84, 94, 103, 157, 246

Time to Play! (Gray), 77, 101, 104, 108, 112, 162

Titch (Hutchins), 79, 101, 103, 113, 158, 162, 167

Treasure (Bloom), 69, 94, 95, 96, 103, 108

"Two Little Blackbirds," 23, 147, 152, 153, 155, 163, 164, 165, 166, 236

We're Going on a Bear Hunt (Rosen), 85, 91, 94, 95, 103, 107, 153, 164

Where Is Baby's Bellybutton? (Katz), 80, 95, 98, 103, 104

"Wiggle Your Fingers," 150, 160, 161, 163, 167, 168

trains. *See* things that go/boats/trains

trucks

Chuck's Truck (Anderson), 68, 92, 101, 111, 113

Duck in the Truck (Alborough), 68, 92, 100, 112, 113

Red Light, Green Light (Suen), 87, 96, 112, 113

Tip, Tip, Dig, Dig (Garcia), 76, 98, 111, 113

Truck Stuck (Wolf), 90, 112, 113

W

water. *See* bathtime/water

weather/clouds/rain/seasons. *See also* *specific seasons*

Bear Snores On (Wilson), 90, 91, 95, 102, 109, 114

The Big Storm: A Very Soggy Counting Book (Tafuri), 87, 91, 99, 106, 108, 113, 114, 166

Blue Sky (Wood), 90, 98, 99, 106, 109, 114, 163

The Busy Little Squirrel (Tafuri), 87, 92, 100, 109, 110, 114

Caterpillar's Wish (Murphy), 84, 96, 97, 109, 111

Chicky Chicky Chook Chook (MacLennan), 82, 92, 97, 101, 109, 111, 114, 158, 165

"Dr. Foster," 163

Duck and Goose Find a Pumpkin (Hills), 78, 92, 99, 100, 108, 109, 154, 163

The First Snowfall (Rockwell and Rockwell), 85, 98, 110, 114

The Five Little Pumpkins (Van Rynbach), 89, 104, 109, 112, 163, 189

"The Great Big Spider," 125, 153, 158, 163, 166, 167, 168, 170

A Hat for Minerva Louise (Stoeke), 87, 92, 97, 98, 101, 109, 114

"I Hear Thunder," 129, 163, 166

In the Small, Small Pond (Fleming), 74, 92, 107, 109, 112, 113, 151, 153, 158, 163, 226

"It's Raining, It's Pouring," 130, 163

A Kitten's Tale (Rohann), 85, 93, 97, 108, 109, 110, 114

Little Cloud (Carle), 71, 98, 109, 114, 163

Maisy Dresses Up (Cousins), 72, 93, 98, 100, 105, 107, 109, 159

Millions of Snowflakes (Siddals), 86, 102, 110, 112, 114, 189

Mouse's First Fall (Thompson), 88, 93, 100, 103, 105, 108, 109, 159

Mouse's First Snow (Thompson), 88, 93, 105, 109, 110, 114

Mouse's First Spring (Thompson), 88, 93, 105, 109, 111

Under My Hood I Have a Hat (Kuskin), 80, 98, 102, 108, 109, 114, 159, 189

Oh! (Henkes), 78, 93, 108, 109, 110, 114

Old Bear (Henkes), 78, 93, 95, 109

"Rain Is Falling Down," 138, 153, 163, 165, 166, 171, 202

Rain (Kalan), 80, 98, 108, 109, 114, 163

"Rain on the Green Grass," 138, 163

"Rain, Rain, Go Away," 138, 153, 163, 202

Raindrop, Plop! (Lewison), 81, 109, 112, 114, 163

"Snow Is Falling Down," 142, 163

Spring Is Here (Hillenbrand), 78, 93, 103, 109, 111

Ten Red Apples: A Bartholomew Bear Counting Book (Miller), 83, 93, 94, 95, 99, 100, 106, 109

"Thumbs in the Thumb Place," 159, 163

"Warm Hands Warm," 148, 159, 163

"Wheels on the Bus" (or Car, Truck, etc.), 149, 162, 163, 164, 165, 166, 167, 169, 250

winter

All You Need for a Snowman (Schertle), 86, 107, 110, 114

Bear Snores On (Wilson), 90, 91, 95, 102, 109, 114

The First Snowfall (Rockwell and Rockwell), 85, 98, 110, 114

A Hat for Minerva Louise (Stoeke), 87, 92, 97, 98, 101, 109, 114

A Kitten's Tale (Rohann), 85, 93, 97, 108, 109, 110, 114

Millions of Snowflakes (Siddals), 86, 102, 110, 112, 114, 189

Mouse's First Snow (Thompson), 88, 93, 105, 109, 110, 114

Oh! (Henkes), 78, 93, 108, 109, 110, 114

Snowballs (Ehlert), 73, 100, 110, 112, 114

Under My Hood I Have a Hat (Kuskin), 80, 98, 102, 108, 109, 114, 159, 189

work

The Busy Little Squirrel (Tafuri), 87, 92, 100, 109, 110, 114

The Little Red Hen (Galdone), 76, 93, 97, 103, 114

Z

zoo

"An Elephant Goes Like This and That," 152, 165

"Here Is a Bunny," 126, 152, 161, 167

"Here Is a Nest for a Robin," 152, 154, 161

"Hickory, Dickory, Dock," 23, 128, 152, 156, 160, 162, 164, 165, 166, 167, 237, 247

Is That an Elephant Over There? (Elgar), 73, 92, 94, 100, 103, 105, 108, 109, 162, 165

"Leg Over Leg," 131, 152, 156, 165, 166

Little Gorilla (Bornstein), 69, 93, 94, 96, 103, 110, 155

"Mama's Taking Us to the Zoo Tomorrow," 153

My Heart Is Like a Zoo (Hall), 77, 93, 98, 99, 102, 106, 110, 114

"Pussy Cat, Pussy Cat," 138, 153, 156, 160

Sam Who Never Forgets (Rice), 85, 93, 100, 102, 114, 152, 157, 165, 246

Splash! (McDonnell), 83, 94, 100, 108, 114, 153, 226

"This Little Piggy," 145, 152, 153, 160, 248

"Three Little Monkeys," 145, 153, 154, 160, 163, 165

"Two Little Blackbirds," 23, 147, 152, 153, 155, 163, 164, 165, 166, 236

Subject Index

A

accessibility of collection, 36, 38
activities
    creative, 191–196, 221–222, 229–231
    early literacy, 38–39
    movement, 198–199, 220
adults
    bonds between children and adults,
        creating, 24
    defined for this book, 16
    ESL (English as a second language), 20–21
    guidelines for, 21
    overview, 20–21
    participation in program, 58–59
age divisions, 16, 54
All Wet! (sample program), 226
arrangement of group, 60
arts and crafts, 192–193, 227, 228
ASL (American Sign Language), 196–197

B

balance and standing, practicing, 23
balls, 199
bells, 181
bilingual families, 25–26
biology and brain development in children. *See*
    brain development in children
blocks, 199–200
body parts, identifying and moving, 24
bonds between children and adults, creating,
    24
bookmobiles, 43
brain development in children
    articles on, 12
    books on, 10–11
    e-resources on, 12–14

    early learning, 8
    language development in children, 6–7
    overview, 5–6
    print resources on, 10–12
bubbles, 200

C

C.A.R. (comment, ask, respond), 18
caregivers. *See* adults
characteristics of books appropriate for ages 12
    to 24 months, 37
child-care providers, 27
children. *See also* brain development in
    children; early childhood
    age groups, defining, 16
    bonds between children and adults,
        creating, 24
    developmental stages, 17–20
    overview, 15–16
collections, 37–38, 42–43
coloring, paper and, 194–195
communication and language development, 7
communication skills, 17–18
community events, 42
creative activities
    arts and crafts, 192–193, 228
    e-resources on, 222
    overview, 191–192
    painting, 194
    paper and coloring, 194–195
    playdough, 195
    print resources on, 221
    puzzles, 195–196
    sample activities, 229–231
    types of, 192–196
    when to do, 192

creative rhyme handout ideas, 232
crowd control, 55–57

D

developmental stages, resources on, 29
dialogue among participants, allowing time
    for interaction and, 64–65
displays
    e-resources on, 222–223
    facts and tips for, 240
    ideas for, 208–210
    overview, 207
    planning, 207–208
door sign, 233
drums, 180–181

E

early childhood
    caregivers, 27
    education, importance of, 3–5
    studies, 3–5
education, importance of early childhood,
    3–5
EFL (English as a foreign language), 25
ELL (English language learners), 25
enhancements. *See also* props
    creative activities, 191–196
    displays, 207–210
    flannel boards, 187–189
    handouts, 210–215
    language activities, 196–197
    media, 181–182
    movement activities, 198–199
    music, 178–179
    overview, 177
    play, 203–207
    print and audio resources on, 221
    puppets, 189–191
    recommended recordings and DVDs,
        183–187
    rhythm instruments, 179–181
    visuals, 182–183
ESL (English as a second language), 25
ESOL (English for speakers of other
    languages), 25–26
evaluation form (sample)
    long form, 234
    short form, 235
eye contact, practicing, 24
eye-hand coordination, 24

F

facilities, 35–36
families
    bilingual families, 25–26
    grandparents, 26
    overview, 22
    special needs family, 22–24
    teen parents, 26
fine motor skills for children ages 12-24
    months, 19
finger paint, 227
fingerplay. *See* nursery rhymes and
    fingerplays
flannel boards
    distributors of flannel-board supplies, 218
    overview, 187–189
    print resources on, 217–218
    sample activities, 236
format for program
    adult education, 64
    bonus section, 64–65
    overview, 61
    setting the stage, 61–62
    storytime, 63
funding, 46–49

G

games, 200
generic template for program, 238
give-away programs, 43
glue or cornstarch paste, 227
grandparents, 26, 30. *See also* adults
grants, 46–49
guides, collection, 37–38

H

hand-eye coordination, 24
handouts and templates (samples)
    All Wet!, 226
    art activity recipes, 227
    craft ideas, 228
    creative play ideas, 229–231
    creative rhyme handout ideas, 232
    displays or filler, interesting facts and
        tips for, 240
    door sign, 233
    e-resources, 222–223
    enhancements, 210–215
    evaluation - long, 234
    evaluation - short, 235

flannel-board fun, 236
generic template, 238
overview, 225
playing, interesting facts and tips for, 242
program guidelines bookmark, 244
program guidelines poster, 245
publicity flyers, program descriptions
    for, 243
quotes to remember, 242
reading, interesting facts and tips for, 241
reading aloud to little ones, 246
rhyme booklet, page 1, 247
rhyme booklet, page 2, 248
rhymes to share, 237
sick sign, 249
singing, interesting facts and tips for,
    241
stories template, 239
talking, interesting facts and tips for, 242
Things That Go, 250
writing, interesting facts and tips for,
    242

I

imaginary play, 204–205, 230
in-house services
    collections, 37–38
    facilities, 35–36
    overview, 33
    programs, 38–39
    staffing and training, 34
infant age group defined, 16
intellect and language development for
    children ages 12-24 months, 19
interaction and dialogue among
    participants, allowing time for, 64–65

L

language
    board books, 196
    communication and language
        development, 7
    e-resources on, 220
    flannel boards (individual), 196
    print resources on, 219
    resources on, 29–30, 219–220
    sign language, 196–197
language-related play, 205–207, 231
latecomers, 57
librarian/presenter, 8–9, 27–28, 59

libraries, early brain research impacting, 8–9
literacy, resources on, 29–30

M

mailing lists, 42
media as enhancement, 181–182
motor skills, 17
movement activities
    e-resources on, 220
    overview, 198–199
    print resources on, 220
music
    distributors of children's media, 217
    e-resources on, 216–217
    overview, 178–179
    print resources on, 215–216
    recommended recordings and DVDs,
        183–187

N

nametags, use of, 57–58
national organizations, outreach programs
        created by, 45
newsletters, 42
non-family members, 27
nonprint materials in collection, 38
nursery rhymes and fingerplays
    audio resources, 175
    e-resources, 175
    list of, 117–150
    methods for teaching, 115
    overview, 114–115
    print resources, 173–174
    resources, 115–116, 173–175
    rhymes to share, 237

O

oatmeal dough, 227
outings, 204, 230
outreach programs
    bookmobiles, 43
    collections created specifically for, 42–43
    community events, 42
    evaluating, 41
    give-away programs, 43
    mailing lists, 42
    national organizations, outreach
        programs created by, 45
    newsletters, 42
    overview, 39

private organizations, outreach
        programs created by, 45
    story programs, 44–45
    target audience, 40–41
    workshops, 43–44
overcrowding at programs, 55–57

P

pace of program, 58
painting, 194
paper and coloring, 194–195
parachutes/scarves/streamers, 201–203, 221
parents. *See* adults
participants, e-resources on, 30–31
partnerships, 46, 48–49
parts of the body, naming, 24
physical development for children ages
        12-24 months, 19
play
    e-resources, 222
    and early learning, 8
    imaginary play, 204–205, 230
    interesting facts and tips for, 242
    language-related play, 205–207, 231
    outings, 204
    overview, 203
    print resources, 221
    water play, 203–204
playdough, 195, 227
preschooler age group defined, 16
pretoddler age group defined, 16
private organizations, outreach programs
        created by, 45
program guidelines
    bookmark, 244
    poster, 245
programming
    adult participation in program, 58–59
    age groups, determining, 54
    annotated bibliography for, 67–91
    arrangement of group, 60
    crowd control, 55–57
    e-resources on, 172
    format for program
        adult education, 64
        bonus section, 64–65
        overview, 61
        setting the stage, 61–62
        storytime, 63
    latecomers, 57

librarian/presenter, role of, 59
    nametags, use of, 57–58
    overview, 38–39
    pace of program, 58
    print resources on, 171–172
    publicity for, 54–55
    registration, 55
    scheduling, 60
    themes, 67
    tips for, 65–66
props
    balls, 199
    blocks, 199–200
    bubbles, 200
    games, 200
    parachutes, 201–202
    scarves and streamers, 202–203
    toys, 203
public libraries, programming and services
        for very young children and their
        caregivers in, 3–4
publicity, 54–55, 243
puppets
    distributors of puppet supplies, 219
    as enhancement, 189–191
    print resources on, 218
puzzles, 195–196

Q

quotes to remember, 242

R

reading, interesting facts and tips for, 241
reading aloud to little ones, 246
recipes, art activity, 227
recommended recordings and DVDs as
        enhancements, 183–187
registration, 55
restrooms, 36
rewards for summer reading program, 39
rhyme booklet
    page 1, 247
    page 2, 248
rhymes, nursery. *See* nursery rhymes and
        fingerplays
rhythm instruments
    bells, 181
    drums, 180–181
    overview, 179
    shakers, 179–180

risk factors for very young children that impede their ability to succeed in life, 4–5

S

safety of facilities, 36
sample program outlines, 164–171
scarves/parachutes/streamers, 201–203, 221
scheduling, 60
seating options, 35
services
  in-house services
    collections, 37–38
    facilities, 35–36
    overview, 33
    programs, 38–39
    staffing and training, 34
  outreach programs
    bookmobiles, 43
    collections created specifically for, 42–43
    community events, 42
    evaluating, 41
    give-away programs, 43
    mailing lists, 42
    national organizations, outreach programs created by, 45
    newsletters, 42
    overview, 39

private organizations, outreach programs created by, 45
    story programs, 44–45
    target audience, 40–41
    workshops, 43–44
  overview, 33
  resources on, 47–48
shakers, 179–180
sick sign (sample), 249
singing, interesting facts and tips for, 241
sitting upright, 23
social and emotional development for children ages 12-24 months, 19
sound equipment, use of, 181–182
special needs family, 22–24
staffing and training, 34
standing and balance, practicing, 23
stories template, 239
storytime books, resources for, 171–172
streamers/scarves/parachutes, 201–203, 221
studies, early childhood, 3–5
summer reading programs, 38–39

T

talking, interesting facts and tips for, 242
target audience, 40–41
teen parents, 26
templates. *See* handouts and templates (samples)

themes, 67. *See also* Theme Index
Things That Go (sample program), 250
tips for programming, 65–66
toddler age group defined, 16
toys, 49–50, 203
training and staffing, 34

V

verbalization skills, 17
visual enhancements, 182–183
visual tracking, developing, 23

W

water play, 203–204, 229
workshops, 43–44
writing, interesting facts and tips for, 242

Y

yoga, 198–199